The Cashless Society:
EFTS at the Crossroads

THE CASHLESS SOCIETY: EFTS AT THE CROSSROADS

August Bequai, Esq.

A WILEY-INTERSCIENCE PUBLICATION

JOHN WILEY & SONS

New York · Chichester · Brisbane · Toronto

Library of Congress Cataloging in Publication Data:

Bequai, August.
  The cashless society.

  "A Wiley-Interscience publication."
  Bibliography: p.
  Includes index.
  1. Electronic funds transfers.   I. Title.
HG1710.B46   332.1′028   80-21517
ISBN 0-471-05654-5

Printed in the United States of America

10 9 8 7 6 5 4 3 2 1

For My Mother and Father

PREFACE

In California, two men were charged by the authorities with the illegal wire transfer of more than $1 million from a Beverly Hills bank. In Canada, several university students reportedly used their school's computer without authorization. Prosecutors charged them with the theft of telecommunications services; the court, however, overturned the conviction, noting that the law had been written to deter unauthorized use of the telephone and not computers. Not to be outdone, three Russian workers employed at a government-owned calculator firm were charged by the authorities with using the firm's computer to steal more than than 78,000 rubles—over $100,000 in U.S. currency. The defendants altered their employer's computerized payroll records and created "ghost employees."

The cashless society—a payment system where computers will replace our present paper-based payment system with "electronic blips"—is upon us. Computers have come to dominate not only our lives but the lives of citizens of numerous other nations. Rudimentary cashless systems make their appearance daily; the automated teller machine, point-of-sale system, and telephone-billpaying service have become common occurrences. Yet the cashless society—based on Electronic Funds Transfer Systems (EFTS)—brings with it problems. As the examples just noted illustrate, EFTS challenge our criminal justice system; they test our social, political, and economic fiber. We live in the dawn of EFTS: a technology at the crossroads.

AUGUST BEQUAI

Washington, D.C.
October 1980

CONTENTS

INTRODUCTION

The 1990s augurs a society where computers will govern every facet of the individual's daily life. Each home will be equipped with a computer terminal; banking will be conducted from the comfort of one's home. By simply using a telephone, the average citizen will be able to pay bills. Funds will be transferred internationally via satellite communications, through a global computerized financial network.

The computer and telecommunications revolution will also have a profound impact on our newspaper industry. Newspaper deliveries and newsstands will become a thing of the past. The reader will simply receive news through a computer terminal located in the home. By simply pressing several buttons, the seeker of news will be able to interrogate the system to any desired depth.

We are now on the threshold of the cashless society, a society in which funds and related financial data are transferred, electronically, with the aid of computers. Electronic Funds Transfer Systems (EFTS), precursors of a pure cashless society, have already made an appearance; rudimentary EFTS are in daily operation.

The cashless society holds vast promises and immense benefits. Armed robberies, forgeries, counterfeiting, and theft of checks will become things of the past in a cashless environment. Currency, coins, and our present checking system will become obsolete. Messages now sent over our mails will be transmitted electronically, relieving the paper glut in our postal system. The savings, in turn, may be passed on to the consumer.

The cashless society, however, will also bring with it a myriad of social, political, and economic problems. A computerized system storing large amounts of confidential data—which are easily accessible at the touch of a button—will give rise to serious invasions of privacy. Inadvertent or deliberate misuse of EFTS will expose personal and financial data regarding an individual to both the private and the public sector. Provisions for liability, for error or malfunction of the system, legal proof of payment, reversibility of transactions, and fraud will have to be defined and clarified under EFTS. Security will also, increasingly, become a problem under

EFTS; in addition, new categories of crime will take shape, and a new class of electronic felons will bilk the public of billions of dollars.

A computerized payments system can prove to be costly; there is concern that only the large financial institutions may be able to afford the needed EFTS technology, effectively excluding the smaller financial institutions. The question of who will bear the real cost for the system has yet to be addressed. The consumer will also lose control over personal financial affairs; the float will no longer be available in an electronic payment system, where funds will be transferred in a matter of seconds.

At the present time 40 percent of our population uses only currency and coins to conduct financial transactions. Several surveys have indicated that a large segment of the public is satisfied with our check payment system. The cashless society raises the key question of choice. How do we accommodate this large group within our population that is opposed to a shift away from our present payments system? EFTS carry not only the potential for economic manipulation but also the real threat of subtle political control of the populace at large by a small, well-organized constituency. A computerized system that can store large amounts of data on hundreds of millions of Americans is also fraught with potential political dangers.

This book is an overview of the social, economic, and legal issues raised by EFTS; it explores and analyzes the forces that have propelled EFTS, and also those that have retarded the growth of EFTS. Chapter 1 explores the need for EFTS, Chapter 2 traces the history of computer technology, and Chapter 3 describes the basic components of the cashless society. Chapter 4 explores the issue of privacy; Chapters 5 through 8 explore the legal problems connected with branching, and also the sharing of EFTS; the serious threats EFTS face from sophisticated criminal groups is also explored. Chapter 9 explores the potential civil liability issues that revolve around EFTS; and Chapter 10 explores the potential impact of this sophisticated technology on our economic fiber. Chapter 11 explores the controversial issue of government ownership of EFTS; the final two chapters deal with the potential international growth of EFTS and the impact of key banking legislation on EFTS.

The cashless society has already made its appearance felt; the requisite technology is available. Rudimentary EFTS have already taken shape in point-of-sale systems, automated teller machines, preauthorized payment systems, telephone-billpaying systems, and automated clearing houses. The question EFTS pose is simple: How do we best address the challenges this new technology will increasingly raise? EFTS will affect every facet of our societal fiber. How we deal with this little understood technology and meet its challenges may, in the long run, determine the outcome of our political, social, and economic institutions. EFTS may constitute one of the more dramatic and subtle developments of the twentieth century.

1
WHY THE NEED FOR
A CASHLESS SOCIETY

The place is Middletown, America; the time is the near future. The Smiths have just returned from their European vacation to discover that their mortgage, utility bills, and auto insurance are due. No problem. Mr. Smith reaches for the touch phone and contacts his bank's computer; he instructs it to transfer funds from his account to those of his creditors. Within a matter of minutes, the bills are paid. Mrs. Smith then instructs the computer to invest some of her funds in 100 shares of the Ding Dong Mutual Fund—her broker had recommended the purchase before the Smiths left for their European vacation.

Mrs. Smith is also reminded that their refrigerator is empty. She drives the family car to the local supermarket. Inflation continues to be rampant. A gallon of milk costs $4.98, a can of tuna sells for $3.50, and a six-pack of her husband's favorite beer costs $9.75. Talk about inflation . . . Wow!

The store clerk rings up her groceries. The old cash register system has given way to a computerized checkout system. A laser reads the stripped Universal Product Code from each item that Mrs. Smith has purchased. "The total is $415.16," the clerk informs Mrs. Smith. "Will it be cashless?" he asks. "Yes," she replies, handing him a plastic card. The clerk inserts the card in a terminal located behind the counter. Mrs. Smith, in turn, presses several buttons on an input terminal (her secret account number) that is connected to her bank's computer through the store's telephone system.

Within a matter of seconds, the bank's computer receives the coded electronic information. It scans its memory banks for the Smiths' account; it computes her credit rating. The Smith's account contains sufficient funds to cover the transaction; the computer relays instructions to the clerk to complete the sale. The clerk then proceeds to finalize the transaction, and the computer automatically deducts the purchase amount from the Smiths' account and credits that of the store. No money has changed hands; the entire transaction is electronic.

The Smiths live in the world of the EFTS—the cashless society—a world where economic transactions are conducted through the use of electronic impulses generated and interpreted by computers.

DEFINING EFTS

Several definitions have been offered to describe the cashless society. The National Commission on Electronic Fund Transfers (NCEFT), established in 1974 by the U.S. Congress (Public Law 93–495) to study EFTS, defined EFTS as payment systems in which the processing and communications necessary to effect economic exchanges and the processing and communications necessary for the production and distribution of services incidental or related to economic exchanges are dependent wholly or in large part on the use of electronics.

EFTS represent a class of related practices and technologies that employ electronic impulses generated and interpreted by computers to debit and credit financial accounts. Each such debit or credit transaction is termed an electronic funds transfer. Electronic impulses, rather than paper, are employed to effect an economic transaction.

EFTS can best be described as a growing array of financial services. Among the services most frequently associated with EFTS are wire transfer of funds, direct deposit of income checks, periodic or authorized payments, check verification, and credit card authorizations. Point-of-sale (POS) systems, automated teller machines (ATMs), and automated clearing house facilities (ACHs) represent a more advanced form of EFTS. These financial services transfer funds through the use of electronic impulses, relying on the computer as their everyday workhorse. These computerized electronic systems have the potential to operate regionally, nationally, or internationally.

This new mode of fund transfers relies on a network of thousands of computers with high-speed mass memory and voice recognition devices, on-line terminal systems, and an army of more than 2 million men and women (computer programmers, operators, engineers, librarians, and managers). At present, rudimentary EFTS of more than 10,000 ATMs, 11,000 POS terminals, and 25 ACHs handle millions of financial transactions and transfer funds daily without the use of checks. By the mid-1980s, a network of more than 30,000 ATMs (each costing $30,000–40,000), 500,000 POS terminals, and 60 ACHs will displace more than 20 percent of our present checking system.

The EFTS revolution has sparked parallel developments in the communications arena. The Electronic Message Systems (EMS), still in an experimental stage, represent an added shift away from our paper society in the communications area. EMS also represent an additional potential array of systems for the electronic transfer of funds.

EMS are defined as data transmission systems that use electronic impulses rather than paper to effect the flow of information. These systems have come to embrace a wide range of services including the Electronic Computer Originated Mail (ECOM), Electronic Message Services (EMSS), and Intelpost. Proponents of the cashless society view these systems as replacements for the present postal, telex, and cable communicating systems.

ECOM is an experimental mailgram-type service; once implemented, it would be limited to mass mailers who send a minimum of 5000 messages a month. ECOM would be run by the U.S. Postal Service (USPS), and would link the nation's 25 largest post offices. The USPS currently is embroiled in a jurisdictional dispute with the Federal Communications Commission (FCC); the FCC takes the position that ECOM and its related services should be regulated by the FCC.

In an ECOM system, messages are recorded initially on a magnetic tape or disk by the user, and then are transmitted, on-line, from the user's premises to each destination post office. Reaching their destination, the messages are converted into hard copy and delivered to the recipient by a mail carrier. Deliveries would be made within a day from the input time. ECOM would also offer a variety of address and text editing features. Deliveries of the same message could be made to several addresses; portions, or even the entire message sent to a specified addressee, could be altered.

Another on-line system currently being developed by the USPS is Intelpost; it is currently undergoing field tests. Similar to ECOM in its workings, it would provide an international computerized transmission service between the United States and several European nations.

Fearful of losing its first-class mail sender to private electronic message systems, the USPS has commenced testing EMSS, a system that electronically transmits first-class mail from origination to destination post offices. A more advanced EMSS is also contemplated; it would provide for the transmission of first-class mail to the recipient's office or home. ITT, RCA, Western Union, and Xerox are currently developing their own private EMSS networks.

There is an array of other experimental systems. Western Union is testing an International Mailgram Service (IMS), and the Xerox Corporation is experimenting with the Telecommunications Network Service (TNS). All are·an outgrowth of the EFTS revolution. In the not too distant future, customers with the needed computer capability will be able to send both messages and funds electronically through EMS.

A rudimentary international EFTS system has also taken shape. The Society for Worldwide Interbank Financial Telecommunications (SWIFT) best illustrates this development. SWIFT is an international organ, created under Belgian law by a group of private financial institutions. It links over 500 institutions in the United States and abroad into an international specialized EFT service; it handles over 100,000 messages daily. SWIFT has replaced the mails, telex, and cables as media for communicating international payments between member institutions.

We are witnessing a subtle, dramatic revolution in our monetary system. For the computer manufacturer, EFTS represent a multibillion-dollar annual market; for store merchants, EFTS represent an array of new services and potentially higher sales. Consumers view them with mixed feelings, and lawyers see in them a panoply of legal problems. EFTS represent a profound technological challenge in our century. The impact of EFTS may have far-reaching consequences for every facet of our societal fiber.

EXCHANGE MECHANISMS TODAY

Attempts to improvise monetary systems traditionally have been linked to the growth of commerce and technology. The simple barter system of antiquity, usually connected with subsistence agrarian societies, gave way, as commerce became more sophisticated, to a modified barter system. A single commodity, widely accepted, came to replace a multitude of commodities exchanged under the simple barter system.

The Age of Metal Coins accompanied the rise of city-states and empires. Ancient Rome came to symbolize the most highly developed metal monetary system. The fall of Rome brought with it a dark era for Europe, with the simple barter system replacing the coin system. However, rising commerce and fear of bandits and pirates sparked the development of what came to be known as the Age of Receipts.

Written receipts (IOUs) came to be widely used by the merchant class of medieval Europe. An Italian merchant selling goods to a French merchant would sell his claim against the French buyer to a fellow Italian merchant who had just made purchases in France. The latter was thus able to repay his French seller by simply forwarding him the IOU he had just purchased from the Italian seller. In turn, the French seller would present the French buyer with the IOU, and be compensated. Bills of Exchange, as these claims came to be known, were instructions by a seller to his buyer to pay the bearer the amount specified. They were the forerunners of our modern checking system.

Banking as we know it has its roots in Europe's Middle Ages. By the early thirteenth century, Italian bankers accepted money from depositors and agreed to repay it on demand. They also payed interest on their deposit accounts.

However, it was the English goldsmith who paved the way for modern banking. Unlike the Italian banker who refused to transfer ownership of deposits from one account to another unless both parties to the transaction appeared in person, the English goldsmith permitted these transfers by allowing his depositors to endorse their receipts. Payment through a goldsmith's receipt became common in the Middle Ages. The goldsmith was obligated to pay in coin anyone who presented him with a receipt. Some goldsmiths even engraved their receipts.

With the growth of the modern state, the monarchs of England and France began to issue paper money. The Age of Paper Money is still with us. Two thirds of all small financial transactions in the United States are conducted through coin and paper currency; 25 percent of the U.S. money supply, over $90 billion, is in coin and paper currency.

It was not until 1861 that the modern checking system made its appearance; it soon gained wide acceptance within the United States and went unchallenged until the 1950s, when new payment systems gained popularity: travelers' checks, money orders, and a multitude of credit cards. More recently, an assortment of electronic payment systems have made inroads.

Coins and Currency

Forty percent of all Americans rely on this mode of exchange to conduct all of their financial transactions. The printing of paper currency is the responsibility of the U.S. Bureau of Engraving and Printing; coins are produced by the U.S. Bureau of the Mint. Both, in turn, are then distributed by the Federal Reserve System, an independent agency, to commercial banks. The banks then distribute the coins and paper currency to merchants, depository institutions, and customers.

The 37 offices of the Federal Reserve act as regional processing centers for both currency and coin. These 37 offices also retire unfit currency from circulation; old and counterfeit bills are destroyed as they are received from commercial banks. More than $3 billion of unfit currency is retired from circulation annually; as the unfit currency is destroyed, damaged and unfit coins are returned by the Federal Reserve to the federal government.

Proponents of the cashless society argue that the present mode of making payments is extremely expensive. There is the cost of production as well as expenses connected with the packaging and distribution of coins and currency. Further, a large army of clerks is required to screen unfit and counterfeit currency.

In addition, a large federal police force (U.S. Secret Service) is needed to both enforce federal currency laws and arrest violators. There is also the additional problem of safeguarding coins and currency from criminals. Financial institutions spend millions of dollars annually to secure themselves from theft and robbery. The cost of supporting the present U.S. coin and currency payment system is said to run in excess of $5 billion dollars annually.

Proponents of the cashless society also point to the high cost of crime, in terms of both monetary losses and physical injury suffered by the citizenry. The annual cost from these losses runs in the billions of dollars in the United States. Supporters of the cashless society also note that in an EFTS environment traditional crimes (robberies, burglaries, larcenies, etc.) will become a thing of the past; with no coins or currency to steal, a thief will have little incentive to rob merchants, financial institutions, or the average citizen.

Proponents of the cashless society further note that EFTS will curtail some organized criminal activity. "Fencing" (the selling of stolen goods) and illegal gambling activities will be adversely affected by EFTS. Law enforcement agencies will have a detailed, computerized record of all illegal transactions (financial transactions, both legal and illegal, will be computerized and recorded by financial institutions under EFTS); these detailed records will lead the police to the culprits. The cashless society will lessen the level of violence in our society.

Checks

Some 14,500 commercial banks with 31,400 branches and 248 clearing houses as well as 12 Federal Reserve Banks with 24 branches are now the processing centers for the entire U.S. check payment system. Numerous thrift institutions also play a role; they provide deposit services in the form of savings accounts and certificates of deposit. Several thrift institutions have also begun to offer checklike access to savings accounts. Some thrift institutions have also played a leading role in the development of EFTS.

The thrift industry includes a myriad of local banking institutions: more than 4800 savings and loan associations and their 11,800 branches, operating in 50 states; 470 mutual savings banks, with 2200 branches, in 17 states; and more than 20,000 credit unions. In addition, there are 175 industrial banking companies, operating 1600 branches, in 23 states. These industrial banks (also known as Morris Plan banks) have no checking account authority but participate in federal direct deposit programs.

The check itself is a demand draft, drawn on an authorized depository institution, directing it to pay a stated amount to the named payee. For the purpose of transferring funds, two deposit accounts and a paper instrument (the check) are required. The payor's institution, when the transfer is effected, subtracts the amount authorized from the payor's deposit account and credits it to the payee's account. If the payee's account is in another institution, clearing arrangements are made. These arrangements may be informal, especially if small local institutions are involved, or highly formal, with written rules and procedures, especially in large metropolitan centers.

The volume of checks has grown by leaps and bounds at an average rate of 7 percent annually. In 1945, the annual check volume was 5.3 million; by 1970 it had grown to 22.5 billion, and by 1980 to 45 billion. Government writes only 7 percent of all checks in the United States, with business and consumers writing the remaining 93 percent; more than half of these are written by the consuming public. Although checks written for more than $10,000 represent 80 percent of the dollar value of funds transferred by check, they constitute only 1 percent of all checks written annually. More than 50 percent of all written checks are for amounts of less than 50 dollars, contributing to the high cost of processing checks.

The cost of operating our present checking system grows daily. It costs an average of 20 cents to process each check. It's estimated that the total bill for handling all the checks in the United States exceeds $11 billion annually.

Proponents of the cashless society note that EFTS could cut these costs by as much as 35 percent. The costs involved in the production, authorization of payment, handling of checks, forgery, fraud, error, as well as costs associated with the float, all would be eliminated under EFTS. Former U.S. Senator Edward Brooke of Massachusetts, addressing an American Bankers Association conference in 1974, best summarized the problem as follows:

> The Federal Reserve Board estimates that the check volume is increasing at a rate that will double during the next decade. The total annual cost of clearing paper checks and using cash in our economy has been approximated at . . . about 1 per cent of our gross national product. . . . Unless there is a large scale transition to electronic funds transfer (EFTS), the growth in check usage may eventually impede the flow of funds in the economy.

However, supporters of our checking system disagree; they point out that EFTS will give rise to new forms of crime. Monetary losses from frauds will increase rather than diminish. They point to the growing problem of computer crime: over $100 million in annual losses. The traditionalists are dubious that the banking industry will pass on savings from EFTS to the consumer; they fear that the cost of developing and implementing EFTS will be borne by the consumer, in the form of higher prices for financial services. Some traditionalists also point to the Alaska Pipeline as an analogy: "They [the oil companies] said that Alaskan oil was needed to keep our fuel costs down. Has it done that?" Rather, they view EFTS as an attempt by the larger financial institutions to monopolize the banking industry.

Credit Cards

Four major types of credit card are now in use: bank cards, such as VISA and Master Charge, travel and entertainment cards, store cards, and gasoline cards. More than 50 percent of all families in the United States use one or more of these cards. The most widely used of these cards is the store card, used by some 35 percent of all American families. Least used are the travel and entertainment cards, which are used by only 10 percent of all families in this country.

There are now more than 5 billion annual credit card transactions; the two major bank card systems alone handle 45 million accounts. Credit cards enjoy great use with middle- and upper-middle-class American families; the poorer classes, however, prefer to conduct the bulk of their transactions in cash—for these elements of our society, the credit card age has yet to arrive.

Federal Reserve Wire

It links the 12 Federal Reserve banks and their 24 branches with 300 member banks in a nationwide network. This network, with its nerve center in Culpeper, Virginia, also links the Federal Reserve System with the U.S. Treasury via a network of high-speed communication lines.

The Fed Wire handles in excess of 50,000 wire fund transfers daily, at 240,000 characters per minute, with a value in excess of $100 billion. The Fed Wire also handles transfers of marketable government securities. This system has been credited with distributing payrolls on time, eliminating theft of checks from mailboxes, and providing better services to the banking community. In addition, it has helped arrest the staggering growth in the use of checks.

Bank Wire

This private communications network serving 115 subscribers, spread out across more than 70 major cities, originated in the early 1950s. The Bank Wire handles 12,000 messages daily, resulting in transfer of more than $25 billion. The computer nerve centers of this electronic network are located in New York City and Chicago. Some Bank Wire subscribers also make use of the Computerized Clearing House for Interbank Payments Systems (CHIPS), for large fund transfers involving foreign financial institutions.

A multitude of other exchange mechanisms have also made their appearance. For example, the Mutual Institutions Nation Transfer System (MINTS) was founded in 1972. Direct deposit programs have also become increasingly popular, especially with federal agencies. However, powerful groups within the financial industry have continued exerting pressure to quicken the pace to EFTS. We have witnessed the rise of the ATM, POS, and ACH. The roots of a sophisticated EFTS have already been laid.

ADVANTAGES OF THE CASHLESS SOCIETY

One of the key benefits to be derived from EFTS will be, without doubt, convenience. The aged and the infirm will value banking from the comfort of their home. A study conducted by the Virginia Bankers Association concluded that consumers from the higher income groups found EFTS of immense value as a time-saving device; professionals, especially, were favorably inclined to EFTS because of the convenience of paying their bills by simply using their telephones.

Personal security is also said to be a key benefit we will derive from EFTS. The incidence of armed robberies and other crimes of violence will decline substantially in a society whose citizenry no longer carries currency. Forgeries and counterfeiting, problems that now plague our society, may also become a thing of the past under EFTS.

The cashless society may also bring with it benefits for our present overburdened Postal Service. EFTS will make it unnecessary for banks and consumers to employ the mails for purposes of making deposits, withdrawals, loan repayments, and a multitude of other financial transactions. EFTS will also eliminate much of the paper work presently connected with payroll and social security checks by directly transferring funds electronically from a business or government account to that of the recipient. In the process, the problem of stolen checks will also be resolved. There should also be an easing of the long bank deposit lines we stand in today. Equally if not more important, the growing costs connected with our checking system will be eliminated.

EFTS may also result in better and increased banking services; store sales may also increase, for customers will no longer have to face long lines. In addition, EFTS will give consumers greater access to their funds, prompting them to spend more. The cashless society may also give the federal savings and loan associations and credit unions a competitive edge over state and national commercial banks, by giving them access to a statewide EFT system.

EFTS will also increasingly give rise to new markets as well as new banking and retail services. They will also tie the multitude of financial institutions into a web of regional and national networks, thus facilitating the transfer of funds.

Critics, however, charge that the cashless society will also give rise to new problem areas. For example, new categories of more sophisticated and complex crimes may take shape. Today's bank robber may give way to tomorrow's electronic criminal. Organized crime may find new opportunities in an EFTS environment. Terrorist groups, a growing international problem, might come to view EFTS as an attractive target—one that, if crippled, could cause serious economic havoc to the target society. Invasions of privacy may also increase in an EFTS environment. The cashless society has its detractors.

OPPOSITION TO EFTS

Some consumer advocates charge that EFTS will open an individual's entire financial history, including his or her most intimate inner secrets, to credit bureaus at the push of a button. The cashless society will augment the dissemination of personal information to third parties. A recent study by the General Accounting Office (GAO) of the U.S. Congress concluded that the threat to privacy under EFTS is a matter of serious concern, one that is founded on a realistic assessment of the present technology. The threat to privacy also carries with it a threat to Constitutional liberties. New crimes, involving the theft of data, will proliferate under EFTS.

Critics also charge that EFTS may reduce competition in the banking sector. The initial costs of the cashless society might prove so high that only a handful of large financial institutions would be able to pay for the expensive technology needed to partake of it. There is justifiable concern that competition in the banking area might be so adversely affected that a handful of banking giants might come to dominate the financial arena. Concern for lessened competition merits serious study.

There is also justifiable concern that EFTS will lessen control over personal finances. The ability to exploit the benefits of the float during the check clearing process will no longer be available to the consumer. EFTS, based on prearranged transfers of funds, limit the individual's ability to manipulate finances. Consumer advocates are also concerned that the canceled check, now used as proof of payment in disputes between consumers and creditors, will no longer be available in the cashless society. In addition, civil disputes may prove difficult and costly to litigate. Evidentiary rules and procedures, such as the hearsay and best evidence rules, may make it difficult to introduce computer printouts, magnetic tapes, or disks into evidence. Today's costly and time-consuming legal process for resolving disputes may become even worse under EFTS.

Consumers now can direct their banks to stop payment on a check, giving them a leverage in their business dealings. In an environment of instantaneous electronic transfers of funds, this leverage will no longer be available to the consumer. There is the added problem of computer error and malfunction. Human error, once entered in the data base, may be difficult to detect and correct.

Fraud, too, is a serious problem. Computer crime is on the increase; computers easily lend themselves to manipulation. A study by the Rand Corporation concluded that there are no major computer defense systems that can withstand a dedicated attack by well-organized and sophisticated criminals. In addition, few law enforcement agencies today have the capability to investigate and bring to prosecution complex computer-related frauds.

Several private and governmental EFTS studies have noted that over 40 percent of the U.S. population is satisfied with the present monetary system. This sizable segment of society shows no inclination to embrace EFTS. On the contrary, many small businessmen, especially those in poor neighborhoods, show little inclination to shift away from the cash economy. The size of this silent opposition raises serious political concerns. Some EFTS critics fear that the powerful financial institutions, in their drive to establish the cashless society, will resort to economic pressure tactics and manipulations.

PRESSURES FOR EFTS

On October 28, 1974, the U.S. Congress established the National Commission on Electronic Fund Transfers (NCEFT), and directed it to conduct a study of the emerging field of EFTS. The NCEFT was also charged with recommending appropriate administrative and legislative actions to the federal government. In October 1977, the NCEFT made a series of recommendations. In large part, these were compromises—attempts to placate the varying competing interests. The NCEFT did not lay the EFTS debate to rest; it continues.

Among other things, the NCEFT noted that the consuming public could benefit if EFTS were developed in an orderly and constructive manner. It recommended that the federal government not involve itself in the operation of any POS systems; rather, these should be left to the private sector. The NCEFT also urged that both large and small financial institutions be allowed to share EFTS facilities where these arrangements would be in conformance with competition.

As regards the implementation of the cashless society, the NCEFT observed that a national EFT system could be supported by as few as 225,000 on-line terminals, installed in general merchandise stores. It also observed that 2800 commercial banks and thrift institutions were already participating in rudimentary EFTS. Consumers were also found to be using EFTS, with varying acceptance. In general, the NCEFT found that in many parts of the United States:

- Bank customers made use of automated teller machines to deposit and withdraw cash 24 hours a day.
- Shopers frequently made use of electronic terminals at retail stores to pay for goods.
- Employees had their pay deposited directly into their checking and saving accounts without ever receiving a paycheck.
- Families payed monthly installments on mortgages and loans by pre-authorized charges to their checking and savings accounts.
- Families paid their regular bills, such as utility and telephone bills, by simply telephoning their bank or thrift institution and authorizing the transfer of funds.

There are currently more than 300 electronic banking programs in the United States. The most common, and probably the simplest, is the check guarantee system, which connects a myriad of terminals in retail stores to a bank's computer. It enables the retailer to determine quickly whether a customer has sufficient funds on account to cover a check; more than 80,000 of these retail terminals are now in operation. Citibank has been a leader in this field, with more than 2500 terminals and investments in excess of $100 million.

Historically, the large commercial banks have been strong proponents of EFTS. The American Bankers Association (ABA), a key organ of the commercial banks, has on numerous occasions voiced approval for EFTS. However, fearful of arousing the ire of the small financial institutions, the commercial banks have, at least publicly, buttressed their support for the cashless society by stressing that EFTS simply represent a new way of delivering old services. They have noted their concern for the rising volume of checks.

However, subtle forces are at work. These have to be further explored to best understand the powerful pressure behind EFTS. Competition from the numerous other depository institutions has prompted the large commercial banks to embrace EFTS; they represent viable technology for a variety of novel banking services. In addition, as the large commercial banks have increasingly made inroads into EFTS, the smaller financial institutions have followed suit for fear of being left out, further stimulating the growth of EFTS.

On the surface, to the unobservant, it would appear that the small depository institutions—among them the savings and loan associations, mutual savings banks, and credit unions—are satisfied with the present payment system and opposed to the establishment of electronic banking. The present system allows the thrift institutions to obtain payment services through a relationship with commercial banks; they need not develop new payment systems and procedures. However, the thrift institutions also regard themselves as second-class citizens; they resent the position of power and strength commercial banks enjoy in the payment process. They view with fear and envy the influx of the large commercial banks into the electronic payment systems. Competitive pressure from the commercial bank sector has prompted the thrifts to follow suit.

Thrift institutions attempted to meet the challenge of the commercial banks initially by offering checking account services. The Wilmington Savings Fund Society of Delaware first took this step in 1971; one year later, the Consumer's Bank of Worcester, Massachusetts, introduced the first NOW account. The mutual savings banks of New York then proceeded to introduce the POW account. In 1974, the Western Savings Fund Society of Philadelphia followed suit with the WOW account. The objective of all these efforts was to allow customers of the bank to draw against their interest-bearing savings accounts.

One of the first efforts by the thrifts to provide a computerized system for the relay of payments messages was the establishment in 1972 of the Mutual Institutions National Transfer System (MINTS) by the National Association of Mutual Savings Banks. Customers of MINTS member banks were issued plastic cards that enabled them to effectuate deposits, withdrawals, and third-party payments through the facilities of other MINTS member banks. In 1974, the First Federal Savings and Loan Association of Lincoln, Nebraska, introduced the Transmatic Money System (TMS); this rudimentary POS system consisted of computer terminals installed in two supermarkets of a local food chain.

In addition to offering the thrifts the opportunity to compete successfully with the large commercial banks, EFTS have also drawn the attention of retailers. The cost of forgery and fraud related to checks is said to run in excess of $5 billion a year. Moreover, costs related to the float, loss of time, and user inconvenience account for an additional several billion dollars in annual losses. Retailers frequently complain that credit verification is both difficult and time consuming; present check verification systems leave much to be desired. The costs related to check cashing operations are also increasing and have become prohibitive for the small retailers. To this must be added the increasing costs associated with clerical help.

The operation of private credit record systems has also become costly and difficult for the retailer. Compliance with privacy legislation has further prompted small retail operations to rely on outside credit organizations and bank credit cards. A growing number of retailers have demonstrated a willingness to embrace EFTS in response to these pressures.

Competition within the retail industry has given further impetus to the rise of EFTS. The influx of large retail institutions into the electronic payments system has prompted the smaller retailers to follow suit. Today's small retailer, prompted by the increasing costs of doing business and also by competition from the large retailers, has shown an inclination to shift to the cashless society.

The business community, too, has shown an increasing willingness to embrace the EFTS. Employers are growing more dissatisfied with the high costs connected with large payrolls; some businesses also find that they must provide their employees with specific time allowances for cashing their paychecks. Banking, clerical, and accounting costs connected with employer payrolls along with losses that stem from frauds, thefts, and bookkeeping errors have all prompted a shift to EFTS. Some firms, especially those that handle voluminous mailings, see EFTS as a simplified procedure that would reduce the massive costs involved in mailing millions of bills to clients.

Pressure for the development and implementation of EFTS has also come from a number of federal agencies. Like the private sector, the federal government finds itself the victim of fraud, counterfeiting, forgery, thefts of checks, and record keeping errors. The federal government, as the country's largest employer, must also bear the increasing costs connected with its massive payroll; many federal agencies encourage their employees to accept a preauthorized deposit system. The agencies are also seeking to automate the billions of dollars in payments they make to more than 40 million Americans, through an array of social programs. However, agencies have also been prompted to act by political considerations; they have sought to safeguard the economic interests of their constituencies.

In April 1974, both the Treasury Department and Social Security Administration (SSA) agreed to implement a direct deposit automated program. The Treasury and SSA programs also found favor within the military branches. In November 1974, the U.S. Air Force commenced its own direct deposit automated program. Authority for these moves was based in Public Law 92-366 (31 U.S. CA 492, as amended August 7, 1972). This statute provides for the making of direct payments to a financial institution selected by the beneficiary. The institution may be a bank, savings and loan association, or credit union. In early 1976, the Treasury, in conjunction with the Federal Reserve System, embarked on a pilot EFTS project; the objective was the establishment of a nationwide EFTS. The Treasury hopes to convert 50 percent of its check volume to some form of EFTS by 1985.

The Federal Home Loan Bank Board (FHLBB) has also studied EFTS and its potential implications for the savings and loan (S&L) industry. It has taken active steps to provide a regulatory climate that will facilitate a shift by S&L institutions (its constituency) to EFTS. The FHLBB has concluded that EFTS offers potential new marketing opportunities for the S&L industry. A large percentage of savings deposits at S&Ls comes from payroll checks, either deposited directly or mailed by employees to their S&Ls. However, the proliferation of ACH systems has increasingly given commercial banks an edge, since only the latter have been allowed to be designated as depositories.

In an effort to improve the competitive stance of the S&Ls, in 1974 the FHLBB accepted over 40 applications from member S&Ls for the establishment of Remote Service Units (RSUs). In March 1976, the FHLBB extended enacted rules to allow federal S&Ls to openly experiment with EFTS.

Savings and loan organizations have attempted, in the last several years, to enter the full-service banking area and attract lucrative customer deposits away from the commercial banks. The S&Ls are now reviewing the entire consumer banking area; especially attractive are such services as consolidated monthly financial statements showing the status of savings, mortgage loans, and consumer loan accounts. EFTS incorporate an array of services, including preauthorized bill payments and point-of-sale systems, offering the S&Ls a medium to compete effectively with commercial banks.

The Federal Reserve System, long dominated by the larger commercial banks, has also displayed an interest in EFTS. In the 1970s, the Fed spent a sizable amount of money in the development of EFTS. It has constructed a nationwide electronic communications network (Fed Wire), which offers a medium for the implementation of a national EFT system. The Fed's member banks have been quick to see the advantages of EFTS, and, with the open support of the Fed, have moved in the direction of automated banking.

The Federal Deposit Insurance Corporation (FDIC) has also encouraged the development and implementation of EFTS. The FDIC has taken the position that EFTS should develop along lines that will maximize competition and minimize unfair trade practices. The FDIC is concerned with safeguarding the interests of its constituency. In an effort to promote the growth of EFTS, the FDIC took the position in the early developmental stages of EFTS that customer-bank-communication-terminals (CBCTs) were not branches. The FDIC has actively encouraged member banks to partake in the cashless society, for fear that EFTS would otherwise fall under the control of the large financial institutions.

On December 12, 1974, the national banks received temporary support from the Comptroller of the Currency in their quest to establish branches nationwide. The Comptroller announced that the National Bank Act did not prohibit national banks from establishing CBCTs nationwide. Under this ruling, the national banks would be allowed to compete and operate in an EFTS environment, free of geographic restrictions placed on them by state law. The ruling would permit the national banks to establish CBCTs within a state, free of branching law restrictions. However, the smaller banks, fearful that the Comptroller's holding would give the large national banks a competitive edge, went to federal court. In January 1975, the Independent Bankers Association of America (IBAA) sued the Comptroller; it asked the Court to invalidate the Comptroller's Interpretive Ruling. The Courts held in favor of the IBAA. The national banks suffered a temporary reverse in their efforts to use EFTS as a tool for nationwide expansion.

The Antitrust Division of the U.S. Justice Department, fearful that EFTS could fall under the sway of the larger financial institutions, encourages competition in the development of EFTS. The cashless society must be free of anticompetitive practices. In the Division's eyes, the private sector must be encouraged to foster the growth of EFTS open to both large and small financial institutions. The Division has also warned that if any banks or other institutions band together to monopolize EFTS, it will charge them with violating federal antitrust laws.

The Federal Communications Commission (FCC) has also become vitally involved in the area of EFTS. Of vital concern to the FCC is whether EFTS are communications systems, which would fall under its jurisdiction. Communications systems that employ wire or broadcast electronic communication have traditionally been under the ambit of the FCC's jurisdiction. However, whether EFTS can be similarly regulated remains to be fully addressed.

The pressures for EFTS are diverse and numerous. Powerful financial interests view EFTS as a medium that offers new marketing and banking opportunities. The smaller financial institutions, fearful that the large banking interests will monopolize EFTS, have also shown interest. Government agencies, in an attempt to safeguard the interests of their constituencies, have also taken steps to facilitate the entry of their constituents into EFTS.

Businessmen and retailers view EFTS as a cost-saving tool that will eliminate much of the present red tape and improve their competitive standing. The giant computer manufacturers see EFTS as a potential multibillion dollar annual market. For the many firms that provide an array of computer-related services, EFTS represents a growing market.

EFTS are technologies made possible by the advent of the modern computer age. They constitute one of the wonders of the twentieth century. The cashless society is upon us; we must understand both the technology and the forces that propel it, lest we suffer its evils.

2
THE AVAILABILITY OF TECHNOLOGY

A large Virginia bank handles more than 2 million transactions, involving $148 million, through its ATM network. In Delaware, a major bank switched to truncation two years ago; in its first year it saved $70,000, and the second year it saved more than $100,000. Further, the bank reduced its staff. It now hires one individual for every 6000 of its accounts; prior to truncation, it employed one person for every 2000 new accounts. In a separate development, the U.S. Postal Service (USPS) has proposed that a computerized mail service be implemented. The system, to be run by the USPS, would allow a sender to enter a message into an electronic message system that would be delivered to its destination the next day.

Computers now are used throughout the United States to streamline bank operations, keep track of parts inventories, design highways, diagnose disease, generate trade names, set type in print, and track airplanes. In 1950, there were only 15 operational computers in this country. By 1960, the number had grown to 50,000. There are predictions that by 1985 it will exceed 500,000. The computer revolution grows daily.

Of the more than 100,000 general purpose computers in use in the United States, over 10,000 are used by the federal government. In addition, a new and expanding market in minicomputers is rapidly growing; there are more than 170,000 of these small, relatively inexpensive units in use in this country. The value of the computer market has also risen dramatically in the last several years. In 1970, government and industry spent in excess of $20 billion on computer-related equipment; by 1985, the figure will easily exceed $100 billion.

The growing number of computers are staffed by an army of several million operators, programmers, technicians, and managers. Computer technology has given rise to the cashless society. The computer has come to constitute the backbone of EFTS; without this workhorse of modern technology, electronic banking systems would be impossible.

DEFINING THE COMPUTER

A computer is a machine that performs complex processes on information without manual intervention. Computers fall into one of two categories: special or general purpose. Special-purpose computers are designed for a specific role; they are wired internally to repeat the same sequence of operations. They are often referred to as limited-purpose computers. Computers employed by airlines to implement reservations are usually special-purpose types. A special-purpose computer cannot be made to perform a new task by simply changing the instructions under which it operates. To change its functions, it is necessary to rewire the computer. Unlike general-purpose computers, special-purpose computers are not programmable.

General-purpose computers can be employed to do any of a variety of tasks by simply changing their instructions (programs). There is no need to rewire the system; the user simply changes the program. By merely changing the program, the operator also changes the tasks the computer performs. General-purpose computers can be employed in a variety of roles because of their flexibility.

Until around 1960, general-purpose computers were divided between those employed in the business world and those employed in science. Business general-purpose computers were initially designed to perform a small amount of computing with voluminous data, whereas scientific general-purpose computers were first employed to perform lengthy scientific calculations using a small amount of data. However, the distinction between general-purpose computers employed in business and science has disappeared.

General-purpose computers can be either analog or digital types. Analog machines have the potential to do many activities in parallel. They can solve a series of equations in the same time it takes to solve a single equation. Digital machines take longer to solve a set of equations than their analog counterparts. However, digital machines have greater storage capacity and can be programmed with greater ease. It is this greater storage capability and programming ease that makes digital computers more attractive to the financial sector. Analog machines, however, prevail in the technical business sector; for example, analog machines frequently are used to design nuclear power plants.

Digital computers are also simple in operation. They will accept data and information presented to them in its required form, carry out arithmetic and logical operations on these raw data, and then supply the required results in an acceptable form. The resulting (output) data produced by these logical operations are fully dependent on the information fed into the computer (input). The sequence of operations required to produce the desired output is specified by a programmer, who prepares a set of instructions that guide the operations of the computer.

Digital computers are characterized as belonging to one of several generations; each generation is distinguished from the other by the electronic components most prevalent in it. First-generation digital computers are distinguished by their extensive use of vacuum tubes and also by their large size. These computers were easily identified by their bulkiness—some so large that they filled several rooms. Second-generation digital computers are often distinguished by their extensive use of transistors and their smaller size, some being no larger than a small office desk. Third-generation digital computers are distinguished by their use of integrated circuits; they are best represented by the IBM System 360. Third-generation computers make use of millions of microelectronic circuits, called solid logic technology. The modern computer is easily identified by both its small size and speed; it may be no larger than a file drawer and thousands of times faster than its giant predecessors.

The computer is largely responsible for the growth and proliferation of EFTS. It is a technology that merits further exporation so that we may best understand its impact on our cashless society.

EVOLUTION OF COMPUTER TECHNOLOGY

The earliest known calculator in the history of civilization is said to be the abacus. It was widely used for more than 3000 years by such diverse people as the ancient Egyptians, Indians, Romans, and the Chinese; it continues to enjoy wide use in Asia. It was not, however, until 1642 that Blaise Pascal, the noted mathematician-philosopher, invented the first modern mechanical adding machine. The most important feature of Pascal's small box-size mechanical calculator was its ability to carry a one to the next column. A wheel within the machine moved from a nine to zero, and then a second wheel to its left advanced one digit. This constituted a radical improvement from previous adding machines.

Thirty years later, the German mathematician Gottfried Leibnitz proposed the construction of a mechanical machine that would perform multiplication by repeated addition. The machine was constructed in 1694, but found poor reception. In 1820, the French scientist Thomas of Colmar constructed a calculator similar in design to the Leibnitz machine. Like its predecessor, the Thomas machine did not prove sufficiently attractive to Europe's business community. However, Thomas did manage to sell some of his machines to the French government. These forerunners of the modern computer were still in their infancy; few businessmen took them seriously.

The experiments continued. Europe's nineteenth-century business community was in need of a mechanical calculator that could enable its army of clerks to keep abreast of its dramatic expansion. Europe's governments, growing more centralized in structure, also needed a tool to enable them to keep track of their increasing populations for purposes of taxation and the census. It was this political and economic climate that sparked Joseph Marie Jacquard to follow in the footsteps of Pascal and Leibnitz.

Jacquard's machine was modeled after an automatic loom first invented by Jacques de Vaucanson to weave tapestries and rugs. To improve the efficiency of his machine, Jacquard used punched sheets of stiff paper as controls; these proved both easy and economical to change. With the assistance of these punched cards, Jacquard's machine could weave repetitive patterns. Jacquard had hoped that his machine would revolutionize the weaving industry. He did not foresee his machine as the forerunner of the twentieth-century's special-purpose computer.

In 1824, Charles Babbage was able to sway the British government to help him finance a calculator that incorporated a punched-card system. The machine would be used to perform algebraic functions and print the results on paper. However, Babbage's machine could handle only simple mathematical problems and proved of little value in handling complex calculations. By 1834, the British government had withdrawn its financial backing. Babbage persisted and sought private backing for his work. In 1871, he completed the construction of his analytical engine.

The Babbage machine was a breakthrough: it had all the basic components of a modern digital computer. It had the capacity to store, control, and input/output. Its memory had the capacity to hold 50,000 digits, and the control function was carried out by the use of punched cards. Babbage's analytical engine had the ability not only to add and subtract but also to multiply—all in less than a minute. His machines inspired other inventors. One of these, Torres y Quevedo, constructed a typewriter-controlled analytical machine.

The 1880s saw the invention of the felt-box machine in America. This was a key-driven calculator, constructed from a wooden macaroni box. About this same time, William S. Burroughs constructed his listening-accountant. This machine incorporated features of both the felt-machine and Pascal's seventeenth-century mechanical calculator. Burroughs's adding machine was the first mechanical calculating machine specifically designed for mass production. It also launched the Burroughs Company into the twentieth-century computer market.

In 1879, Herman Hollerith was graduated from Columbia College; soon afterward, he went to work for the U.S. Census Office. In 1882, he left the Census Office and took a job at the Massachusetts Institute of Technology; it was here that he commenced construction of his census machine. Eight years later, in time for the national census, Hollerith constructed a mechanical calculator that proved highly successful; it incorporated some of the principles of Jacquard's automatic loom machine and made use of an automatic card-feeding mechanism.

Hollerith's census machine soon found great applicability in the accounting area. By the turn of the century, his machines were widely used by large railroads to keep records concerning their boxcars, insurance companies used them in their actuarial work, and large retail stores employed them to keep track of their inventory. Even the government of Czarist Russia called on Hollerith to help it with its census.

In 1896, Hollerith founded the Tabulating Machine Company (TBC); in 1917, TBC merged with two other growing computer companies and changed its name to International Business Machines Company, Ltd. (IBM). By 1920, Hollerith's computing machines had won great acceptance in both the United States and Europe. In 1927, one of his machines was used to compute the positions of the moon for the remainder of the twentieth century. The astronomical data were punched into 500,000 cards; the computations proved accurate and of great value to both astronomers and mariners.

Punched-card machines became very popular in the 1930s, when they were employed by major corporations. Users increasingly called on computer manufacturers to develop faster and more accurate machines. In 1937, Professor Howard Aiken of Harvard University approached IBM with a proposal to construct a giant computing machine. The machine was finally constructed in 1943 at IBM's laboratories and was known as the Mark I (Automatic Sequence Controlled Calculator). This giant computer, which used a perforated paper tape program, could multiply two 23-digit numbers in six seconds.

Technological breakthroughs permeated the computer industry in the 1940s. In 1940, the Bell Telephone Laboratories constructed their giant Model I computer and commenced operating it in their New York offices. The Bell computer was capable of adding, subtracting, multiplying, and dividing complex numbers faster and more accurately than any of its predecessors. The Bell Company followed its success with the Model V computer; this model was a general-purpose computer, which proved to be both efficient and accurate. The Model V found wide acceptance in both business and government.

During this same period, computer science was also progressing in Europe. In 1944, Konrad Zuse constructed the Z-3 machine in Germany. The Zuse computer was constructed with telephone relays; it could store 64 floating-point binary numbers and was faster than IBM's Mark I. Zuse also constructed the Z-4, a highly efficient and versatile computer.

Another major computer breakthrough took place in 1946. Two American scientists, John Mauchly and J. Presper Eckert, working at the Moore School of Electrical Engineering at the University of Pennsylvania, constructed the giant ENIAC computer. The Mauchly machine was a general-purpose computer; it had the ability to perform 5000 arithmetic operations per second. The ENIAC was by far the most complex and reliable computer yet constructed; it was 1000 times faster than the Mark I and made use of more than 18,000 vacuum tubes.

A series of other computers, forerunners of the modern computer, also made their appearance during this period. In 1947, IBM came out with its Selective Sequence Electronic Calculator (SSEC). The SSEC made use of 23,000 relays and 13,000 vacuum tubes, and it soon became one of the most widely used commercial computers of its day. During this same period, John von Neumann constructed the EDVAC. Although smaller than the

ENIAC, the EDVAC had a larger memory capacity and made use of fewer tubes. The EDVAC marks the first generation of modern general-purpose computers. It became a model for the computer industry.

In 1949, a team of British scientists constructed the first stored program computer. This was followed in 1950 with the construction of the Standards Electronic Automatic Computer (SEAC) by the National Bureau of Standards. SEAC was designed primarily for use by the military. SEAC made use of only 750 vacuum tubes; it also employed a manual keyboard for direct input, and a teletypewriter for direct output. SEAC proved itself to be a sturdy workhorse and was not retired until 1964.

About this same time, the Whirlwind I computer made its appearance; it employed paper tape input/output devices and used only 6800 vacuum tubes. In 1951, the Remington Rand Company constructed the Universal Automatic Computer, (UNIVAC I). The UNIVAC computer was much smaller than ENIAC; it used only 5000 vacuum tubes and could add in 2 microseconds. It also made significant use of magnetic tapes as an input/output medium. In 1952, it was used to analyze the outcome of the Presidential election, predicting that Eisenhower would be the winner.

Competition between computer manufacturers increased dramatically in the 1950s. General Electric, RCA, NCR, Sperry Rand, Honeywell, and Control Data Corporation also entered the market. Honeywell introduced its Datamatic 1000 series, and an NCR subsidiary introduced the CADAC 100 model. IBM, however, soon took the lead in 1953 with its 701 model; it reinforced that position two years later with the introduction of its 702 model.

This first generation of computers made wide use of vacuum tubes. However, the invention of the transistor in 1948 made it possible to construct a new generation of computers. This second generation of computers made its appearance in 1959; these computers were smaller, less bulky, and more efficient than their predecessors.

RISE OF SUPERCOMPUTERS

A key reason for constructing faster computers is to achieve high processing speeds. This allows a user to complete tasks faster and engage in new and more complex computations that would have proven impractical with slower machines. The first generation of modern computers, like the Mark I, used fewer than 10,000 electrical relays and performed arithmetic operations at a rate of one per second. In the 1940s, the vacuum tube was first used in the ENIAC; this led to an increase in performance by a factor of 1000.

By 1950, many of the complex features that we associate with the modern computer had made their appearance. The speed of computers has increased dramatically each year since the construction of UNIVAC I. We now are approaching speeds in excess of 1 billion operations per second. The first generation of modern computers had a maximum primary memory of 1000 words; today's supercomputers have primary memories that easily exceed 1 million words.

The second generation of computers appeared in 1959; the transistor supplanted the vacuum tube as the active component of the computer. IBM manufactured the 709 TX computer; Philco Corporation engineers constructed the TRANSAC S-2000, and NCR introduced its 315 series. NCR's computers featured a shift to a magnetic card cartridge auxiliary memory. The Burroughs Corporation introduced the 5000 System, and Manchester University constructed its Atlas computer. Some of these second-generation computers were ahead of their time in design and served to bridge the technological gap needed to shift to a more advanced phase in computer technology.

In 1964, the third generation of computers made their appearance. IBM introduced its System 360; Control Data introduced its 6600 System, and RCA introduced the Spectra 70 series. Not to be outdone, Sperry Rand introduced its 1108 System. Many of the features of the IBM 360 soon became the standard of the industry, further assuring IBM's leadership in the computer industry. Texas Instruments developed its Advanced Scientific Computer (ASC), and Burroughs introduced its 5500 series. General Electric made its third-generation entry with the 600 series, as did Honeywell with its 200 system.

The late 1960s also witnessed the use and proliferation of the minicomputer. Minicomputer manufacturers relied heavily on microprogramming techniques to increase the versatility of their machines. The Digital Equipment Corporation was quick to see the potential of the minicomputer market; in 1968, it gained a dominant position with the introduction of its PDP-8 System. The PDP-11 Digital System, a more powerful minicomputer, was introduced two years later. Data General Corporation also made its entry in the minicomputer market with its NOVA and super-NOVA series. Hewlett-Packard and Inter-Data followed suit with their own models. The modern computer era has also witnessed the rise of microcomputers.

Increasingly, laser technology holds the promise of dramatic improvements in the capability of our modern computers. Computer service bureaus now offer both national and international hook-up services. Corporate giants now link their numerous offices in elaborate data processing networks; both national and international reservation and credit-checking systems have taken shape. All this has been made possible largely by the rise of computer technology. The abacus of antiquity has given way to a generation of supercomputers.

BASICS OF A COMPUTER OPERATION

The key elements of any computer system can be divided into (1) equipment elements (hardware) and (2) program elements (software). The hardware components of a computer system consist of the central processing unit (CPU), input-output devices, and auxiliary storage; the software components consist of a collection of computer programs associated with the computer.

The computer program itself is a planned procedure for solving a problem or series of problems; it consists of a series of instructions to the computer, to be performed on the data. The instructions are prepared by a programmer and fed into the machine. Without the software (programming elements), the computer is a helpless giant without direction.

The CPU is the heart of the computer. It consists of the circuitry, which controls the input and output units, and also the auxiliary attachments. The CPU interprets and executes the instructions it receives from the program elements; it also contains fast memory or storage devices that can hold a program and data. It is the focal point of the system; it receives data from input units and file storage units and then carries out a variety of arithmetic and logical operations on these data. The CPU also transmits the results to the output and file units.

A CPU consists of three key components: the memory unit, the arithmetic and logic unit, and the control unit. The function of the memory unit is to store data; the CPU's operations are carried out within the arithmetic and logic unit; and the control unit ensures that the computer operates in accord with the instructions it receives from the program.

The input unit of the computer accepts the raw data that the machine uses; input devices read the information from such media as paper tape or punched cards. Typewriterlike devices are also used to communicate with the computer.

It is the input unit that converts the data from the written language to a form understandable to the computer. The data may be punched into cards or paper tape; the information is then read off the card or tape by a special electromechanical device known as a reader. The reader then converts the data from the cards or tapes into electronic impulses, which are then communicated to the computer. Modified electric typewriters or teletype machines are also frequently used as input devices. Teletype machines are most frequently employed by an operator to communicate with the computer.

The output unit takes information as directed by the computer's program from the CPU, and then records those data on some medium, such as a printer, display unit, paper tape, or punched card. Typewriterlike devices are often preferred for low-volume printed output; they may be situated within the computer facility or at a remote terminal. Video-display units have also gained acceptance as output units. In the latter case, the output data appear on a televisionlike tube. The advantage of the video-display unit is that it can handle a large volume of data and generate additional information very rapidly. The disadvantage, however, is that unlike the printer, the video display unit does not produce a hard copy or a permanent record.

Paper tapes and punched cards have also been used increasingly as output units. In addition, magnetic tapes are also gaining favor as output units. Magnetic tapes can operate at higher speeds than their paper counterparts.

However, paper output units continue to be favored because they are less costly.

The auxiliary storage unit is the filing cabinet of a computer system. Computerized records may be held in one of several storage devices; the commonly favored are magnetic tapes, disks, and drums. These storage units differ in both performance and price. Data stored on magnetic tape files must be maintained in some predetermined sequence; new input data must also be stored in the same sequence.

Magnetic disks have increasingly gained favor within the industry; they are more efficient than magnetic tapes. Data on disks can be easily corrected, changed, and modified. However, disks are more costly than tapes. Magnetic drums have also gained wide acceptance as storage mediums. Data stored on a drum can be retrieved faster than is the case with either disk or tape storage. However, drums are more expensive than tapes or disks, and this factor has stifled their growth as storage devices.

Every computer program must meet two basic tests: it must have instructions that specify to the computer the operations it must perform, and it must also specify and identify the location of the information that is to be referenced or manipulated. There are several types of program; one of the more common types, especially in areas involving inventory, payroll, and accounting, is the application program. A more widely used set of instructions, especially in routine processing, is the generalized or packaged program. This last program frequently is modified by the computer user to accommodate the needs of the organization.

Two additional types of program, usually supplied by the manufacturers themselves, are the compiler and assembly programs. These programs are often employed to translate application programs into computer language. Moreover, the computer manufacturers have themselves created an array of additional programming languages. Common languages are ALGOL (Algorithmic Language), FORTRAN (Formula Translater), and COBOL (Common Business-Oriented Language). FORTRAN has traditionally been favored by the military services, whereas COBOL has gained greater acceptance within the business sector. This array of programs, program languages, and computers has retarded attempts to establish uniform standards within the industry.

Computer technology is still in its infancy; today's supercomputers will soon be dwarfed by a new generation of machines. It is this technology that has made the cashless society a possibility.

3
UNDERSTANDING EFTS

In several states—New York, Pennsylvania, and Minnesota, for example—bank customers are able to pay their bills by simply dialing their bank's computer. Customers of the Farmers and Mechanics Savings Bank in Minneapolis can pay their bills electronically with the aid of a touch-tone phone. The customer simply punches in a secret identifying code and the amount of money to be paid. Each month, the customer is supplied with a statement and a payment register book.

In the suburbs of Washington, D.C., a credit union member enters one of the many People's Drug Stores and pushes a plastic card into an electronic teller machine located inside the store. The card, in turn, activates a computer located in Valley Forge, Pennsylvania, that keeps records for 10 major credit unions that are participating in the program. The network is the first off-premises system of automated teller machines for credit unions; it enables more than 30,000 credit union members in the Washington, D.C., area to transact business without the need to go to their local credit union offices. The credit unions provide the more than $200,000 needed to operate the system.

EFTS terminals can be found everywhere; they perform a variety of banking services. They accept deposits, dispense cash, transfer funds, authorize credit or check transactions, make credit purchases, and even provide data concerning the status of a customer's account. Terminals located in retail stores assist in collecting information that can be valuable for purposes of inventory control and marketing.

EFTS represent the application of computer technology to the financial arena. EFTS constitute an array of automated payment systems, in which the merger of computer and telecommunications technology is employed to improve the efficiency of our present payments system. The basic components of this electronic payments system are with us; the quiet EFTS revolution is here.

BASIC ELEMENTS OF EFTS

Many Americans pay their utility, insurance, and department store bills without using cash or checks. Our paper payment system is undergoing a subtle transformation. The basic components of this revolution take on various forms: automated clearing houses, point-of-sale services, automated teller machines, preauthorized credits and debits, and telephone-billpaying services, among others. These basic elements constitute the needed pillars for the coming cashless society. To understand the EFTS revolution, we begin by scrutinizing the components of the electronic banking revolution.

Automated Clearing Houses

Jane Jones recently received a $500 stock dividend from the Ding Dong Company. She wants the dividend credited to her sister's account and instructs her financial institution to take appropriate steps. The financial institution proceeds to record the amount involved on a magnetic tape, which is then delivered to an ACH. The ACH debits the account of the Ding Dong Company for $500, and credits that of Ms. Jones's sister.

Ms. Jones also instructs her financial institution to pay her $50 utility bill. The financial institution records the amount Ms. Jones wants debited on a magnetic tape; the tape is then delivered to an ACH, which credits the utility company's account for $50.

The ACH constitutes one of the most fundamental forms of EFTS; it is also one of the first operational forms of EFTS. The ACH is a computerized, interbank transfer system through which an originating bank transmits payment orders electronically or on computer tapes. These payments are then routed by the ACH to designated receiving banks.

A typical process commences with a computerized list of payment orders from one or more payers. On the list are recorded the names and account numbers of the payees, those of their banks, and also the amount to be paid each. The list is transmitted, electronically, by the payer's bank computer to the ACH computer; the latter sorts out the information and directs the payment orders to the appropriate receiving bank.

The ACH process has replaced check clearing facilities with electronic entry systems, which clear by means of electronic impulses. The key advantage to an ACH is the increased speed by which balances can be adjusted at a common clearing bank, freeing these balances for other uses more quickly than under the manual system employed by many check clearing facilities.

The ACH movement originated in April 1968, with the establishment of the Special Committee on Paperless Entries (SCOPE) in California. SCOPE was founded and organized by the Los Angeles and San Francisco Clearing House Association with the objective of studying ways to reduce the increasing paper glut facing the financial community. That same year, the ABA established its own Payments System Planning Committee (MAPS) in the hope of improving the efficiency of our monetary system.

In 1971, MAPS recommended the establishment of automated clearing houses. A year later, the California Automated Clearing House Association, a private banking group made up of California banks, commenced operation. Several months later, the Georgia Automated Clearing House Association commenced similar operations on the East Coast. ACH systems were designed primarily to replace checks as mechanisms for making insurance, mortgage and other recurring payments by consumers. The ACH also provides for the automation of wages, dividends, and other recurring payments to consumers.

By December 1974, ACH facilities were operating in such major cities as San Francisco, Los Angeles, Minneapolis, Atlanta, and Boston. During this same period of time, the National Automated Clearing House Association (NACHA) was established; its original membership included population centers in all Federal Reserve districts. The NACHA was established with the objectives of promoting the ACH concept and establishing guidelines and standards for the exchange of payments between ACHs.

To ensure consistency with the rules and policies of the Federal Reserve, ACH associations often coordinate with the Fed operating rules they establish for their members. The success of the ACH system is in large measure an outgrowth of several factors. The needed technology is readily available, at an acceptable cost; for example, the initial start-up cost for the average ACH is less than $1 million. ACH operations traditionally have had strong backing from the Fed; a number of other federal agencies also view ACHs as a medium for direct deposit programs for recurring benefits and payrolls.

The very simplicity of the ACH operation makes it attractive. An ACH system involves only a small number of financial actors, among them a private ACH association, corporate and individual customers, and the Fed. The ACH facility offers participating depository institutions numerous services, including direct deposits of payrolls and preauthorized bill payments. ACH facilities are extremely useful in processing direct deposits of federal recurring payments such as social security payments. ACH facilities parallel, in many respects, check clearing operations; they differ only in that ACH financial data are exchanged on magnetic tape rather than on paper checks. Clearing, delivery, and settlement services for ACH payments are currently provided by the Fed, without any specific charges to the depository institutions using the system.

The Fed's interest in EFTS began in 1915, when the Federal Reserve Board first authorized use of the telegraph system to transmit the Fed's financial data. Banks have been able to integrate ACH operations at a fraction of the cost; ACH's employ the same Fed computer and delivery systems that are used to process and deliver paper checks. The Fed's ACH operation is simple; Fed banks receive private sector originated ACH payments on computer tapes from member banks and member associations, including thrift institutions. The Fed banks then distribute these items to member banks and member ACH associations.

Where federal recurring payments are involved, the Fed acts as the fiscal agent of the government. Fed banks provide clearing, settlement, and delivery functions under rules jointly established with the U.S. Treasury. These regulations provide for the delivery of these payments to all depository institutions, regardless of whether they are ACH members.

There are now more than 30 ACHs in operation; by the mid-1980s the number will grow to 50. Hundreds of major corporations (among them Xerox, Dow Chemical, and Hewlett Packard) now electronically deposit the salaries of their employees directly into their bank accounts. Further, more than 50 percent of the Air Force's payroll is deposited automatically through the use of ACHs. By the early 1980s, more than 25 million federal government employee salaries will be deposited through a checkless payroll system employing ACHs.

The ACH is designed to handle a number of transactions. It can handle debit and credit transfers, where corporate customers instruct depository institutions to pay or collect funds from consumers. An ACH can also process fund transfers in cases where a consumer instructs a depository institution to make payments on his or her behalf. A consumer can also direct a depository institution, through a terminal located at a retail establishment, to make payments to specific individuals or retailers. The depository institution records these payment orders on computer magnetic tape for deposit at an ACH; the latter clears and settles the payments on those dates listed in its instructions.

Point-of-Sale Systems

One of the first POS efforts occurred in 1974, in Nebraska. A small thrift institution, the First Federal Savings and Loan of Lincoln, set up electronic terminals in two Hinky Dinky supermarkets. First Federal customers were issued cards and were authorized to make deposits and withdrawals at these two stores, even when First Federal offices were closed. In addition, these pilot POS transactions could be handled at a cost of $0.05 per transaction as compared with the manual teller cost of $2 for a similar transaction. The system proved so successful that First Federal attracted more than 100 new accounts each week.

The POS system has been described as the purest EFT system now available; the ultimate success of the cashless society may depend on the widespread acceptance and use of POS systems by the public at large. In a POS system, a terminal is installed at a location where the sale will be transacted; the terminal, in turn, is linked to the computer of a financial institution. A POS terminal can be used to process deposits, withdrawals, and interaccount transfers, and also to verify account balances and pre-authorized credit extensions. In a POS, on-line electronic messages involving the instantaneous verification of accounts and the transfer of funds from customers to merchants replace present traditional paper flow systems. POS terminals eliminate, in large part, the requirement of paper flow in the initial payments transaction.

A POS also electronically captures and transmits payments information originating at a merchant's location; this is accomplished by transmitting a message from a terminal located at a merchant's counter to a data base in a depository institution's computer. The object is to transfer funds or to provide an information service such as verifying or guaranteeing a check of authorizing a draw against a preestablished line of credit.

Unlike an ACH transaction, which is preauthorized by the customer and initiated by the company or by the customer through his depository institution, POS transactions are initiated individually at an electronic terminal by the customer through a merchant or other terminal operator. POS transactions also require immediate and unique authorization by the depository institution where the customer's account resides. Whereas most ACH transactions are initiated by employers (of corporations or government agencies) and may entail regional or national distribution, POS transactions are more local in nature. They frequently occur in local stores, involving a customer doing business with a local merchant.

One of the pilot POS projects was carried out in 1971, by the Hempstead Bank of Long Island, New York. Bank customers were issued coded cards and terminals were installed in 35 local stores. A customer making a purchase at one of these participating stores would hand the coded card to the store who, in turn, would enter it into a terminal. The customer then keyed in a secret code, and the bank's computer would electronically debit the customer's account and credit that of the store. About this same time, the City National Bank of Columbus, Ohio, undertook a similar POS pilot project. POS terminals were installed in several suburban stores in the Columbus area. The system was most frequently used to obtain credit authorizations.

In 1973, the First National City Bank of New York issued more than 700,000 cards to its customers. These Citibank cards were intended to be used primarily for credit authorization purposes. One of the more extensive POS systems was constructed in St. Louis, Missouri. In 1977, POS terminals were installed in 42 Schnucks markets; eight area savings and loan associations partook in the project. The pilot POS system allowed customers of these participating S&Ls to make deposits or withdrawals from their savings accounts at the 42 Schnucks stores, eliminating the need for trips to the offices of the participating S&Ls.

To date, three types of POS systems have taken root. The first, and most rudimentary type of POS system, is the *simple model*. In this system, the customer and the store have accounts at the same bank. When a customer makes a purchase at a participating store, data from his or her card and the customer's secret code (PIN) are transmitted to the bank's computer via conventional telephone lines. Additional data, such as the item purchased, date of purchase, amount of the sale, and the store terminal number are also transmitted to the bank's computer. The computer compares the value of the transaction with the balance in the customer's account; if there are sufficient funds in the account, the computer authorizes completion of the sale. It automatically debits the customer's account and credits that of the store. The customer immediately receives a printed receipt at the store; the bank will later send them both the customer and the store a regular monthly statement that lists the transactions conducted.

This one-bank POS, however, is neither realistic nor capable of handling regional or national EFTS transactions. A more sophisticated type of POS is needed to handle a multibank operation; this second type of POS is the *transition model*. This system involves two or more banks; the customer's account is often not with the store's bank.

When the customer makes a purchase in the transition POS, the store (as with the simple POS) dials the customer's bank's computer; the computer scans the customer's account to see if sufficient funds exist to cover the sale. If sufficient funds exist, the computer authorizes the sale. However, unlike the simple POS, the credit entry into the store's account is delayed; the entry is made on a magnetic tape, for later delivery to an ACH. At the ACH, separate (secondary) tapes are prepared from this tape. These secondary tapes consist of credit entries destined for specific banks (among them, the store's bank). Each secondary tape is then delivered to its respective (store) bank; at the bank; the data center makes the credit entry into the appropriate (store's) account.

A third POS, more sophisticated than the previous two systems, is the *network model*. The requisite technology is available to make the network POS both possible and feasible. This third type of POS is distinguished from the other two systems by the inclusion of switches (special subsystems). A *network switch* is a large computer system designed to perform complex communications processing. The system's computer is housed in a facility called the Switching and Processing Center (SPC). An SPC will serve all member system stores and banks in a given locality. A regional or national POS system would consist of multiple switches, each switch servicing a designated locality.

POS systems have found great acceptance among merchants. A POS enhances the merchant's inventory control; the ability to record sales of individual products enables the merchant to maintain an up to date inventory record. POS systems also represent savings for the merchant; it minimizes losses from errors on charge sales and eliminates the need for a large staff for purposes of credit authorization. POS systems also increase customer satisfaction because of the reduced checkout time; they improve the efficiency of the sales force and provide control over merchandise ticketing (when tickets are generated by the computer).

POS systems, however, also suffer from some serious drawbacks. They are vulnerable to security breaches in key areas: customer identification, communication links, the switching and processing center, and the system's computers. Customer identification is accomplished with dual keys, consisting of a magnetic striped card and a secret code (PIN). The security risk to the PIN is great in a POS; for example, at a crowded checkout counter, other customers would be in a position to observe the transaction and discover the PIN. In some POS systems, the customer verbally gives his PIN to the sales clerk, thereby running the risk of a nearby customer hearing the secret code, or a corrupt sales clerk breaching the system for personal gain.

POS communication links are highly complex, especially when compared to those of a rudimentary EFT system. A complex POS network offers criminals numerous opportunities to penetrate any of its critical communication links. Several electronic tools can also be used by criminals to penetrate the system; the most common of these is the spoofer. This is an electronic device that is undetectable by any of the system's interfaces. The spoofer simulates the customer's bank computer; it can thus be employed to issue instructions to POS terminals in retail facilities to okay particular transactions. The spoofer, by authorizing the transaction, results in great losses to the retailer.

The POS is also open to electronic penetration through use of an imposter terminal; through use of this device, a criminal can access the records of the system. The imposter terminal can also be used to fraudulently manipulate the data within the computer. In addition, the computer itself in a POS system is also open to criminal attack. The input data can be altered, the output data can be stolen, and the computer itself is open to physical destruction. POS systems also raise serious questions regarding the privacy of a customer's records; both users of the system and outsiders pose a threat to privacy, if the system's security is lax. The customer may, in turn, become the target of blackmail. Invasions of privacy are a serious threat—one that POS designers must seriously address.

Automated Teller Machines

Kentucky's Jefferson County is fast becoming the seat of a banking network of automated teller machines (ATMs); more than 200,000 bank customers transact around-the-clock banking in 128 locations throughout the county. The Citizen's Fidelity Bank and Trust of Louisville, Kentucky, provides customer-operated terminals in 59 food and retail stores in the Louisville area. It also operates 14 ATMs, 24 hours daily, at branch locations and remote shopping centers. There are now more than 10,000 ATMs in the United States; they have also proliferated in Europe (with 4500) and Japan (with 5000).

ATMs (occasionally referred to as customer-bank communication terminals, or CBCTs) are defined as machines capable of processing a variety of transactions between a depository institution and its customers. The ATM can perform a variety of functions; it can, for example, accept deposits, provide withdrawals, transfer funds between accounts, and accept instructions to pay third parties in a transaction. An ATM may be either an on-line or off-line category; it may be located either on or off the premises of a depository institution. Some ATMs permit customers access 24 hours a day, seven days a week.

A more primitive type of ATM is the cash dispensing machine (CDM). This type of ATM only permits a customer to make withdrawals of currency and coin. CDMs are more popular in Europe and Japan, where depository institutions keep shorter hours and employ fewer tellers; the CDM assists the teller during peak hours. CDMs serve, as do all ATMs, as an alternative to the construction of expensive branch offices.

ATMs, however, provide a more elaborate system of services for bank cusotmers; they are also more expensive, so that a utilization rate higher than that of CDMs must be maintained to justify the investment they require. The newer generation of ATMs cost an average of $35,000 each. The modern one-line ATMs provide a customer with the ability to access an account, thus answering a balance inquiry. When a customer makes such a request, his account is accessed; its balance is determined and then displayed in the ATM's numeric display panel.

The majority of ATM devices today operate in the off-line mode. Off-line ATMs are not connected to a computer but rather operate independently. They are equipped with the necessary logic to read and decode a customer's entry card. Bank clerks are assigned the daily task of reviewing services performed by these off-line ATMs. A printed receipt usually is generated for all customer transactions; the customer receives the original document through the ATM cash drawer, and a duplicate is retained by the machine for bank proofing and posting operations. An off-line machine may also be equipped with an internal (magnetic core) memory to store lists of delinquent (hot-card) accounts and stolen cards; these lists are updated for each ATM belonging to a particular bank.

The on-line ATM represents the newer and more sophisticated generation of CBCTs. An on-line machine frequently is directly connected, through the use of telephone communication lines, to the bank's central computer. This newer generation of ATMs is more expensive than the off-line type; however, on-line machines provide the customer with the capability of making an account balance inquiry. In addition, they are less vulnerable to attack by unsophisticated criminals, and they provide a means for computer file updating. However, it should be pointed out that on-line machines are vulnerable to attack by sophisticated white-collar criminals; by simply manipulating the bank's central computer, a criminal can alter, fabricate, or destroy records. On-line ATMs can also keep more current hot-card lists than can their off-line counterparts.

For the customer, the mechanics of an ATM network are simple. Customers are issued plastic entry cards by a financial institution; on the card is printed a special magnetic code for purposes of identifying the customer and preventing unauthorized entry. Included in this magnetic code are such data as the customer's account numbers, limitations on customer withdrawals and credit transfers, and also the number of daily transactions allowed the customer. The plastic card is a key to the system; it is both the device that activates the ATM and, together with the PIN, identifies the user to the machine.

In a typical ATM transaction, the customer inserts his card into the card input/reader; he is then instructed to enter his PIN on a numeric keyboard. He is generally allowed several attempts (usually three) to perform this step. If the customer is unable to complete this operation successfully, the plastic card (as a security measure) is retained by the ATM. Once the customer enters the correct PIN, he is then instructed to select both the type of transaction and also the amount on the machine's keyboard.

Deposits can also be made with the machine simply by placing a check or cash in an envelope, inserting the envelope into the machine, and instructing the machine on the sum deposited. A customer may also transfer funds from his savings to his checking account, or pay his mortgage, simply by pressing the appropriate keys on the ATM's keyboard.

An ATM offers numerous benefits to a bank's customer. The customer is able to bank 24 hours, seven days a week, just by going to his bank's local ATM. Some banks install ATMs so that a customer can use them without ever getting out of a car. The ATM offers a customer both convenience and security; at the same time, it frees personnel to conduct more important customer services. The ATM also represents an inexpensive alternative to building and staffing a branch office; for a bank with a shortage of operating space, it offers expansion possibilities. Banks also find ATMs less expensive than the costs of hiring and training several tellers to perform the same operation; in addition, ATMs represent a vehicle for cutting down the manpower needs of a bank.

The ATM revolution, however, has also brought with it distinct disadvantages. ATMs frequently malfunction, for example. They are open to criminal attack, especially by bank insiders. The number of banking services they provide is limited; many ATMs have a $100 limit on withdrawals. ATMs are also impersonal; some bank customers refuse to use them because the technology frightens them, and members of the lower economic strata have displayed a resistance to using ATMs. In addition, many bank employees have not been fully trained in the use of ATM technology.

ATMs also are subject to potential breaches of security. Fraudulent authorizations pose a problem; a criminal who gains access to a customer's card and PIN can easily access the system. Many customers, fearful of forgetting their PIN, keep a written record of it, carrying this in their wallet or purse with their card. Counterfeit cards also represent a problem. In addition, ATM facilities can be bugged by a concealed electronic listening device; also, a felon may simply post himself across the street and use binoculars to observe a customer using an ATM and witness the PIN typed on the keyboard. Some sophisticated criminals have resorted to skimming techniques, whereby the data from the card's magnetic strip are transferred to a second card.

Criminals have also demonstrated an ability to penetrate the more sophisticated on-line ATMs by simply employing a spoofer. This is a device that is inserted in the communications lines that connect the ATM to the central computer at the bank. The spoofer is employed to direct the ATM to dump cash until the cash hopper is empty. ATM communications lines are also vulnerable to taps; the felon, through use of a tap, can intercept key financial data. ATMs are also subject to physical attack; criminals may attempt to break into them. They also lend themselves to extortion schemes; criminals can threaten to blow up the ATMs unless a bank surrenders to their demands. Dishonest bank employees, however, pose a more serious problem, as do vendor installation and service engineers.

The ATM technology represents an effort on the part of the modern banking community to bring its services to its customers at convenient locations on a 24-hour basis. It must be viewed as a first and major effort in the evolutionary process to a cashless society.

Preauthorized Credits and Debits

The payment of payrolls (credits) and bills (debits) by corporations, government, and the average citizen is an everyday banking phenomenon; it is a major component in the shift to an EFTS. This rudimentary EFTS allows for recurring payments to be made electronically rather than manually. The process is a simple one, often used in conjunction with ACH services.

Preauthorized credits are direct payments into the recipient's account; the most common are direct payroll and social security deposits. An employee who wants to participate in a preauthorized credit program simply signs an authorization form with his employer. Before each payday, the employer's computer records on a magnetic tape the employee's bank number, bank account, and amount to be credited to this account. The magnetic tape is then sent, before the date of payment, to the employer's bank, which debits the employer's account for the entire deposit payroll and credits the accounts of any employee who has an account with it. Remaining credits on the magnetic tape are then transmitted to an ACH for distribution to the financial institutions where the other employees have accounts. Each participating employee in this program is supplied with a statement as evidence of deposit. Several government agencies and private concerns now participate in an elaborate preauthorized credits program. These direct deposit programs are attractive for several reasons: they provide security and convenience and lower the handling costs involved in payroll programs. They also cut down the paper glut by decreasing the number of checks written.

More than 40 percent of all checks written by an individual are for the purpose of making payments to credit card companies, utilities, retailers, mortgage companies, and financial institutions for auto loans. A preauthorized debit system constitutes an electronic mode of paying periodic bills. The system usually is simple and is employed in conjunction with an ACH. The bill payer signs an authorization form, which preauthorizes his bank to pay any bills submitted by specified companies or individuals. The authorization data are stored by the bank on a magnetic tape that contains all preauthorizations in effect for its customers. When the bank receives a bill from a specified creditor, its computer reviews the authorization master file to see if payment is authorized; the computer will then charge the bill payer's account for the amount of the bill and credit that of the company or individual (creditor) in question. The information is recorded on a tape, which is later forwarded to an ACH for settlement with the creditor's bank. The bill payer generally is supplied with a written statement for his own personal records.

Pilot projects for both preauthorized credits and debits have been undertaken in the 1970s. The preauthorized credits system has gained favor with both the federal and local governments. The Equitable Assurance Society, in 1974, commenced a preauthorized debit program; more than 20,000 entries were processed each month by computer. Preauthorized credit and debit programs are key ingredients in the evolutionary process toward EFTS.

Telephone Billpaying

Banks in New York, Connecticut, Pennsylvania, and other states, have installed computerized equipment that enables their customers to pay bills by simply dialing the bank's computer. In Minneapolis, a customer of the Farmers and Mechanics Savings Bank simply telephones the bank's computer (at a special number) to pay the bills of more than 1000 participating businesses. If the customer's phone is of the dial type, he merely feeds the information to a bank teller who in turn passes it on to the computer. The customer with a touch-tone phone simply punches his secret account number (an identifying code printed on the bottom of the bill he received from his retailer) and the amount he wishes to have paid. This telephone-billpaying service costs the customer merely 10 cents per bill. The customer receives only a monthly statement in a payment register book—generally kept near the telephone.

In Seattle, the state's largest mutual savings bank and seven other thrift institutions have formed a holding company that offers telephone-billpaying services. For a small fee of two dollars a month, a customer can open a passcard-plus account; through it, he can pay bills to more than 1600 participating merchants and credit card companies by simply dialing his telephone. Customers with dial phones can telephone their banks from their home or office; they give the teller their secret pass-code number and tell the teller to whom and how much they want to pay. Bank customers with touch-tone phones need only punch a seven-digit number, which will gain them access to the bank's computer. After the customer has gained entry, the computer (in a soft voice) requests the customer's account number. After the customer gives his account number, the computer requests the secret pass code (a four-digit number). The computer also asks for the payment code (the number assigned the store to be payed); the customer then tells the computer the amount to be paid the merchant. If the customer catches a mistake he need only hit the asterisk; the computer automatically cancels the entry and requests the correct information.

The private and public sectors are increasingly employing ACHs to make many of their recurring payments: salaries, commissions, dividends, annuities, social security, welfare, and retirement payments. Consumers similarly are exploring new technologies to make many of their recurring payments to businesses. Payments such as mortgages, utility bills, insurance premiums, and auto loans easily lend themselves to payment by telephone. The bank customer simply calls his depository institution, provides identification information, and directs the institution to make payments to specified individuals or businesses. Telephone-billpaying systems are presently employed by more than 50 depository institutions in numerous states. However, these telephonic payment systems have met with some consumer opposition. One bank vice-president best verbalized it as follows:

> Customers are used to dealing with paper and getting canceled checks. Many customers are not eager to experiment with telephone bill paying systems. Our hope is that the younger generation, which has grown up with computers and trusts them, will partake in the system.

In 1973, the Seattle First National Bank introduced its touch-tone billpaying system. By using a touch-tone phone, a bank customer could pay creditors from the convenience of home or office. The cost to the customer: a fee of less than seven dollars per month. However, only 100 merchants signed up for the program, and First National was not able to enlist the participation of the necessary number of its customers. At its peak, the system enlisted the support of only 500 paying customers, far from the necessary number. First National's telephone-billpaying project was a short-lived failure.

As with other EFTS technologies, telephone-billpaying systems are viewed by the older and more traditional bank customers with skepticism. However, they have increasingly gained adherents among younger bank customers and professionals. Telephone billpaying is a prelude to the development of cashless society.

REGIONAL VERSUS NATIONAL EFTS

The first federal effort to develop EFTS came in late 1973; the Federal Reserve Board of Governors announced its proposed amendment to regulation J, the regulation that governs the procedures for the collection of checks through the Federal Reserve banks. The Board indicated that the objective of the proposed amendment was to further the development of electronic payment systems. The FHLBB subsequently enacted regulations that would allow federal savings and loan associations to participate in EFTS. In December 1974, the Comptroller of the Currency declared CBCTs outside the scope of the McFadden Act, which prohibits national banks from constructing branches where state chartered banks are prohibited from so doing by state law. At present, some 17 states view CBCTs as branches.

As a result of this federal impetus, many of the states, fearful that the federal government would preempt the field of EFTS, began in 1974 to enact an array of laws and regulations in this area. The approach of the local legislatures has varied from state to state. However, the objective of the states has been to preserve the competitive parity between the national banks and small, state-chartered institutions. Some states have endorsed and given their full backing to the development and implementation of EFTS. In 1974, Washington, Massachusetts, and Oregon enacted EFTS legislation that would permit the installation of CBCTs (remote electronic banking facilities) within their respective jurisdictions. Subsequently, New York, New Jersey, and other states, enacted similar EFTS legislation.

To date, some 32 states have enacted EFTS-related laws. Many of these states have empowered their state banking commissions to enact whatever regulations are needed to enhance the competitive parity of state banks with their federally chartered competitors. Some 30 state legislatures, under increasing pressure from powerful state banking interests, have enacted laws that limit or prohibit bank branches. State branching laws (to be fully discussed later in the book) will play a key role in determining whether EFTS develops along local or national lines.

Another stumbling block to the development and implementation of a national EFT system is our privacy laws, both state and federal. In an EFTS environment, the consumer will increasingly find his privacy threatened; a black market in stolen data may become a serious problem. Several states and the federal government have enacted laws that attempt to curtail EFTS-related privacy abuses. However, this array of legislation, although well-meaning, has created an avalanche of red tape for the banking community. Some of the smaller financial institutions have found the costs of compliance with privacy legislation prohibitive. As an example, the federal Bank Secrecy Act, which requires the maintenance of records and the reporting of individual financial data by financial institutions to the federal government, has resulted in added compliance-related costs for banks. The patchwork of privacy laws found in numerous local jurisdictions and at the federal level, at times inconsistent and costly to comply with, may retard the rise of a national EFTS.

Sharing the EFTS technology has also become an issue of concern. Some financial institutions have already established rudimentary EFTS but permit their competitors to have access to them; others seek to franchise their EFTS. A few of the larger banks have entered joint EFTS ventures. This has prompted fears among many of the smaller banks that unless they are able to share the EFTS technology with the larger institutions, they will be unable to compete or participate in the cashless society. If kept out of EFTS, the smaller institutions will certainly succumb to the banking giants.

The small merchants have displayed similar concern. To date, more than 25 states have attempted to address the issue of sharing; 19 of these states have made sharing of EFTS, in one form or another, mandatory. State sharing laws and regulations vary in great degree with respect to what must be shared, which institutions are mandated to share, and also the degree of sharing. For example, Washington makes sharing mandatory between commercial banks but not between savings and loan associations. However, some states have enacted laws that would apply equally to both federal- and state-chartered institutions.

Critics of mandatory sharing laws, however, argue that these mandates retard the development of EFTS; further, that they perpetuate inefficiency and increase the cost of doing business. They also charge that state sharing legislation does not promote but inhibits competition. The U.S. Department of Justice appears to side with the critics; it has publicly taken the position that mandatory state sharing statutes may be a violation of federal anti-trust laws. The sharing issue remains to be fully addressed.

An array of issues remains to be resolved. The investigation and prose-cution of EFTS-related crimes, to be discussed later in greater detail, will increasingly become a serious problem for law enforcement. Many of our present legal evidentiary rules may prove difficult to adapt to a cashless environment. The investigation of these electronic crimes may also prove difficult for our more than 40,000 police agencies; at present, both federal and state police agencies are ill-trained and equipped to handle complex EFTS-related crimes.

The issue of liability also merits consideration. The Uniform Commercial Code (UCC) regulates disputes arising out of the processing of check col-lections and deposits. Liability under the UCC is based on the handling and examination of checks; for example, a bank bears the loss for forged signatures on checks. The UCC thus defines the legal liabilities and obliga-tions of each party under our present check system. However, the UCC's application under EFTS remains, at best, in dispute.

Whether EFTS assumes a local/regional or national character will, in large part, depend on the ability of its architects and that of society to accommodate the needs of one another. Rudimentary regional EFTS net-works already have taken shape. These regional systems often encompass sev-eral financial institutions and businesses connected by local communication networks. A regional system offers its users switching services that enable messages to enter at any point and be transmitted electronically to the addressee.

A national EFT system can be defined as being a national computerized payments network linking numerous regional systems into a national grid (cashless society). A national EFT system would provide for the transfer of funds and related data over vast distances. At present, the Fed Wire and Bank Wire are rudimentary examples of a national electronic banking network. National bank card systems also provide a skeletal outline of the structure a national EFTS could assume. The form EFTS assumes will, in large measure, depend on the ability of its architects to surmount present problems.

CURRENT TRENDS

In 1973, only 15 percent of the telephones in this country were touch-tone types. Today, more than 60 percent of all installed telephones are of the touch-tone type; as a result, pay-by-phone systems are increasingly making their appearance felt. The Union Commerce Bank, one of Cleveland's largest banks, with assets in excess of $1 billion and more than 30 branches, has met with great success in the introduction of its pay-by-phone system. The communications revolution has made it possible for bank customers to pay an array of bills from the comfort of their homes.

The minicomputer revolution has also enhanced the development of EFTS in the retail industry. Minicomputers, employing integrated circuits, provide more power than did many of their giant predecessors, and at a fraction of the cost. Minicomputers connected to large central computers through a network of telephone lines form a sophisticated electronic transmission network that can handle and process large amounts of data. Minicomputers located in retail establishments enable large armies of sales clerks to control EFTS terminals in their stores and communicate with a central computer in a matter of minutes, making it possible for them to conduct large numbers of transactions daily.

Sears, Roebuck and Company, the nation's largest retailer, recently entered into an agreement with the National Credit Union Association to electronically accept and clear share drafts for its customers. Sears has installed optical character recognition readers in some of its cash registers; these, in turn, transmit transaction information to the company's central computer. This electronic network makes it possible for Sears to receive payment within 24 hours, rather than wait a week for the present share drafts to clear. At the same time, the Transaction Management Company has announced the marketing of its model 1021 retail transactor; this new POS terminal is reported to handle nearly 300 different types of transactions and costs $2395 per terminal.

The computer and telecommunications revolution is largely responsible for the advent of the cashless society. Microprocessors are widely used in computer systems and terminals; there are also plans to install them in telephones in the near future. Scientists plan to employ the magnetic properties of material to store data. This development in the computer and telecommunications industries hold great promise for EFTS.

The current developments in the EFTS realm must be viewed from both the technological and societal perspective. Technologically, the computer and telecommunications revolution has made it possible for scientists to construct the needed scientific edifice for EFTS. The new technology has made it possible to handle large amounts of data with greater certainty, and at a lower cost. However, the societal fiber has been slow to respond; our political, economic, and social institutions, when confronted with EFTS, constitute an amalgamation of inner contradictions. A society that fails to adequately respond to the challenges of its technology may find itself swept aside.

4
THE THREAT TO PRIVACY

The American Medical Association, concerned that the instances of theft and misuse of medical patient information may increase in the near future, has recommended the establishment of 15 guidelines for safeguarding the confidentiality of computerized medical data bases. More than 60 percent of the respondents in a poll of 1500 Americans were seriously concerned about invasions of their personal privacy; the major threat, they noted, came from finance companies, credit bureaus, insurance companies, and the Internal Revenue Service. The survey included civil servants, legislators (both state and federal), businessmen, and professionals. These same fears are also shared by their Canadian cousins. In a separate poll, a large percentage of Canadian citizens (including government officials) likewise noted a concern for their personal privacy. Some feared that computers based in the United States, and used to process data gathered in Canada, could pose a serious threat to the personal and financial privacy of Canadians.

These fears are not entirely without basis. A study of the Social Security Administration (SSA) by the General Accounting Office (GAO), the watchdog agency of the U.S. Congress, has found that the medical and financial files of millions of Americans stored in SSA computers were not adequately safeguarded from potential destruction, loss, or misuse. The GAO study concluded that the SSA computers were lacking in adequate security.

There is justifiable concern by a number of consumer groups that the cashless society will augment the ability of the private and public sectors to invade the privacy of the average citizen. We have ample evidence of abuses of privacy by credit bureaus, insurance companies, private investigators, and numerous police agencies. As a result of these abuses, target individuals were often denied credit; they frequently were given no reason for the denial. Further, consumers could do little to remedy any inaccuracies in the files of reporting agencies.

However, businessmen often complain, with some justification, that they are inundated with government regulations. They fear that EFTS will increase pressure for additional costly and time-consuming legislation; for example, banking officials point out that compliance with a recent federal privacy law may cost them in excess of $1 billion annually. The concerns of both the consuming public and the business community must be balanced if EFTS is to prove a viable medium.

PRIVACY THREATENED

The growing sophistication of computer technology has given rise to questions about whether privacy can be adequately safeguarded in a cashless society. Data about an individual will come from numerous sources and in large quantities. The highly mobile nature of current society and our decentralized data base make it difficult to construct any detailed consumer profile. However, this will all change in an increasingly sophisticated EFTS environment. Information will be highly centralized; numerous institutions will share the system, thus having access to in-depth confidential and personal data. It will be possible to secure much more detailed information regarding the time, place, and character of an individual's financial transactions. The consumer's daily EFTS transactions will leave a trail for both private and government investigators to follow.

Behaviorists have long held that an individual is best characterized by his spending habits. Knowing what he buys, where he buys it, and to what political and social groups he contributes financially will provide a composite profile of his behavior. It can also open the individual to political blackmail or manipulation. Supreme Court Justice William O. Douglas, in his dissent in the *California Bankers Association* case, best summarized the problem as follows:

> A person is defined by the checks he writes. By examining them the [government] agents get to know his doctors, lawyers, creditors . . . and so ad infinitum. . . . [T]hese . . .items will . . .make it possible for a bureaucrat—by pushing one button—to get in an instant the names of 190 million Americans who are subversives or potential and likely candidates.[1]

Former Senator Sam Ervin, Jr. (of Watergate fame) specifically addressed the potential for privacy-related abuses under EFTS, noting:

> It has become increasingly clear that unless we take command now of the technology [EFTS] with all that it means in terms of substantive due process for the individual who is computerized, we may well discover someday that the machines [computers] stand above the law.

In the past, informational privacy was not as seriously threatened at it is by our present computer technology. The data gathered was often super-

---

[1] *California Bankers Association* v. *Schultz*, 416 U.S. 30, 85.

ficial in nature and maintained on a decentralized basis; access generally was costly and difficult. EFTS, however, will change this; Americans will find themselves scrutinized, measured, watched, and counted by thousands of computers. Financial data will take the form of electronic blips; personal data will be stored and transmitted, at the push of a button, over a vast communication network. EFTS raise the Orwellian specter of a totalitarian society where privacy ceases to exist. It is imperative that we understand the implications it holds in store for our privacy.

LAW OF PRIVACY

If you ask the average citizen what privacy is, he will respond that "it is the right to be left alone." Privacy, however, is more than that; it is a legal right rooted in our common law and Constitution. In addition, an array of court decisions and legislative acts have further solidified the right to privacy within our societal fiber. However, the right to privacy is not absolute; it is qualified. An individual has a right to "be left alone" only some of the time; it is important to know when the right to privacy comes into play.

The framers of our federal Constitution explicitly guaranteed the citizenry their freedom of speech, religion, and assembly. These Constitutional freedoms, when viewed in their totality, constitute a shield of privacy. For example, our Bill of Rights prohibits the quartering of soldiers in private homes without the consent of the owner (Third Amendment). Citizens are also protected against unreasonable searches and seizures of their persons, papers, homes, and effects (Fourth Amendment). The government is also prohibited from forcing the individual to be a witness against one's self in a criminal investigation or trial (Fifth Amendment). Our Constitution also ensures that the citizenry will have a champion in the form of legal counsel to do combat in the courts of our land (Sixth Amendment).

However, the framers of our Constitution limited these safeguards to the individual and his physical property; further, these Constitutional privacy protections are directed only at governmental action. They do not apply to the acts of private citizens or corporations. There is no Constitutional privacy shield vis-à-vis credit bureaus, insurance companies, or financial institutions. The Founding Fathers, living in an agrarian society, were ill-prepared for the privacy problems that have arisen in our information-oriented society. The Bill of Rights did not extend its privacy protections to invasions or unwarranted intrusions by the private realm. Questions dealing with such issues as when, how, and under what circumstances personal confidential data can be communicated to third parties were not addressed by the framers of our Constitution. These issues were left to be resolved by the common law.

The common law of negligence (torts) deals with wrongs committed upon a person, his family, or his property. To sustain a successful action under the law of negligence, an individual must demonstrate the following:

- He (the wronged party) enjoyed a legal right.
- His right was violated by another.
- As a result, he suffered damages.

Under the law of negligence, a wronged party can bring an action against an individual, a corporation, and even a charitable institution. The courts also have occasionally allowed injured parties to recover losses from municipal corporations and government employees.

The wronged party may recover under one or more of three categories of damages: compensatory, nominal, punitive. He may recover compensatory damages where he can demonstrate physical injury resulting from the acts of another. Many courts allow recovery for mental and emotional anguish, where it is the outcome of the willful or malicious conduct of another. If the injured party is unable to show any physical damages, he may still recover nominal damages; these usually do not exceed one dollar. Courts also allow for punitive damages, as a form of punishment against a wrong-doer whose acts are willful or malicious. In a civil action for invasion of privacy, a wronged party may recover one or more of these categories of damages.

Until the turn of the century, privacy-related actions were brought only under the law of defamation. To succeed in a defamation action, a wronged party must demonstrate the following:

- False statements were made about him.
- These were willful or malicious.
- They were made to others (published).
- The wronged party suffered damage(s).

Defamation can take the form of a writing, picture, or image (libel); or it can be an oral statement (slander). Defamatory acts can take on numerous forms; for example, a writing (libel) that Mr. Smith committed a serious offense when, in fact, this is false. Truth is always a defense to defamation. In addition, an absolute or qualified privilege may also constitute a defense to a defamation suit. Attorneys, witnesses, and judges engaged in a judicial proceeding enjoy an absolute privilege; all statements made by them within the contents of that proceeding are privileged. Legislators, government officials, and law enforcement officers often enjoy a qualified privilege; it extends to all communications made by them in good faith, and on a subject in which the party has an interest or duty to speak.

In any action for defamation, however, the aggrieved party must demonstrate injury to his character or reputation; and it must be proved that the statement (written or oral) made was false. Privacy-related invasions, however, often involve an injury to an individual's feelings rather than to his character or reputation. As a result, the law of defamation is of limited value in privacy suits.

It was this specific limitation in the law of defamation that prompted Louis Brandeis (later to become a U.S. Supreme Court Justice) and his friend Samuel S. Warren, in 1890, to write their now classic treatise on the law of privacy, "The Right to Privacy."[2] The treatise grew out of a series of scandalous newspaper articles that dealt with the social activities of Warren's wife. These articles were not actionable under the law of defamation, since Mrs. Warren was unable to demonstrate injury to her character or reputation. In their treatise, however, Brandeis and Warren argued that there was a fundamental right to personal privacy, a right imbedded in numerous earlier decisions of the U.S. Supreme Court. In the years that followed, courts and legal scholars came to embrace the Brandeis-Warren treatise on the law of privacy, and it became the nucleus for the present law of privacy.

At the heart of the law of privacy lies the concern for the feelings—the mental anguish and distress—of the individual. In an action for invasion of privacy, an individual must demonstrate three key elements:

- There is a private affair in which the public does not have a legitimate interest.
- There is a publication of this affair.
- The individual's feelings suffered, as a result, injury.

Actions involving invasions of privacy have taken on numerous forms. The following are prevalent:

- An individual (or corporation) that appropriates the likeness or name of another for purposes of personal profit is liable for damages.
- An individual who is placed in a false light may sue.
- If private facts regarding an individual are disclosed to another, the party responsible for the disclosure is liable for damages.
- If there is an intrusion on the right of another to be left alone, the intruder has invaded another's privacy.

In privacy-related suits, injured parties have recovered damages where personal data of a private nature have been disclosed in an unreasonable manner. Courts have also allowed recovery in instances involving illegal taps or bugs. The classic case (in this latter instance) involved a consumer advocate and the nation's largest auto manufacturer. Private investigators for the large corporation tapped the consumer advocate's telephone lines. He sued, and the court ruled that his right to privacy had been violated.

[2] 4 *Harv. L. Rev.* 193 (1890).

In an EFTS environment, errors in the collection, storage, or dissemination of data by a financial institution may be covered by both defamation and privacy laws. However, civil litigation can prove to be both time consuming and costly. In addition, the injured party must demonstrate that the financial institution was responsible for the activity that caused the injury. In shared EFTS, this may prove difficult to demonstrate in a court of law. Further, the doctrine of qualified privilege has been applied in privacy cases where financial institutions and credit bureaus have provided erroneous information to subscribers who had a legitimate business interest. To overcome this privilege, the injured party would have to demonstrate either malice or reckless disregard.

The qualified privilege can also be vitiated if it can be demonstrated either that a subscriber who gained access to the data did not have a legitimate right to do so or that the data were distributed to the general public. However, this may prove technically difficult to demonstrate. As computers become increasingly complex and sophisticated, they will be able to make evaluative judgments as well as direct feedbacks based on stored data. Testing a computer's judgment in a sophisticated EFT system could place an inordinate burden on the consumer to prove liability, as he would have to establish that the computer was maliciously or recklessly misguided in its evaluation by employees of the financial institution or credit bureau.

PRIVACY LEGISLATION

The inadequacy of the common law to remedy serious abuses of privacy in a complex computerized environment led Congress, in 1970, to pass the Fair Credit Reporting Act (FCRA).[3] The FCRA was designed to protect the consumer by requiring that reporting agencies adopt reasonable procedures to assure the confidentiality, accuracy, and proper use of credit-related data. The jurisdiction of the FCRA is broad; it covers banks, credit card companies, and an array of credit reporting agencies. It regulates the release of all financial reports to third parties.

The FCRA requires financial institutions and credit bureaus to maintain current files. A consumer, upon request, must be informed of the contents of his file; if the consumer has reason to believe that the information is inaccurate, he can request a reinvestigation. The financial institution must comply, unless the request is frivolous. If a consumer is denied employment, credit, or insurance as a result of the information provided by a financial institution or credit bureau, the user of the credit report must inform the consumer of this fact and must also supply him with the name and address of the source of the report.

[3] 15 U.S.C. 1681 *et seq.*

A key advantage of the FCRA is that it was drafted specifically for a computerized financial environment. The FCRA specifically directs that:

> Consumer reporting agencies employing automatic data processing equipment, particularly agencies that transmit information over distances by any mechanical means, must exercise special care to assure that the data is accurately converted into a machine-readable format and that it is not distorted. . . . Procedures must also be adopted that will provide security for such systems in order to reduce the possibility that computerized consumer information will be stolen or altered.

The FCRA also imposes criminal sanctions against individuals (or corporations) that obtain data from a consumer reporting agency under false pretenses. Civil remedies are also available to the consumer against a reporting firm that willfully or negligently fails to comply with the FCRA.

The FCRA, however, suffers from some serious drawbacks. It places no limitations on the type of information that can be collected or reported by a financial institution. Consumers are not allowed to have physical access to or copies of their files. In addition, government agencies can have access to consumer reports under specified conditions. The FCRA also exempts credit bureaus from civil suits involving invasions of privacy, negligence, and defamation. The FCRA exempts medical records from its jurisdiction. Finally, the FCRA leaves the brunt of the enforcement of its provisions to the injured party. Few consumers can afford costly litigation.

In 1973, Congress passed the Crime Control Act (CCA).[4] The CCA regulates the use and dissemination of criminal history records. These records frequently contain such information as arrest data, court dispositions, and appeals. Under the CCA, an individual has the right to review his criminal history file and correct any erroneous information. The object of the CCA is to ensure that criminal history records are not misused. Further, the CCA also seeks to ensure that these records are accurate and updated. However, the CCA exempts investigative files from its provisions; an individual may have no access to such files, nor any opportunity to correct errors in these files.

The Equal Credit Opportunity Act (ECO) outlaws credit discrimination on the basis of age, race, color, religion, national origin, sex, or marital status.[5] A creditor, however, may request, as part of any application, information that relates to any of these areas. However, the ECO requires that an applicant be informed by the creditor of any government requests for this information. A creditor must maintain current files and must notify a consumer if any adverse credit-related action is taken based on these

---

[4] 42 U.S.C. 3771.
[5] P.C. 93–495, as amended by P.C. 94–239.

records. The consumer must also be given specific reasons for the refusal to grant him credit.

Of similar value in safeguarding the accuracy and confidentiality of private records is the Family Educational Rights and Privacy Act of 1974 (FERPA).[6] The legislation addresses the privacy of information collected, stored, and disseminated by educational institutions. Educational institutions must allow a student or former student (or his parents, if the student is under 18 years of age), to inspect his personal file. A student may challenge the accuracy of the data contained in his file and may also request that a written statement outlining his version of the facts in dispute be added to the file. However, FERPA does not permit a student to review his medical or psychiatric records, although a physician of his choice may do so. Personal data about a student may not be released to a third party without first obtaining the student's written consent. Educational institutions are also directed to keep a detailed record of all individuals and organizations that have requested or obtained access to the student's personal file.

More than 50 percent of the states have enacted similar legislation. Like federal privacy legislation, state statutes also attempt to regulate access to financial and criminal history records. The individual, under these state statutes, has a right to review his personal records; he also has a right to challenge the accuracy of the records, and can submit written recommended changes. He may also request that the financial institution or government agency provide him with the names of all users that received the data.

In an EFTS environment, these privacy statutes should prove of some value in limiting access to an individual's records. When employed with the laws of defamation and privacy, they should constitute a credible deterrent to those who would misuse confidential consumer data.

STATUTORY LIMITATIONS ON GOVERNMENT

In an effort to safeguard the privacy of the personal data collected, stored, and disseminated by the federal government, Congress enacted the Privacy Act of 1974 (PA).[7] The statute specifically directs that federal agancies may not disseminate personal data as regards an individual, unless they first obtain his consent. In addition, the PA prohibits federal agencies from collecting and maintaining more information about an individual than is necessary under their mandate.

Federal agencies are also directed to keep a detailed record of all disclosures that they make and to whom these are made. The agencies must also keep a record of the purpose for which these disclosures were made. Further, the accounting must be readily available to the individual upon

[6] 12 U.S.C. 1232g.
[7] 5 U.S.C. 552a.

request. An individual who discovers errors in his files may also take steps to remedy them.

The PA, however, does not provide for the disclosure of personal data to agency personnel who need the information so that they may perform their delegated duties; the data may also be made available to the Bureau of the Census. Law enforcement agencies, with legitimate police objectives, may also have access to the data. Congressional committees with jurisdiction over the subject matter similarly have access. All "routine" information may be readily disseminated to third parties, and the agency itself decides what is routine information. By giving an agency such broad latitude in defining its own system of records, the PA opens Pandora's box. Agencies can circumvent it by simply labeling as routine any data they wish to pass on to third parties.

The PA provides for both civil and criminal sanctions against government employees found violating it. However, enforcement of these provisions has proven to be extremely lax. As with other privacy-related legislation, enforcement is left to the private individual.

On July 27, 1978, in an attempt to ensure the confidentiality of data stored in federal computers, the Office of the Management and Budget (OMB) issued Circular A-71 to all heads of the federal Executive agencies. The circular directed all federal agencies to take all necessary measures to establish personnel and physical security programs, to safeguard the operation, maintenance, and integrity of their computer facilities. OMB also called the federal agencies to conduct periodic audits and evaluations to test the integrity of their computer systems.

Congress has also passed the Trade Secrets Act (TSA), which prohibits federal employees from disclosing to unauthorized third parties any information that relates to trade secrets.[8] The TSA also prohibits the disclosure of any data regarding the source of any income, profits, losses, or expenditures of any person, partnership, or corporation. The TSA provides for fines of up to $1000 and/or imprisonment of up to one year for any federal employee convicted of violating its disclosure provisions. However, the provisions of the TSA have not been enforced by the government, and leaks of confidential data by federal employees continue unabated.

In 1976, Congress passed the Tax Reform Act (TRA) in an effort to curtail privacy abuses connected to IRS investigations. Under the TRA, a bank customer must be notified, in writing, by his financial institution if the IRS issues a subpoena for his financial records. Before 1976, banks generally surrendered a customer's financial records without notifying the individual in question—many times even without the IRS issuing a subpoena.

The Financial Privacy Act of 1978 (FPA) prohibits federal agencies from gaining access to the financial records of a bank customer, unless:

---

[8] 18 U.S.C. 1905.

- The customer has authorized disclosure.
- The financial records are disclosed in response to a subpoena or summons.
- The financial records are disclosed in response to a search warrant.

In addition, the FPA requires that the records sought be reasonably described.

EFTS could easily become tools for monitoring the activities of political dissidents and critics, by both the private and public sectors. Congress has enacted a series of laws to curtail the exchanges of data between government and the financial community. In the past, such exchanges often resulted in flagrant abuses of an individual's right to privacy.

LEGITIMATE ACCESS TO RECORDS

Not all disclosures of information in the cashless society need be illegal or constitute an invasion of an individual's right to privacy. Some disclosures will be necessary and permitted by law, lest our financial institutions cease to function. For example, when a consumer makes a purchase with an EFTS debit card the merchant will want to be assured that the card is not stolen or counterfeit. Further, depository institutions, for legitimate business purposes, will find it necessary to exchange data with credit grantors or credit bureaus. Depository institutions and credit bureaus now exchange voluminous data regarding an individual's income, loan activity, general assets, and buying and payment habits. Occasionally, financial institutions also exchange data concerning delinquent or otherwise misused accounts. These constitute legitimate uses of financial and other personal data, provided they are carried on within the ambit of the law.

The courts have also acknowledged the right of the government to conduct, for legitimate purposes, periodic intrusions in the private affairs of the citizenry. Privacy is a qualified right. Government investigators, armed with a court order, may conduct electronic surveillances. However, the Supreme Court, in the case of *Berger* v. *New York,* was quick to point out that state statutes that provide for electronic eavesdropping cannot be overbroad.[9] The Supreme Court has permitted invasions of the right to privacy by police armed with a proper court order; thus the Supreme Court has left it to local and federal courts, at least in criminal cases, to determine if the invasion of an individual's privacy was legal.

However, government investigators need not always apply for a warrant to conduct a search (intrude on the privacy of a citizen). In 1970, in an attempt to curtail organized criminal activity, the Congress passed the Bank Privacy Act (BPA).[10] The BPA empowers the Secretary of the Treasury to

[9] 388 U.S. 41 (1968).
[10] 12 U.S.C. 1829 g.

order banks to retain financial records of the identity and financial activities of their customers; the Secretary has ordered banks to retain microfilm records of all checks written for more than $100 by a customer. The financial institution is also obligated to record the identity of the party for whose account the check is to be deposited or collected.

The BPA has been employed, with mixed results, by the IRS to uncover tax evaders. In 1974, the constitutionality of the BPA came under attack in the case of the *California Bankers* v. *Schultz*.[11] The Supreme Court, however, ruled that the BPA did not violate a bank customer's right to privacy. Two years later, in the case of *United States* v. *Miller,* the Court reiterated its position, ruling a second time that the BPA was not in violation of a bank customer's right to privacy.[12] Bank records, the Court held, are for the benefit of the financial institution and not for the benefit of its customers. A bank customer cannot expect complete privacy, the Court noted; the government has an occasional interest in the financial records of its citizens. The BPA raises serious questions regarding the government's power to access EFTS customer records without a court order.

EFTS raise concerns about the privacy of financial and other personal data. The potential for abuse is great. Attacks may come not only from the private and public sectors, but also, increasingly, from organized crime. Criminals have demonstrated an interest in confidential records. Data-related thefts will be on the increase in the cashless society; specialized criminal fencing networks will make their appearance. Our privacy will be under daily attack. However, a society ruled by ethical considerations and a vigilant citizenry has little to fear; it can take adequate steps to ensure that its privacy will prevail against a technological onslaught.

[11] 416 U.S. 21.
[12] 425 U.S. 435.

5
SHARING EFTS
CAN BE A PROBLEM

The legislature of an Eastern state has considered legislation that would make it mandatory for out of state banks to obtain permits from the state's Banking Commissioner before operating ATMs, POSs, or electronic equipment in stores for purposes of approving credit card purchases. Several large national banks have threatened to take the state to court if such legislation is passed. A Texas bank, in order to construct a drive-in window at its main office, had to first get a city ordinance passed and an easement approved—retaining the services of a battery of lawyers and lobbyists in the process.

In Washington, D.C., the Justice Department reviewed a proposed joint venture among several commercial banks in Nebraska. The banks are planning to construct a statewide EFT system. However, Justice Department lawyers have indicated to the banks that the proposal could violate federal antitrust laws.

Increasingly, the financial community has come to view EFTS as a medium for offering its customers an array of banking services. However, bankers, retailers, and others, are finding that the road to the cashless society is not an easy one. The technology to construct EFTS is readily available. However, businessmen are increasingly confronting a legal quagmire. Computer technology has progressed so rapidly that our legal system has failed to keep pace. Our banking and antitrust laws, enacted many years ago to ensure the survival of the small banker and businessman, now threaten the growth of EFTS.

EARLY BANKING IN AMERICA

Ours is a dual banking system. Banks are chartered by both the states and the federal government. Two-thirds of the banks in the United States are state chartered and subject to numerous state banking regulations. Some 32 states place some form of limitation on branching by banks. Eleven of these states have outright legal prohibitions against any form of branching. Only one state, Wyoming, has not passed any bank branching laws. Some of these states look on ATMs, POSs, and other components of EFTS as branches and prohibit their construction. Branching laws make it both costly—as was the case with the Texas bank that wanted to consruct a drive-in window at its main office—and difficult to construct a cashless society.

Bank branching laws have their roots in the early history of this country, in an era when Americans lived a rural and isolated existence and feared the tentacles of the urban Eastern banking establishment. The ideological disputes between the Jeffersonian and Hamiltonian schools of thought best illustrate these fears. Nineteenth-century rural America was an agricultural society; communications between communities were poor. The small local bank was viewed as an integral part of the community; it constituted the financial lifeblood of rural America.

However, post-Civil War America changed dramatically, increasingly turning urban and industrial. The railroads brought the borders closer together; the large Eastern banking interests grew and expanded. A national banking system began to emerge. An increasingly urban and mobile society needed convenient and accessible banking services; the small local banking interests saw themselves threatened. Under increasing pressure from these small banking interests, the Congress, in 1864, passed the National Bank Act. Section 8 of the act required that banks conduct their transactions only at the office specified in the bank's organizational certificate.

The majority of nineteenth-century Americans were accustomed to local banking practices; bank branches were a rarity. Few Americans were willing to entrust their funds to financial institutions located in other states. By the early 1900s, several states had passed legislation that allowed only state-chartered banks to establish branches within the state. The national banks, however, saw these state branching laws as subtle efforts to limit their ability to compete effectively with state-chartered banks. In 1923, under increasing pressure from the large national banks, the Attorney General of the United States issued a legal opinion on branching. He noted that national banks were not prohibited from establishing branches for the purposes of transacting routine business, such as deposits, withdrawals, and the cashing of checks. The Attorney General, however, also noted that branches could be established only in those states that had no prohibitions.

The Comptroller of the Currency soon issued his own opinion on the subject of branching, and authorized the national banks to construct teller windows. The Comptroller's ruling gave the state-chartered banks cause for concern. They feared that the national banks would inundate their communities with branches. The local banks decided to take their challenge to court. In 1924, the Supreme Court of the United States handed down an important ruling on the issue of bank branching.[1] It held that national banks, like their local counterparts, were subject to the branching laws of the states in

---

[1] *First National Bank* v. *Missouri,* 263 U.S. 640 (1924).

which they operated. The national banks had argued that state branching laws threatened their operations and efficiency; that they impaired their ability to conduct their business in accord with their federal charters.[2] The Supreme Court, however, disagreed; it noted that state branching laws served a legitimate state interest and were no threat (as the national banks had argued) to the survival or the financial well-being of national banks.

BANK BRANCHING LAWS

The national banks, fearful that local branching laws would place them at a disadvantage vis-à-vis the state-chartered banks, lobbied Congress for legislation. In 1924, one month after the Supreme Court's adverse decision on branching, Congressman McFadden introduced legislation to permit national banks to establish branches. In 1927, after long debate and lobbying efforts by both sides, the Congress passed a compromise version of the original bill. The McFadden Act allowed national banks to establish branches within a city, town, or village in which the bank was located, provided this did not violate state branching laws. The act did not supplant state branching laws, as the national banks had hoped it would; rather, it struck a compromise. Those laws would now have to be applied equitably to both state-chartered and national banks. They could no longer be employed to discriminate against national banks, as they had been in the past.

Although the 1927 McFadden Act was subsequently amended, its tenor remained the same. It constituted a compromise position. The act and its amendments form the basis of Section 36(c) of the National Bank Act. This key section provides, in part, as follows:

> A national banking association, may with the approval of the Comptroller of the Currency, establish and operate new branches: (1) within the limits of the city, town, or village in which said association is situated, if such establishment and operation are at the time expressly authorized to state banks by the law of the state in question; and (2) at any point within the state in which said association is situated, if such establishment and operation are at the time authorized to state banks by the law of the state in question and not merely by implication or recognition, and subject to the restrictions as to location imposed by the law of the state on state banks.

Section 36(f) of the amended act goes on to define a branch as follows:

> Any branch bank, branch office, branch agency, additional office, or any branch place of business located in any state or territory of the

---

[2] National banks are federally chartered banks, regulated by the Comptroller of the Currency.

United States or in the District of Columbia at which deposits are received, checks paid, or money lent.

The act maintains the delicate balance between the national and state-chartered banks. The objective of the McFadden Act was to recognize and safeguard the "competitive equality [balance] between state and national banks." National banks could establish branches only to the same extent that state-chartered banks could. The act sought to ensure that if state-chartered banks were allowed to establish branches, the states would not discriminate against the national banks.

In 1932, the Senate considered an amendment to the McFadden Act that would have allowed national banks to branch anywhere within their own states, without regard for state branching prohibitions. The amendment would have also allowed national banks to establish some branches outside their states. However, opponents argued that the amendment would invade the sovereignty of the states and create a national banking system dominated by a small number of financial giants. Senator Wheeler, an opponent of the amendment, argued that the amendment to the act would allow the "national banks to go in there [the state] and establish branches against the will of the people." Senator Norbeck, also an opponent, noted that the "bank owned and managed by the home folks of a community" was the "American kind of bank," and that the proposed amendment would threaten the existence of small banks. Congressman Luce, of the House Conference Committee, best summarized the position of the opponents as follows:

> In the controversy over the respective merits of what are known as unit banking and branch banking systems, a controversy that has been alive and sharp for years, branch banking has been steadily gaining in favor. It is not, however, here proposed to give the advocates of branch banking any advantage. We do not go an inch beyond saying that the two ideas shall compete on equal terms and only where the states make the competition possible by letting their own institutions have branches.

During the Great Depression many of the small, state-chartered banks found themselves in financial difficulties. The Comptroller of the Currency suggested that the larger banks should be allowed to acquire them as branches. Many of the small banks were undercapitalized; their financial future looked dim. However, the powerful Congressional supporters of the state banking interests opposed any federal legislation that would enable the national banks to establish branches. The rural Congressional interests were fearful that any amendment to the McFadden Act would only serve the interests of the large urban Eastern banking groups. They were fearful, with some justification, that through geographic expansion the national banks would gain a dominant foothold over the economy.

However, the Roosevelt administration took steps to assist the state banking interests. Banking reforms assured many of the localities that their deposits in state-chartered banks would be insured by the federal government. The local bank survived the economic turmoil of the Depression, and the branching issue continued to plague the national banks.

Some of the states, however, took measures on their own initiative to relax their branching restrictions. Iowa, for example, relaxed its absolute prohibitions against branching and instituted a limited branching policy. Other states began to permit branches within the city or county of a bank's main office; still others allowed banks to establish branches within a 100-mile radius of their main office. Some permitted branching within a city or county that is contiguous to the city or county the bank's main office is located in. A small number of states went so far as to permit banks to establish branches outside the state and even in foreign countries. Branching laws have undergone some modifications to accommodate some of the banking needs of our highly mobile technological society. However, critics of branching argue that more is needed, and that branching laws merely serve the needs of inefficient bankers.

BRANCHING AND THE COURTS

Our commercial banking system is composed of four categories of banks, each regulated in a different mode. National banks are regulated primarily by three agencies: the Federal Deposit Insurance Corporation (FDIC), the Federal Reserve Board (FRB), and the Comptroller of the Currency. Branching by national banks is under the control of the Comptroller's Office. A second category of commercial banks is that of the FDIC-insured, state-chartered banks. These are regulated by both the FDIC and state agencies. Member FRB state banks constitute the third category; these are regulated by the FDIC. Branching issues concerning these banks are dealt with by the FRB's Board of Governors. The state-chartered banks constitute the fourth category; these are not insured by the FDIC and are regulated solely by their respective states.

The regulators, however, often do more than regulate; they also take up the cause of the regulated. Students of regulatory agencies often note that the survival and existence of the regulated frequently come to depend on the zeal with which the regulator takes up his cause. The Comptroller of the Currency has on numerous occasions displayed such zeal. In the area of branching, the Comptroller's Office has done battle with the states on behalf of its constituency.

One of the first major branching cases that made its way to the Supreme Court of the United States involved the First National Bank of Logan, Utah (a national bank). First National had applied to the Comptroller for a certificate of authorization to establish a branch office in Logan. The Comptroller issued the certificate; soon afterward, the Walker Bank and Trust Company (a state-chartered bank) filed suit in court in an attempt to block the Comptroller's authorization. Lawyers for the Walker Bank argued that the Comptroller and First National had violated Utah's branching laws. The Comptroller, in turn, argued that it had the power to authorize national banks (First National) to establish branches. In 1966, the case made its way to the Supreme Court, where it was ruled that the Comptroller was in error: Congress, in enacting the McFadden Act, left it to the states to decide the question of branching.[3]

Subsequent to the decision in the First National Bank case, the Comptroller issued a number of interpretive rulings that authorized national banks to operate off-premise deposit machines. The First National Bank in Plant City, Florida, pursuant to the Comptroller's authorization, established a stationary receptacle for customer deposits. Florida law, however, prohibited branching; the question, then, became whether First National of Plant City had violated Florida's branching laws. Rather than wait for the state to act, the bank took the initiative and brought the case to federal district court. The court upheld the Comptroller's ruling, and noted that since no deposits were received, checks paid, or money lent at these off-premise facilities, they could not be held to be branches within Florida's branching laws.[4] The case made its way to the Supreme Court, and in 1969 the Court rendered its decision.[5] It took exception with the Comptroller's rulings and held that First National's off-premise receptacles were branches. A branch, the Court noted, includes any facility where deposits are made. Further, the Court was concerned that the Comptroller's rulings gave national banks an undue advantage over state-chartered banks: they were disruptive of the competitive equality the McFadden Act had established.

The next major test for branching laws came in 1974, in the form of a federally chartered savings and loan association (S&L)—not a national bank—which had installed computer terminals in two Hinky Dinky stores in Nebraska. The EFTS terminals were connected, through telephone wires, to a computer at the home office of the S&L in Lincoln. This rudimentary EFT system enabled the S&L customers to make deposits and withdrawals at the two stores. The Attorney General of Nebraska, however, saw these activities as being in violation of the state's branching laws. He filed suit in state court.[6]

The Nebraska case, however, differed somewhat from the Utah and Florida cases. In this instance, the financial institution in question was not a national bank, but rather a federally chartered S&L. Attorneys for the Hinky

[3] *First National Bank of Logan* v. *Walker Bank and Trust Co.*, 385 U.S. 252 (1966).
[4] *First National Bank* v. *Dickinson*, 274, F. Supp. 449 (1967).
[5] *First National Bank* v. *Dickinson*, 396 U.S. 112 (1969).
[6] *State of Nebraska, ex. rel. Clarence A. H. Meyer* v. *American Community Stores*, 228 N.W. 2d 299 (1975).

Dinky stores argued that the S&L fell under the regulatory jurisdiction of the Federal Home Loan Bank Board (FHLBB); further, they argued that the FHLBB had the legal power to authorize federally chartered S&Ls to operate as it wished. The Nebraska Supreme Court agreed; it held that if the FHLBB authorizes a federally chartered S&L to install computer terminals in retail stores, the owner or operator of the store is not engaging in bank branching activities. The decision can have far-reaching consequences for branching laws as they apply to FHLBB member S&Ls.

The FHLBB has been empowered by the Congress to regulate the federally chartered S&Ls in this country. It can enact rules and regulations for their organization, operation, and incorporation. Although it has no specific authority to allow member S&Ls to establish branches, courts have interpreted this as being the case. Like the Comptroller of the Currency, the FHLBB has taken the position that member S&Ls can employ EFTS terminals for purposes of deposits, withdrawals, and the transfer of funds. It also, like the Comptroller, takes the position that EFTS terminals are not branches. However, unlike the Comptroller, it has not met with any strong opposition to its stance; nor have the courts overturned its rulings. Unlike in the case of the national banks, Congress imposed no branching limitations on FHLBB member S&Ls. Congress left this decision entirely to the discretion of the FHLBB.

Traditionally, state-chartered banks have viewed federally-chartered S&Ls with little of the trepidation with which they view national banks. Courts also, as the Nebraska case illustrates, have not imposed any branching limitations on FHLBB member S&Ls. FHLBB member S&Ls were established for the purpose of providing funds for the construction and purchase of housing. Unlike commercial banks, they have not been permitted to accept demand deposits. Branching laws were not directed at FHLBB member S&Ls largely because state-chartered banks did not view them as competitors. With the advent of EFTS, and the advantages FHLBB member S&Ls enjoy through branching laws, this may change.

EFTS have already sparked rivalries between the national banks and FHLBB member S&Ls. The national banks regard the branching restrictions imposed on them as discriminatory. They argue that these same restrictions should apply to federally chartered S&Ls. The national banks fear that while they are constrained from constructing EFTS terminals, FHLBB member S&Ls may gain an advantage in the area of EFTS; as FHLBB member S&Ls have increasingly made their way into areas traditionally the domain of national banks, this rivalry has become more intense. It first surfaced in the EFTS area in Illinois. In 1974, an Illinois national bank went to federal court and challenged the ability of FHLBB member S&Ls to establish branches.[7] Lawyers for the national bank argued that national banks were

---

[7] *Lyons Savings & Loan Association* v. *Federal Home Loan Bank Board, et. al.* 1377 F. Supp. (1974).

being discriminated against. However, the court disagreed; it noted that national banks were regulated differently and subject to different regulatory provisions from FHLBB member S&Ls. Since they were established to perform different roles, it could not be said that they were being discriminated against. The court's decision gave federally chartered S&Ls a blanket immunity from branching prohibitions. They could establish EFTS terminals, free of branching prohibitions.

When confronted with charges of discrimination, the FHLBB member S&Ls note that they pose no present economic challenge to either state-chartered or national banks. However, EFTS may open new markets for them—perhaps even bring them in a head-on confrontation with the national banks. The FHLBB has taken the position that it will allow its members to establish branches; competitors fear that FHLBB members may eventually, because they are immune from branching prohibitions, establish a monopoly over EFTS.

Several other major branching court decisions have been handed down; these merit some analysis because they are indicative of near future legal trends in the area of branching. All these cases have proven consistent on one point: national banks must comply with branching restrictions. In a well-publicized Colorado case, the Comptroller's Office authorized a Colorado national bank to establish EFTS terminals at a shopping center several miles away from its home office. The EFTS terminal allowed bank customers to make withdrawals and deposits and transfer funds. The case made its way to federal court, and the judge ruled that the bank had violated the state's branching laws.[8] He noted that there was little, if any, difference between an automated terminal operated by the bank and a stationary deposit facility; the automated terminal, he held, was similar to a branch and could be held to be a branch.

In an effort to remove the limitations placed on EFTS terminals owned and operated by national banks, the Comptroller, in 1975, issued a ruling that sought to exempt EFTS terminals from the branching prohibitions. The Comptroller's ruling provided, in part, as follows:

> A national bank may make available for use by its customers one or more electronic devices or machines [EFTS terminals] through which the customer may communicate to the bank a request to withdraw money either from his account or from a previously authorized line of credit, or an instruction to receive or transfer funds for the customer's benefit. The device may receive or dispense cash in accordance with such a request or instruction, subject to verification by the bank. Such devices may be unmanned or manned by a bona fide third party under contract to the bank.

---

[8] 394 F. Supp. 797 (1975).

This ruling was soon challenged by the Independent Bankers Association of America.[9] The court held that it saw no difference between the way a customer makes a deposit at an EFTS terminal and at a stationary receptacle. In the court's view, both were branches and fell within the ambit of the branching prohibitions. National banks, the court noted, cannot escape the sway of these laws by simply substituting an electronic terminal for a branch office constructed out of mortar and brick.

PROS AND CONS OF BRANCHING

Supporters of branching argue that unrestricted branching will result in the demise of the local state bank. The banking industry, they note, will fall into the monopolistic grips of the banking giants. They point to the auto industry as an example, and they decry the decline of the small "mom and pop" store in America. Small banks, they will tell you, know the community and its needs; they understand the towns and cities they operate in, and know how to serve them best. Further, they are an integral part of the community; they do not live in faraway places. Their needs and those of the community they serve are one and the same. The financial giants, they report, neither care nor understand the needs of the thousands of small communities in this country; they bear these communities no loyalty, and look upon them as simply another market.

Branching supporters also note that without branching laws, deposits will be concentrated in a few large banks. Such a concentration of economic power, they fear, will lead to higher (rather than lower) prices for credit. Further, the giant banking interests will find it more profitable to finance large corporate ventures rather than small community needs. Branching laws, we are told, serve to stave off an alliance between the banking giants and the multinational corporations; such an alliance would not only imperil small banks but would also pose a threat to small business in general.

Opponents of branching, however, argue that the fears of diminished competition are exaggerated. They question whether state branching laws do, in fact, curtail the concentration of deposits in a few large banking institutions. They point to Texas in support of their argument. Texas is the third largest state, it is the home of 10 percent of this country's banks, and state law prohibits branching. However, branching prohibitions have not stifled financial concentration; 15 banking institutions in Texas control more than 50 percent of that state's deposits.

Critics also charge that branching laws promote inefficiency and give small banks monopolies over local communities. These communities are thus denied access to modern banking services. Branching laws, critics also note, hinder the development of EFTS; by defining EFTS terminals as branches,

---

[9] *Independent Bankers Association of America* v. *Smith,* 402 F. Supp. 207 (1975).

state branching laws deny their citizenry access to a convenient method of banking. Small communities are denied the benefits of modern banking technology. The object of branching laws, critics will tell you, is to ensure that well-entrenched local financial interests continue to enjoy their local banking monopolies. By placing limitations on the expansion of the large national banks, branching laws have created safe havens for inefficient, monopolistic, and antiquated state-chartered banks.

Few banking-related disputes match that of branching in emotions. It pits not only small against large banks, but also states' rightists against aggressive federalists; the roots of the conflict lie in the early history of this country. For the states' rightists, branching laws symbolize a bulwark against encroaching federalism; for their opponents, branching prohibitions exemplify an antiquated mode of banking that can no longer be justified in an electronic society. Regardless of which side one selects in this battle, there can be no dispute that branching laws do retard the growth of EFTS.

These arguments, regardless of their merits, pose no solutions. "Where do we go from here?" you ask. At the crux of the dispute lies the small banker's fear (and with some justification) that the large banks will absorb him. EFTS must not be closed to the small banking interests. It is this fear that must be addressed: how to ensure that the small banker has an interest in EFTS. Both large and small banks have a role to play in EFTS.

ANTITRUST IMPLICATIONS

In April 1977, the federal government filed suit against the Rocky Mountain Automated Clearinghouse Association, charging it with violating the federal antitrust laws. The government, in its complaint, alleged that the association had deprived the small financial institutions access to key financial facilities. In a separate action, the federal government charged the American Telephone and Telegraph Company with violations of the Sherman Act because of its dominant market position within the communications industry. Trade associations representing more than 150 computer-related firms charged that the nation's largest computer manufacturer violated a 1956 consent agreement with the Justice Department requiring the company to make its computers and other equipment available to purchasers on the same terms as to lessees.

These cases highlight some of the antitrust issues that have had an impact on the growth of EFTS. Higher operating costs, increased customer demands for quality services, and a shift to EFTS by some of the larger financial institutions have led many within the banking community to view the cashless society as a key factor in their economic survival. EFTS technology, however, is expensive; to finance the needed terminals, communication links, computer processing facilities, and switches for routing messages among participating depository institutions, many financial institutions have entered into joint ventures. Others have established franchise arrangements.

However, both governmental and private sources have raised concern that some of these EFTS-related sharing arrangements may be in violation of the federal antitrust laws. These sources point out that sharing arrangements restrain competition, restrict the activities of their members, and establish monopolies that discriminate against nonmembers. There is justified concern that many of these sharing arrangements may result in diminished competition. In addition, the smaller banks, unable to construct their own systems, fear that they will fall prey to the larger institutions. Our economic history amply justifies their concerns.

POTENTIAL ANTITRUST VIOLATIONS

The theoretical objective of the federal antitrust laws is to maintain a free marketplace in which the forces of free competition reign, the private sector produces in accord with the needs of the free marketplace, and consumers are allowed to have freedom of choice. Artificial barriers to the entry of other businesses into this free marketplace are viewed as being illegal monopolistic constraints. These monopolistic practices, blatant in the late nineteenth century, led Congress to act: in 1890, it passed the Sherman Act.

Section 1 of the Sherman Act makes all contracts, combinations, and conspiracies in restraint of trade illegal; it also outlaws combinations and agreements between competitors formed for the purpose of fixing prices. Section 1 of the act also makes it illegal for firms engaged in the same business to agree to divide up the marketplace. Section 2 of the act prohibits monopolies or attempts to establish a monopoly over any area of interstate or foreign commerce; this includes any conspiracies or combinations to establish a monopoly. Monopolists who employ predatory practices or coercive tools to gain a dominant position within a market would find themselves prosecuted under the Sherman Act.

In 1914, under increasing public pressure to take additional steps to curtail corporate predatory practices, Congress passed the Clayton Act. Among other things, the Clayton Act prohibits a business from acquiring stock in a company if the outcome of such an acquisition would be to lessen competition. The act also empowers an individual or firm that has been injured as a result of violations of the antitrust laws to bring a civil action for damages. Subsequently, Congress passed additional antitrust legislation; the gist of the antitrust laws is to preserve and safeguard the free marketplace and ensure competition.

Joint EFTS ventures involving several large institutions thus could find themselves in violation of the antitrust laws. These laws require that an EFT system be open to both large and small firms alike—that there be no discrimination. The antitrust laws also require that a business refrain from inhibiting competition among participants in a venture by compelling them to adopt uniform prices, allocate markets, and force unnecessary standardizations. Three key areas of any EFTS joint venture will come under scrutiny by prosecutors: who will have access to the system; whether entry will be closed to nonparticipating members; and whether the venture discriminates against competitors or the consuming public at large.

Access

EFTS ventures will be scrutinized in terms of who has access to the system. Access will be determined in terms of whether a nonmember can gain access to the system by payment of reasonable fees. Our courts have long held, in analogous industries, that access by nonmembers must be nondiscriminatory. The classic case in this area came before the Supreme Court in 1912. In the Terminal Railroad Association case,[10] a group of large railroad companies had established an association with the objective of monopolizing all access routes across the Missouri River. Nonassociation railroads found themselves discriminated against, since they could utilize these access points controlled by the Terminal Railroad Association only if the association's members gave their unanimous consent. The federal government brought suit, charging the association with violating the Sherman Act. The Supreme Court found that the association had, indeed, discriminated against nonmembers, and had also established a monopoly over the access routes across the Missouri River. The Court found the association to be in violation of the antitrust laws. The case illustrates two key points regarding joint EFTS ventures: first, they must not discriminate against nonmembers; and second, they must not negate or hinder competition.

Entry

Joint ventures also must not limit entry to an EFT system only to participating members. To exclude nonmembers would negate competition. The 1964 Penn-Olin case amply illustrates this point.[11] It involved a joint venture by subsidiaries of two large chemical firms; the objective of the venture was to produce sodium chlorate for the southeastern U.S. market. At that time, only two other firms manufactured sodium chlorate for that same market. The federal government, however, brought an action under the Clayton Act; it charged that the joint venture had the effect of lessening competition in the southeastern market. The Supreme Court agreed with the government and held that the joint venture did, in fact, negate competition and was in violation of the Clayton Act, The case illustrates a key question regarding joint EFTS ventures: does this venture negate competition? If it does, it constitutes a violation of the antitrust laws.

---

[10] *United States* v. *Terminal Railroad Association,* 224 U.S. 383 (1912).
[11] *United States* v. *Penn-Olin Chemical Company,* 378 U.S. 158 (1964).

Discriminatory Practices

Joint EFTS ventures must not result in discriminatory practices against either competitors or consumers. The classic case in this area involved the Associated Press (AP); in 1945, the case made its way to the Supreme Court.[12] In the AP case, federal prosecutors charged that AP had discriminated in the dissemination of its news reports by forbidding its members to disseminate these reports to nonmembers. In addition, non-AP members found it difficult to join. The Court held that AP had discriminated against its competitors. The case should suffice as indicia that joint EFTS ventures likewise must not discriminate against their nonmembers.

STATE SHARING LAWS

To insure that the smaller financial institutions are not denied access to EFTS, more than 24 states have attempted to address the issue of sharing through legislation. Fourteen states make sharing arrangements mandatory; several states have enacted legislation that permits sharing but does not make it mandatory. Other states have sought to expand their sharing statutes to include both state- and federally-chartered financial institutions.

State sharing laws require that large financial institutions share their EFTS services or components with their smaller counterparts. The object of these state laws is to ensure that the smaller financial institutions will not be placed at a competitive disadvantage in an EFTS environment. They seek to ensure that the EFTS technology is equally available to both large and small financial institutions. However, questions have been raised whether these state sharing laws are in violation of the federal antitrust laws. To date, the Justice Department has brought no prosecutions involving state sharing laws. However, some Justice Department sources have noted, informally, that some of these state sharing laws could possibly constitute a violation of the antitrust laws. The political overtones of these state laws have restrained federal officials from taking any antitrust action.

STATE REGULATION DOCTRINE

Our courts have long held that the federal antitrust laws were not drafted with the objective of restraining legitimate regulatory action by the states. Where state regulations specifically direct the acts of private individuals or firms, these individuals and firms are immune from liability under the antitrust laws.[13] Private individuals or firms, acting within the ambit of these state regulations, are immune from antitrust prosecution; but private

---

[12] *Associated Press* v. *United States,* 326 U.S. 1 (1945).
[13] *Parker* v. *Brown,* 317 U.S. 341 (1943).

firms acting outside the scope of these regulations and engaging in discriminatory and monopolistic behavior can be prosecuted successfully.

Some government sources, however, take the position that not all EFTS state-mandated sharing arrangements are immune from prosecution under the antitrust laws. They note that many state sharing laws do not establish any state agencies to enact any rules and procedures and oversee the workings of these EFTS sharing arrangements. Rather, these state laws only direct that access and entry to an EFT system be open to large and small financial institutions alike—that small banks are not discriminated against. In addition, these sources also note that for state sharing laws to provide immunity from prosecution, they must establish regulatory procedures and a state agency to oversee compliance. The NCEFT, in its study of EFTS, noted that state sharing laws retarded the growth of EFTS and recommended that steps be taken to ensure competitive EFTS. However, save for the NCEFT's allusion that state sharing laws created a noncompetitive EFTS environment, the federal government has taken no official stand in regard to whether private activities mandated by state sharing laws fall within the state regulatory doctrine and thus are immune from prosecution under the federal antitrust laws.

The form and direction EFTS will take will be determined, in large mesure, not only by our technology but also by our branching and antitrust laws. Branching laws appear to be in conflict with the needs of modern banking; our antitrust laws appear to deter efforts to safeguard the interests of the small financial institutions through EFTS sharing arrangements. Both branching and sharing laws evoke emotional responses well beyond the realm of banking. If a sophisticated EFTS edifice is to become a reality, these issues must be resolved. A first step would be to assure the smaller institutions that they, too, have a role to play in the cashless society.

6
THE RISE OF ELECTRONIC CRIMES

It has taken the chief accountant of a large firm several months of overtime to build a complete model of his company's financial operations on its computer. It was time well spent; at least Mr. Wrong thought so, for over the last several years, he has slowly and methodically embezzled more than $5 million from his employer. The computer told him that by making each phony payment within the normal 10 percent level of inventory shrinkage he can continue, undetected, leisurely pilfering a little at a time until the company gives him his retirement party.

In a large eastern city, the chief teller of a well-known financial institution is charged with stealing in excess of $1 million from his employer by simply using the bank's computer. He was able to transfer funds electronically from legitimate accounts in the bank's computer to fraudulent accounts he controlled at several other financial institutions. Not to be outdone, a group of white-collar felons with ties to organized crime copy key financial and personal data stored in the computer of a large retail chain.

The cashless society, with millions of subscribers and the bulk of this country's economy dependent on it, could easily prove an attractive target for criminals and terrorists. Computer-related crimes are on the increase. They pose a serious problem for both the private and public sectors. Computer felons are said to steal in excess of $100 million annually; some law enforcement sources place the figure as high as $500 million. The average computer "caper" is said to be in excess of $400,000 and the probability of apprehending this electronic felon is said to be 1 in 100. Even if convicted, the likelihood of the electronic criminal going to prison is 1 out of 500. The cashless society—with its several hundred thousand computers, millions of terminals, and an army of several million men and women needed to operate it—will face a serious threat from the electronic criminal.

EFTS CRIMES

Thieves with a knowledge of computerized bank codes and how to transfer funds electronically nearly stole $2 million by simply transferring these funds over various communication circuits stretching from Florida to Mexico. A civilian pay clerk for the military is charged with embezzling more than $40,000. He allegedly programmed a government computer to print out dozens of checks drawn on accounts from the various military agencies. The checks were made out to several of his associates, who, in turn, cashed them and shared the proceeds with him.

These cases illustrate the ease with which computerized financial systems can be bilked by highly motivated felons, armed with the necessary technical know-how. EFTS-related crimes will pose a serious problem for both government and the private sector. Electronic criminals will find that preying on these systems can be both easy and rewarding. Lax security, ill-trained police forces and prosecutors, and antiquated legal procedures will pose little deterrence to this new breed of criminal. EFTS computers, terminals, and communication lines will find themselves the objects of attack by an array of electronic criminals: dishonest employees, extortionists, organized crime, sophisticated white-collar criminals, and terrorists.

EFTS-related crimes will take on various forms. The majority of these crimes will be financial in nature. By simply manipulating the input data, felons can create phony earnings, ghost employees, and assets. There are ample examples of computer-related financial crimes. For example, the biggest fraud in American history involved the Equity Funding Company of Los Angeles. In the Equity Funding case, top management (assisted by other company employees) played an instrumental role in defrauding the investing public out of more than $1 billion. In 1969, Equity's tax management embarked on a massive falsification of insurance policies and corporate assets. Two-thirds of the company's more than 97,000 life insurance policies were fabricated; these fictitious policies were then recorded in Equity's computer. These phony policies were assigned a secret computer code: Department 99. The "99" designation enabled the company's computer billing programs to skip the bogus policies when bills were sent to the real policyholders. When government auditors requested documentation of the life insurance policies, Equity's officers supplied them with forged hard copies. The massive fraud surfaced only when a disgruntled former employee "blew the whistle." Had it not been for this, the fraud might have continued undetected for several more years.

Data-related crimes will also be on the increase in the cashless society. Valuable programs, mailing lists, personal records, trade secrets, and other valuable confidential data will become the target of criminals. Confidential data can be copied or intercepted; the technology is readily available to accomplish this. In addition, lax security (both physical and personnel) will make it easy for criminals to gain access to data stored in EFTS. Employees at a computer facility can easily be bought, blackmailed, or frightened into cooperating; organized crime has shown an uncanny ability in subverting corporate employees. Specialized fencing networks will be established by criminals to handle valuable stolen data.

Theft of services will also be a problem for EFTS. This type of crime may take the form of unauthorized use of a bank's computer, or other EFTS components, for the personal gain of the felon(s). For example, computer operators have been known to use their employer's facilities to run computer services for personal gain. Felons have also used bank and university computers for their own direct mailings. One government study disclosed how an engineer, no longer employed at a computer installation, continued to make unauthorized use of his former employer's computer long after he had left. It's been estimated that he used in excess of $4,000 worth of the company's computer time. The classic theft of services case involved a midwestern bookmaker who used the computer of a local university to calculate his bets. Unauthorized use (theft of services crimes) of EFTS by employees and others will pose a growing problem in the cashless society.

Property-related thefts will also be a problem in an EFTS environment. These types of crime will usually involve the theft of merchandise or other property through the simple manipulation of an EFT system. Criminals can easily employ stolen or counterfeit EFTS cards to pay for the merchandise; or, through the simple manipulation of an EFT system's computer, they can arrange for the payment or diversion of valuable property. An analogous case in this area involved the computers of the Pacific Telephone and Telegraph Company. An engineering student gained access to the company's computers and was able to steal more than $900,000 worth of valuable merchandise from the company. In a similar case, a group of felons (allegedly tied to organized crime) diverted more than 200 freight cars from the Pennsylvania Railroad Company to a small railroad terminal in Illinois; they did this by simply manipulating the company's computer. These analogous cases serve to illustrate the ease with which corporate computers can be manipulated by felons with the requisite technical know-how to steal valuable merchandise and equipment.

EFTS will also become the targets of sabotage and vandalism. Terrorists, disgruntled employees, and felons may seek to cripple or retard the ability of an EFT system to function adequately; the motives may vary from politics to economics. Competitors may also attempt to sabotage the computer facilities of a competing financial institution. In addition, labor–management disputes may also result in attacks (sabotage or vandalism) vented against EFTS. The sabotage of a key EFT system could bring about political and economic chaos in any of our large cities, where the populace would find it difficult to conduct its everyday financial transactions.

A series of major attacks resulting in the destruction of key EFTS computer nerve centers could bring about political and economic upheaval. Experts estimate that the destruction of several hundred key computers in the

United States could deal a severe blow to its economic fiber. The destruction of key EFTS computer facilities could similarly deal a severe blow to the cashless society. Sophisticated criminals and terrorists could hold an EFT system hostage. Adequate security measures can play a key role in deterring such acts.

POTENTIAL EFTS FELONS

An employee at a key federal agency was charged with embezzling more than $500,000 by simply manipulating the agency's computer. The agency's computer issues more than $1 billion in disability checks to more than 4 million workers and their dependents each month. Federal prosecutors allege that the defendant processed disability checks under numerous aliases, using real social security numbers; the defendant then proceeded to erase all records of payments from the computer before it produced a regular audit of claims and payments. Government investigators also allege that the defendant was not acting alone, and may have been taking orders from members of a religious cult. The investigator in charge of the case summarized the alleged crime as follows: "This was a very sophisticated scheme and the . . . lack of safeguards at (the agency) is alarming. There's a potential that we're sitting on the tip of an icebreg."

TABLE 1. CHARACTERISTICS OF THE ELECTRONIC FELON[a]

Age	18 to 30 years
Race	Caucasian
Sex	Male
Skills	Professional technician
Personal traits	Intelligent
	Highly motivated
	Seeking adventure
	Views crime as challenge
	Fears ridicule
	Usually works alone
	Middle class
	Can justify crime
	Robin Hood syndrome
	Living beyond means
	Thrill seeker
Prior criminal history	None

[a] These represent the more common traits and characteristics attributed to the electronic felon by the popular mass media. Although they do for interesting reading, they bear little semblance to reality.

The news media and some studies of computer-related crimes often portray the electronic criminal as young, aggressive, adventuresome, arrogant, and a modern-day Robin Hood. His or her acts frequently are interpreted as being those of the individualist striking back at technology.[1] Crime, for the electronic felon, becomes a game; he matches his wits against the computer, and comes out winning. Monetary gain, we are told, plays a secondary role.

Although the "Robin Hood syndrome" serves the needs of the popular media when portraying the electronic felon, it bears little semblance to reality. The real threat to EFTS will come from organized crime and its associates, white-collar felons, and terrorists (especially in cases of international EFTS). Adequate security measures can go a long way in deterring the illegal acts of the lone electronic felon: the disgruntled employee, the mentally unstable, and the traditional felon, who now turns his attention to EFTS. It is the professional and sophisticated felon, armed with the requisite technical know-how, that poses the real threat; his motivation is gain, and crime for him is a business rather than a game. The political zealot, technically sophisticated and motivated by blind adherence to ideology, also poses a formidable challenge. In Italy alone, terrorists have sabotaged more than 20 computer facilities, some with serious consequences for their victims. Crime in the cashless society will become the preserve of the professional criminal. It is his challenge that we must address.

One of the more serious criminal threats to EFTS will come from organized crime. The modern "Syndicate" is sophisticated, well-versed in the ways of the financial world, and has the requisite financial and technical resources to infiltrate and subvert the cashless society. It controls immense wealth and owns (directly or through legitimate fronts) a number of businesses and financial institutions; it has also demonstrated an ability to commit complex and sophisticated white-collar crimes. For example, the Syndicate is said to be behind the theft, counterfeiting, and manipulation of billions of dollars of securities. Organized crime also controls and has access to sophisticated fencing networks that can find buyers for its EFTS-related capers; for example, it could easily dispose of valuable mailing lists, confidential corporate or personal data, trade secrets, and other EFTS-selected valuables.

Increasingly, white-collar crime has become big business in America; white-collar felons are said to steal in excess of $40 billion annually. White-collar felons have been engaged in an array of sophisticated frauds: complex payoff and kickback schemes, massive embezzlements, insurance and bankruptcy frauds, and an array of government program and contract frauds. White-collar criminals have also made their way into the EFTS arena (especially the computer). Sophisticated, highly motivated, well-

---

[1] We increasingly find women making their way into the arena of electronic crime.

TABLE 2. ROLE OF ORGANIZED CRIME IN THE STOLEN SECURITIES AREA[a]

Main Targets for Theft of Securities	Techniques to Attack Targets	Techniques to Convert Securities[b]	Conversion of Stolen Securities
Brokerage houses	Direct infiltration by the mob	Thieves turn stolen securities to syndicate elements or their associates (fences)	Stolen securities are converted to cash for the benefit of organized crime by:
Banks	Persons under pressure to steal securities:	Fences sell the securities to legitimate sources	Resale through brokers
U.S. mail			Placement in banks as collateral for loans
Individuals	Gambling debts		Placement in portfolios of insurance companies
	Loansharking debts		Transfer outside the United States, where they are:
	Narcotic addiction		Resold
	Strongarm		Placed in banks as collateral
	Thieves who depend on mob for conversion		Used to establish trust accounts, which are used to make letter of credit or certificates of deposit for return to United States

[a] Based on the findings of the U.S. Senate Permanent Subcommittee on Investigations.

[b] Securities which are stolen include corporate stocks and bonds and U.S. notes and bonds. These securities are either in "street name," bearer instruments, or names of companies or individuals.

organized and funded, white-collar criminals pose a serious threat to the cashless society.

Terrorism is a growing and serious problem in many parts of the world. In a number of European, African, and Asian countries, terrorist groups have caused serious injury to computer facilities and the personnel that man them. The cashless society, with its computers and terminals, will prove to be both an attractive and a vulnerable target for terrorists. Destroying a nation's electronic banking system could prove more damaging than kidnapping its business and political leaders. Holding the economy hostage can have a devastating psychological impact on the victim. The terrorist has both the tools and motivation to attack an EFT system. The terrorist adds to the sophistication and motivation of the white-collar criminal a willingness to use violence, posing a formidable economic and political threat for EFTS. His actions can lead the government to employ draconian measures, which, in turn, can rob a democracy of its freedoms. Thus terrorism poses not only a physical threat but also a political one. Given the present global instability, terrorism enjoys a fertile environment to grow in.

Supporters of EFTS have long noted that they will rid society of many traditional crimes; banks and street robberies may become a thing of the past. However, EFTS will also spawn new and more sophisticated crimes that may pose a greater threat to society. Further, the advent of the electronic criminal may tax the resources of our criminal justice system to a point beyond which it ceases to be effective. We should take serious note of these matters as we design the cashless society.

THREAT OF ELECTRONIC PENETRATION

Electronic penetration of EFTS poses a serious threat to the integrity of the cashless society. Computers and communication lines in EFTS will be open to an array of electronic attacks. However, electronic entry tools require a degree of technical know-how that only a limited number of professional criminals may possess; but in their hands, electronic interceptive tools can pose a formidable threat to EFTS.

One of the more widely employed electronic interceptive tools is the wiretap. Taps can easily be connected directly to the communication lines of an EFT system, thus enabling a felon to intercept and record messages. Another mode of electronic interception is the electromagnetic pickup. Electromagnetic devices are readily available which are designed to intercept the radiation generated by an EFT system's telephone and teleprinter lines. Criminals can also connect an unauthorized terminal to a valid private line and enter the system whenever the legal uses is inactive but still holds the communications channel. This technique, known as the between-the-lines entry, can also be employed to access an EFT system.

TABLE 3. ANNUAL INCOME OF ORGANIZED CRIME IN FLORIDA[a]

Areas	Sources	Value
Gambling (bookmaking)	Only for Dade County	$ 44,000,000
	Profits only from nine operations in Dade and Broward counties	$ 4,650,000
Bingo frauds	Profits only from eight operations in Broward County	$ 8,000,000
Narcotics	Property losses from crimes committed to support heroin habits	$ 276,000,000
Financial frauds	In 34 Florida counties	$ 950,000,000
Total		$1,282,650,000

[a] Does not include the annual national income of the Syndicate estimated by the Chamber of Commerce of the United States to be in excess of $50 billion.

TABLE 4. ANNUAL COST OF WHITE COLLAR CRIME

Type of Crime	Sources ($ in billions)			
	U.S. Small Business Administration	Chamber of Commerce of the United States	American Management Associations	Joint Economic Committee
Arson			1.3	
Bankruptcy fraud		0.08		
Bribery, kickbacks, payoffs		3.0	3.5–10.0	3.85
Burglary	0.958		2.5	
Check fraud	0.316	1.0	1.0–2.0	1.12
Computer-related		0.10		0.129
Consumer fraud		21.00		27.0
Credit card fraud		0.1	0.5	0.500
Embezzlement		3.0	4.0	3.86
Insurance fraud		2.0	2.0	2.50
Pilferage/employee theft	0.381	4.0	5.0–10.0	4.84
Robbery	0.77			
Securities theft/fraud		4.0	5.0	0.291
Shoplifting	0.504		2.0	
Vandalism	0.813		2.5	
Receiving stolen property		3.50		
Total	$3.05	$41.7	$29.3–41.8	$44.2

Another common electronic interceptive tool that can be employed to penetrate an EFT system is browsing. This involves the tying of an unauthorized terminal into a system that does not authenticate terminal entry. The browser gains access to the system. Criminals can also probe a system for unprotected entry points caused by error, malfunction, or lax security. This technique is known as trapdoor entry. Criminals have also employed the piggyback-entry technique; messages in the transmission stage are selectively intercepted and altered. The modified message is then released to the valid user. EFTS could prove extremely vulnerable to these interceptive techniques.

The foregoing electronic interceptive tools are readily available; sophisticated criminals, with the needed technical know-how, can easily employ them against EFTS. The threat from organized crime and white-collar criminals is a serious concern in this area. Technology has provided the professional criminal with the necessary electronic tools to attack the cashless society.

INVESTIGATING EFTS CRIMES

Historically, every society has employed its police agencies to deter criminal activity. Deterrence very often is gauged by the effectiveness of a society's police forces, its prosecutorial tools, and its judicial system to deal effectively with criminal behavior. It is also judged by the penal and rehabilitative machinery of its correctional institutions. Prosecutors, by necessity, must rely on the police agencies to go forth and investigate criminal acts. It is the investigatory arm that must develop bits of evidence into a credible case for use by prosecutors in a criminal trial. In our federal system police agencies fall into one of two camps, local or federal. However, our local police agencies, to date, are ill-trained and ill-prepared to deal effectively with sophisticated EFTS-related crimes. Many of our federal police agencies fare no better.

At the local level, our police agencies face a serious problem when confronted with complex EFTS crimes. Local police forces are small and fragmented. There are more than 40,000 local police departments in this country; more than 50 percent of these employ fewer than 10 full-time police officers. The local trend is not toward a merger of resources but rather toward a proliferation of smallness. The President's Commission on Law Enforcement and the Administration of Justice described local law enforcement in America as composed of small forces, each acting independently within the limits of its jurisdiction. Cooperation between this myriad of local police agencies frequently is nonexistent.

EFTS crimes will call for new police investigatory tactics and strategies. Their complexity will necessitate cooperation between the many local police forces, and also new training programs to develop the in-house technical know-how within these forces. Whether local law enforcement can meet the threat and challenge of the EFTS criminal remains to be seen.

Many of our federal police forces fare no better than their local counterparts. Cooperation between the federal agencies often is the exception rather than the norm; few of these agencies share their investigatory findings with other federal investigators. In addition, cooperation between local and federal law enforcement leaves much to be desired. Local police complain that their federal counterparts "do little of the footwork, and take all the glory." Further, some federal agencies—for example, the Internal Revenue Service—are prohibited by law from exchanging investigatory data with other investigatory units(federal or local).

The federal police forces, like their local counterparts, suffer from petty jealousies and rivalries, lack of progressive leadership, and lack of adequate training to deal effectively with complex EFTS crimes. Save for the Federal Bureau of Investigation and the U.S. Secret Service, few federal agencies have taken steps to train their investigators in this area. In addition, many federal investigative units (among them the SEC, FDIC, and FHLBB) have only civil jurisdiction; criminal cases must be referred to other agencies for criminal prosecution. Jurisdictional rivalries may well dissuade such cooperation.

The federal police forces, like their local counterparts, need training and a new strategy in this area. Further, many of their archaic bureaucratic practices must be streamlined to conform to the needs of the cashless society. The eletcronic criminal, armed with intelligence and technical know-how, poses a formidable challenge; it is one that the federal police agencies can ill afford to neglect.

PROSECUTING ELECTRONIC FELONS

The prosecutorial machinery consists of an army of local and federal prosecutorial agencies. The local prosecutorial machine consists of an array of rural, urban, and suburban prosecutors; these go under such names as state attorneys, district attorneys, county attorneys, and state attorney generals. At the federal level we also have a wide variety of prosecutorial agencies; however, save for the U.S. Justice Department, these other agencies have only civil and administrative powers. For example, commodity frauds would fall within the jurisdiction of the Commodities Futures Trading Commission (CFTC), but the CFTC has only civil and administrative powers. It must refer all criminal cases to the Justice Department for action. However, like the investigatory apparatus, the prosecutorial agencies may prove ill-equipped and ill-trained to handle complex EFTS crimes.

The local prosecutorial machine fares no better than the local police agencies in meeting the challenge of the electronic felon. It finds itself handicapped by a lack of resources, training, and the needed jurisdiction to investigate complex EFTS frauds. For example, fewer than 50 percent of all state attorney generals have annual budgets in excess of $1 million. It should be pointed out that complex EFTS frauds, especially when perpetrated by such groups as organized crime or white-collar criminals, could easily cost several hundred thousand dollars to investigate and bring to prosecution. It is not unusual for a complex fraud to cost an added several hundred thousand dollars to bring to a successful conclusion. Problems connected with lack of resources are further magnified when prosecutors are under community pressure to prosecute traditional street crimes. The local prosecutor may also find his options limited by the jurisdictional limitations placed on him by our federal system. For example, a small city prosecutor would not be able to subpoena witnesses and records located in other states. He may also find it difficult to obtain the assistance of other local prosecutors.

Criminal prosecutions at the federal level are confined to the Justice Department and its 94 U.S. Attorney Offices. However, save for the U.S. Attorney Offices located in our large metropolitan centers, the majority of these local federal prosecutors' offices are small and lack the expertise to handle sophisticated EFTS crimes. Even the large offices, with their specialized Fraud Units, have severe limitations placed on their manpower and resources to commit the necessary efforts in complex EFTS crimes. For example, the average Fraud Unit may average 10 attorneys; the total number of all prosecutors employed by these units numbers about 300 men and women. At the present, this small prosecutorial force would be called on to bear the brunt of the federal effort in the EFTS area. Lacking adequate resources and training in this area, the U.S. Attorney Offices would find themselves unable to adequately handle the criminal referrals from the numerous federal agencies, or even those brought to their attention by the FBI and the Justice Department in Washington, D.C.[2]

Adequate funding and training and better utilization of existing resources by the prosecutorial arm of our criminal justice system can assist in combating complex EFTS crimes. However, even an adequate investigative and prosecutorial arm will not prove a sufficient deterrent, unless the other components of the criminal justice system are brought into the fold of modernity. There are statutory, evidentiary, judicial, and penal issues that remain to be addressed.

EFTS CRIME LEGISLATION

Only a handful of states have enacted legislation to address some of the problems connected with computer crimes. There is also a federal Electronic Fund Transfers Act (EFTA) that attempts to address some of the criminal

---

[2] The Justice Department often acts as a clearinghouse; the bulk of the federal prosecutions are handled by the U.S. Attorneys and some specialized units.

problems related to the cashless society.[3] The act makes it a crime for anyone to:

- Knowingly use or attempt or conspire to use for any counterfeit, fictitious, altered, forged, lost, or fraudently obtained debit instrument to obtain money, goods, services, or anything of value.
- Knowingly transport or attempt or conspire to transport in interstate or foreign commerce a counterfeit, fictitious, altered, forged, lost, stolen, or fraudulently obtained debit instrument knowing the same to be counterfeit, fictitious, altered, forged, lost, stolen, or fraudulently obtained.

The act addresses crimes that make use of EFTS cards to gain entry into the system; how the courts will interpret the act remains to be seen. In addition, it remains to be seen whether courts will expand it to cover EFTS frauds that do not rely on EFTS cards.

At the state level, prosecutors have employed traditional criminal laws to combat EFTS-related crimes. Arson statutes have been employed in cases involving a burning; burglary, embezzlement, and larceny statutes have also been used where an illegal taking of property has occurred. Conspiracy, forgery, and false pretense statutes have also been used with some limited success.

At the federal level, an array of Title 18 United States Code statutes have been employed, with mixed success, in the area of computer-related crimes. The wire fraud and mail fraud statutes have proven of value only when felons employ the wires or the mails in interstate or foreign commerce to perpetrate the fraud. The Omnibus Crime Control Act, enacted to deal with illegal electronic interceptions of oral communications, would prove of little value here since EFTS transmissions are not oral. Forgery laws have proven of some limited value. Some efforts are currently on hand to enact specific legislation to address some of the EFTS-related problems.[4] However, legislators both at the local and federal level must take added steps to address specific EFTS-related problems, lest prosecutors find themselves without an adequate legal arsenal to deal with the electronic felon.

Prosecutors and investigators will also encounter procedural and evidentiary problems when dealing with complex EFTS crimes. Although simple cases such as EFTS-related arsons and vandalisms should pose no greater problem than other traditional criminal cases, complex EFTS frauds raise serious investigatory and prosecutorial problems. One area of serious concern is that of search warrants. Traditionally, courts require that a search warrant be as specific as possible as regards the following:

[3] 88. Public Law 95–630.
[4] In January 1980, Senator Abraham Ribicoff introduced S. 240 (the Federal Computer Systems Protection Act) in the 96th Congress.

- Records to be seized.
- Time period in question.
- Number of persons whose records are sought.
- Area(s) to be searched.
- Credibility of source.

A search warrant must not be overbroad, lest it be open to challenge and all the evidence seized under it be excluded from the trial. In an EFTS environment, it may prove difficult for the police to be specific about the records to be seized, the time period in question, the number of persons involved, and the areas to be searched. The police will have to call on experts to assist them in drafting the search warrant so as to meet the legal criteria outlined by the courts. Prosecutors issuing subpoenas will face many of these same problems.

Further, police searches of EFTS facilities will necessitate that the authorities bring an expert with them to assist them; they need a guide. Using employees at the EFTS facility as guides could prove ill-advised, since many could be suspects in the investigation. It might also be necessary to suspend operation of the facility so as to conduct the needed search; shutdowns could prove costly for the system, and there is also the danger that investigators destroy or erase EFTS records in the process. Law enforcement agencies will, by necessity, have to train and establish specialized units to handle complex EFTS frauds.

Technical experts will also have to be called in when wiretaps are being considered. Before a court issues a wiretap order, the police must first convince a court the following:

- There is probable cause that an individual(s) has committed, is committing, or is about to commit a crime.
- Communications about that offense will be obtained by the surveillance.
- Those communications will occur at a specified time.
- Normal investigative procedures have failed.

To withstand a successful court challenge, the wiretap order must be specific as to the communication, location, and time. Once again, the police must call on experts for assistance lest the evidence they gather be successfully challenged. However, even with the aid of experts it may be difficult to meet the specificity test; in addition, there is the real possibility that the authorities might inadvertently threaten the privacy of nonsuspects.

Law enforcement agencies will also encounter serious evidentiary difficulties in the area of complex EFTS frauds. Present evidentiary rules would make it difficult to introduce into evidence such things as computer printouts, magnetic tapes, magnetic disks, paper tapes, and punched cards.

Prosecutors, especially those at the local level, will encounter such objections as the Best Evidence Rule, which calls for the introduction of the original document into evidence in a trial. Prosecutors will also encounter some problems with the Hearsay Rule, which excludes oral or written statements made out of the court as evidence in a trial. The New Federal Rules of Evidence attempt to facilitate computer- and EFTS-related litigation; however, many states continue to adhere to archaic evidentiary rules and procedures. These evidentiary rules and procedures will pose a problem for complex EFTS prosecutions.

JUDICIAL AND PENAL ISSUES

Judges act as referees. They are called on to decide what evidence will be admitted in a trial and the procedures to be pursued, and they render their verdict at the conclusion of a trial. Some experts are fearful that our present judicial apparatus may prove ill-equipped to deal effectively with complex EFTS-related prosecutions. Complex white-collar prosecutions amply document this problem. Further, many local judges are hard pressed for time; they handle a large number of cases and lack the requisite time needed to become well versed in complex electronic frauds.

Compounding the problem of judges is that of juries. The Seidlitz prosecution in Maryland amply illustrates the problem.[5] The case involved a simple fraud by computer. However, the federal prosecutors were fearful that the jury might not understand the technical evidence presented in the trail and that in its confusion it would find in favor of the defendant. Prosecutors face a serious problem when confronting juries with these new technological crimes. Juries may prove unable to grasp the intricacies of EFTS crimes. As we venture into the cashless society, traditional crimes will increasingly become outmoded; EFTS crimes will become the wave of the future.

These EFTS crimes will also call for a reassessment of our present penal philosophy; we may have to alter our penal system to accommodate this growing class of electronic criminals. Confinement is often a last-resort measure. In deciding whether to confine or release (probation or parole) an individual, judges and parole boards often look at his prior history: his role and status in society, family and community ties, involvement in drugs, prior criminal history, type of crime (whether violent or not), and so on. This is the traditional penal model, geared to deal with offenses committed by the lower strata of our society. However, we should ask whether such a model can realistically serve us in an environment inundated with EFTS crimes.

[5] *United States* v. *Seidlitz,* U.S. District Court for the District of Maryland, Criminal No. 76–0794.

This new breed of criminals may call for a drastic reform of our present penal system. Personnel in our penal facilities may have to be retrained; our counseling and halfway house programs may also have to be modified. Sentencing and parole guidelines will have to be altered. Hard-core EFTS criminals—for example, organized crime types—may prove difficult, if not impossible, for any penal system to reform. In addition, there is a real possibility that with the advent of EFTS crime, two types of penal system may take form: one for our traditional criminals, and the other for our electronic felons.

We are told that the invention of gunpowder had a profound effect on crime. Murders and robberies took on new form; the lone felon, armed with this new technology, became a fearsome adversary. EFTS similarly will give rise to new crimes and call forth new solutions. Crime in the cashless society will pose a challenge and test our ability to adapt our criminal justice system—in a democratic manner—to this new technology.

7
SECURING EFTS

A computer programmer employed by a savings and loan association trans-ferred over $4000 from bank customer savings accounts into that of his wife. A magnetic-tape librarian when informed by her employer that she was fired replaced all of the computer master file tapes with blank tapes. A bank employee stole all of his employer's computer programs and documentation and held them for ransom. Two employees of a federal agency breached a $500,000 security system with the aid of a screwdriver; they unhinged the door to the computer facility and proceeded to steal carts of magnetic tape. A study of a large federal agency whose computers store confidential data on millions of Americans concluded that its com-puter security program did not even meet the minimum standards for data security.

Security in a computerized environment is an area of growing concern for both the public and private sectors. The cashless society—with its army of computers and terminals—is extremely vulnerable to criminal attack. The Federal Reserve System, concerned about EFTS security, has commenced testing encryption equipment to guard its EFT system against unauthorized access and fraud. The Fed's 40,000-mile communications net-work, centered in Culpeper, Virginia, is comprised of a series of switches located at Fed banks and branches; these switches link member commercial banks to their respective Fed district banks. The Fed's EFT system handles an average of 80,000 messages daily; securities and funds, valued in excess of $150 billion, are transferred through the system to the Fed's more than 5000 member commercial banks. The Fed is concerned that the system may be vulnerable to sabotage and other forms of criminal attack.

EFTS VULNERABILITIES AND SECURITY

For many years, the evolution of computer technology was based on the assumption that it operated in a benign environment; the army of men and women that operated this technology were viewed as honest and trustworthy.

Computers were stored behind glass doors and storefront windows; their high visibility was desirable and interpreted as a symbol of corporate efficiency. Both the private and public sectors took pride in their newfound technology. The computer became a status symbol; few, if any, steps were taken to safeguard the assets and confidential data stored in its electronic data banks. Although some experts noted concern that errors and omissions could impair the system's efficiency, scant attention was paid to the potential criminal threat posed by individuals both within and outside the computer facility. In 1973, the massive Equity Funding fraud disrupted this euphoria; it caused great concern for data security. The honeymoon was over.

EFTS security may be defined as the safeguarding of the data in such systems against unauthorized disclosures, modifications, or destruction. An adequate security program encompasses deterrence, prevention, detection, and recovery techniques. A security program is said to consist of three categories of safeguards:

1. A physical security program, which seeks to safeguard the integrity of the system, its components, environment, and access controls.
2. A personnel security program, which encompasses operational and procedural security tasks to oversee the tasks performed by the individuals who operate the system and also to test their trustworthiness.
3. A communications security program, which safeguards the transmission of data from illegal interception, modification, or destruction.

An adequate security program must also identify and classify the data it seeks to safeguard, the resources it has available to safeguard that data, and the potential threats to those data. In addition, a threat analysis of the system should be conducted to determine the natural forces (fire, water, and earthquakes) and potential felons that could pose a threat as well as the probability of that threat becoming a reality.

EFTS are vulnerable in three key areas: (1) the computer facility that operates the system; (2) its terminals; and (3) the communication lines that link the system's components. The computer is said to constitute the central nervous system; all the data and assets stored in an EFT system are recorded in its computers. Although computer technology has grown in sophistication and storage capacity, the computer itself continues to be extremely vulnerable to criminal attack at any of the following four operational stages: input, programming, CPU, and output.

At the input stage, a computer is fed the basic data it must process and store. At this stage a criminal can introduce false data, alter the data, or destroy them; many computer-related frauds are committed at the input stage. False accounts can also be created at this stage, and fictitious deposits and withdrawals entered. The computer can also be manipulated at the programming stage. At this stage, instructions are given to the computer in the form of programs; the computer can use only those data the program instructs it to use, and can perform only those operations the program directs it to perform. Since programs can easily be altered, the computer is open to manipulation at the programming stage. Programs can also be stolen or destroyed, either at the computer installation itself or through a remote terminal. Further, a program's safety devices can be manipulated, with changes continuing undetected for an extended period of time.

The CPU constitutes the central nervous system of the computer; it guides the computer by following the instructions it receives from the program. It retrieves the required data and directs the computer to perform the necessary functions with respect to those data. Destruction of the CPU can deal an EFT system a serious blow. Of equal concern, for purposes of EFTS security, is the output stage. At this stage, data are received and translated into intelligible forms. Crimes at this stage may take the form of thefts of mailing lists, customer lists, and confidential financial data.

An EFTS terminal is also open to criminal attack. Customers' plastic cards have been counterfeited by criminals through a method called skimming. This process involves the transference of magnetically encoded data from one card to another. Criminals can also resort to the buffer recording technique to produce better quality counterfeit cards. The process, however, is more complex and expensive than that of skimming. Criminals have also been known to use stolen or lost plastic cards to penetrate an EFT system. Unfortunately, many bank customers also write their PINs on their plastic cards, thus facilitating criminal abuse of the system. Employees of EFTS have also been known to assist criminals. Bank tellers, retail cashiers, and terminal maintenance personnel can prove of invaluable assistance to professional felons.

The communication links of an EFT system are also open to fraud and abuse. Both off-line and on-line systems have been penetrated by criminals. In an on-line system the terminal is not directly connected to the system's computer by communication lines. Rather, the data are stored in magnetic tapes or punched cards and physically delivered to the computer facility. A criminal can defraud the system by simply altering, deleting, or destroying these instruments.

In an on-line system, the terminal is connected to the system's computer by telephone lines. Criminals can employ imposter terminals to penetrate the system and intercept confidential data or customer PIN numbers. Imposter terminals can also be employed to alter or delete information. These wiretap devices frequently are simple to operate and inexpensive, and they pose a serious threat to the system's communication links. A complex EFT system often employs communication switches, which enable computers within the system to communicate directly with one another. These switches, however, are also vulnerable to criminal electronic penetration and manipulation.

Adequate security measures could play a key role in curtailing many EFTS criminal attacks. Unfortunately, for too long both the private and public sectors have shied away from adequate security programs. When lax security is added to our poorly equipped investigatory and prosecutorial machineries, the criminal finds an inviting environment. Security can play a key role in safeguarding the cashless society.

PHYSICAL SECURITY

Investigators for the General Services Administration found during one of their surprise inspections at a supposedly secure federal computer installation that access was simple. One of the investigators described their surprise visit as follows:

> We entered that [computer] center. We wore no visible identification and were unknown to the employees at the center. We moved about the installation freely. None of the employees we met challenged us nor did anyone ask for our IDs.

A study of another federal agency found that the average compliance with its own security standards was only 36.9 percent. Access to the computer facility was on the basis of "just knock, and you'll be let in."

The objective of any meaningful EFTS security program is to implement measures that can safeguard and preserve the integrity of informational, physical, and human assets by minimizing the exposure of the system to an array of threats that can disrupt or nullify its ability to provide services. An EFTS physical security program seeks to minimize, and when possible prevent, injury to the system by intentional, accidental, or natural events. An adequate physical security program must encompass not only the computer installation itself, but also the tape library, magnetic volume control, terminals, and other components of the system.

Physical security programs will vary from system to system; they must be sufficiently flexible to meet the needs of the equipment and the environment in which the system functions. The program must accommodate not only the needs of the system itself, but also everyday economics. Physical security employs a series of physical barriers, visual and electronic surveillance tools, and procedures that limit access to the system's protected areas. An in-depth program makes wide use of an array of technical tools: perimeter barriers(both natural and structural), perimeter entrances, protective lighting, intrusion alarm systems, detection systems, and closed circuit television systems. The objectives of these physical barriers can be summarized as follows:

- To safeguard the data and assets recorded in the system.
- To insure the integrity of the magnetic media on which the data reside.

- To provide the needed documentation for both investigatory and prose-cutorial purposes, should security be breached.

However, no EFTS security system—regardless of the sophisticated tools it employs—can guarantee 100 percent security for the system or any of its components. Security can only make access more difficult, discourage unauthorized entries and electronic interceptions of the system's communication links, and possess the capability to detect intruders.

Adequate physical security, however, must be structured not only to meet the challenge of illegal penetrations of the system but also to address problems connected to the physical environment itself. Natural disasters, such as fire and flooding, can also seriously impair the ability of the system to function adequately. Physical security programs thus must employ an array of fire detection and extinguishing systems. They must also be geared to deal with flood-related problems. Power failures and mechanical breakdowns can shut a system down; even a brief shutdown can prove costly. An adequate security program must take note of such eventualities. Standby equipment and reserve power services must be readily available to ensure that the system will continue to function efficiently.

Power- and equipment-related breakdowns can also be a cause of major concern for an EFT system. A security program must address such problems; for example, the loss of a system's air conditioning can result in temperatures and humidity changes that can shut down the system. Standby air conditioning systems may be necessary. Further, problems may develop with the system's ventilation equipment. This can result in hazardous rise in heat. Backup equipment and also alarm systems will be needed to address these threats. Lightning bolts can produce problems for the system. They may give rise to electrostatic fields, which can create serious problems for the system. Antistatic equipment may be needed. In addition, it may be necessary to survey, in advance, the physical environment in which the system will operate to ensure that such natural events will be of minimal occurrence. Atmospheric ions have also interfered with the operations of EFTS; ions have been found to retard the performance of computers. Even dust and smoke particles can affect sensitive EFTS equipment.

Man-made phenomena such as magnetic fields caused by radar and high-power transmitters can also affect EFTS. In designing a security system, both natural and man-made phenomena must be taken into consideration. Both environmental and intentional acts by individuals can seriously hamper the operations of an EFT system.

The facilities selected to house the computers that run the system must be of sufficient structural integrity to provide adequate and effective physical security for the system. Site selection for a computer facility and EFTS terminal can prove important. The facility should not be housed in heavily populated areas or in structures that are open to members of the general public. Criminals and terrorists must not be afforded easy access. The computer facility should be located at the center of a building; glass doors and windows, which invite entry, are discouraged. Locations subject to accidental floodings should also be avoided. Access to tape libraries, data preparation areas, and the computer itself should be regularly controlled by barriers and electronic detection devices.

A windowless and solidly constructed structure is the ideal site for a computer facility. Glass doors and windows should be replaced with impenetrable plastics or masonry. Ground floor windows should be equipped with alarms and the glass should be replaced with some durable plastic. Doors should be metallic, and door hinges should be mounted on the inside. Doors should also be secured from the inside; an alarm system should be employed to detect illegal entries. Hinge pins should be brazed to make their removal difficult.

Physical access controls are also necessary to control the flow of human traffic into the facility and discourage illegal entries by unauthorized personnel. Access to restricted areas can be controlled by such physical barriers as counters and locked doors equipped with electrical releases. A badge system should also be employed whenever possible, and guards should be stationed at key entry points. Emergency entrances should be controlled and have alarms. A system of identification numbers may be employed to control access to the facility and identify authorized personnel. Logs and strict accountability over key entry tools should be integrated in the security program. The loss of keys, badges, and identification cards should be immediately investigated. Key access points should be monitored by closed circuit television. Access to the computer facility and other sensitive components of the system must be limited to authorized personnel; visitors, equipment maintenance personnel, and others must be restricted in their movements. In addition, an in-house guard force (or contract guards) should be employed.

Access to the system's libraries must also be limited. Magnetic tapes, disks, paper tapes, and punched cards are stored in the library. A librarian must be assigned the specific responsibility for volume labeling, access control, and accountability for all the volumes stored in the library. The library should be located, whenever possible, adjacent to the computer facility or at least within a protected area. Safeguards against fire, floods, and other natural phenomena must be implemented. Essential software must be safeguarded from both criminal attack and natural disasters. The electrical facilities that support the system—such as electrical closets and transformer vaults—must also be secured.

Terminal security is also of paramount importance to an EFT system. Terminals must be secured from both intentional and accidental disasters. A terminal should be located in a secure environment; terminal usage should be carefully monitored, and illegal intrusions should be investigated. Access to the terminal must be restricted to authorized personnel; sensitive output data should be removed from the terminal location only by authorized employees. Power control locks should be used to prevent misuse, and terminals located in general office areas should be removed when not in use. Terminals should be located only in secure areas.

All physical security measures, however, should be coordinated with police and fire departments. Their assistance can be called upon in designing a physical security program. Physical security, when adequately planned and implemented, can play a key role in safeguarding an EFT system and its crucial components from intentional, accidental, and environmental acts.

PERSONNEL COUNTERMEASURES

The employee of a large engineering firm—with the assistance of the company's computer—was able to steal some $20,000 before the fraud was uncovered. He simply pocketed cash receipts and destroyed the related computer input documents. An executive with a major manufacturing firm took his employer for about $1 million by simply creating "ghost" suppliers and employees. Checks were issued to the fictitious accounts; the executive and his fellow conspirators simply pocketed the funds.

Physical security can play a key role in deterring the unsophisticated felon; it can serve to secure the system from external attacks. Personnel security, however, is directed at the insider; the dishonest and disgruntled employee, who misuses his position of trust and authority for personal gain. Breaches in personnel security have played a key role in enabling organized crime, white-collar felons, and terrorists to penetrate a computer facility. Computer-related crimes should be sufficient indicia of potential difficulties that a complex and advanced EFT system can face; personnel security can play a key role when employed in conjunction with other security measures to deter these crimes by insiders.

EFTS personnel security is concerned with sabotage, vandalism, frauds, and the theft of data by insiders. It seeks to screen and evaluate present and prospective employees and others with access to sensitive equipment and key operations of the system. Personnel security programs are specifically geared to individuals with regular access to data input and output media or data processing equipment. In an advanced cashless society, where records on millions of Americans will be available at the push of a button to individuals who operate the system, the potential for great abuse and fraud must be given serious consideration.

At issue in designing a personnel security program is not only the technical competence of the individuals who will man the system but also their dependability, maturity, and mental state. An individual with access to key financial and personal data must also, by necessity, be one with a strong sense of ethics. Criminals and the mentally unstable pose a threat to the integrity of the system. Background checks will be necessary for personnel with key and sensitive positions; those with past histories of criminal misuse of EFTS facilities must not be allowed access to sensitive EFTS operations. Individuals with a long history of gambling, drugs, repeated indebtedness, and personal behavior that opens up an individual to potential blackmail and extortion should also be barred from having access to key and sensitive equipment and operations of the system. Those with a history of heavy alcoholism should also be barred from such positions.

All EFTS personnel should be made aware of their great responsibilities and of the need for adequate security. The role of security and its importance to the integrity and viability of the system must also be outlined to EFTS personnel. Training programs should be established to make EFTS employees security conscious and to familiarize them with security equipment and procedures and the steps to take in an emergency. Personnel should also be told whom to call in case of accidental (fire) or intentional (sabotage) damage to the system. In addition, they should be told which sectors of the system are closed to unauthorized personnel. Instructions to personnel, whenever possible, should be detailed and in writing; further, no one individual should have the authority to process a job from start to finish.

Duties among EFTS personnel should be separated; no one individual should have access to all phases of the operation. An employee with the responsibility for data preparation or error control should not also have responsibility for programming or systems analysis. Individuals with the responsibility for the accounting of assets should not also have custody of these assets. Such practices often invite fraud. Work assignments should be rotated randomly, whenever possible; these random rotations often facilitate the detection of frauds. Enforced absences can also be employed to detect frauds; such absences should be for one or more weeks. Adequate supervision should also be integrated within a personnel security program. Supervisors can play two key roles: first, they can oversee overall operations and employee work performance; and second, they can encourage positive and ethical attitudes among system employees. Employee dissatisfaction and low morale are frequently cited as causes of sabotage and vandalism.

Logging should also be employed in key and sensitive areas of the system; employees should be directed to log the time, date, and the assignment they last performed. Access to sensitive system facilities and equipment should be only on a "need-to-know basis." Whenever possible, outsiders performing maintenance or repairs on the system should be accompanied by authorized personnel. A terminated employee should be required to sign an affidavit in which the employee states that he will not make known to outsiders any confidential or proprietary data he has learned at his place of employment, and that he has not removed any property (hardware or software) from the facility. All stoppages and interruptions should be logged and explained. A register of errors should also be maintained; this should include a detailed record of any and all action taken to remedy the error. Planning and programming personnel should be barred from having access to any tapes used for processing. Program changes should list the dates on which changes were made, who made the changes, and who authorized them. All changes should be tested and properly authorized by a supervisor in charge.

Dishonest employees have been known to alter and destroy master records, manipulate payrolls and accounts, and steal valuable data. Programs, memory devices (tapes and disks), and files have been favorite targets of disgruntled employees. Personnel security can play a role, when employed in conjunction with other security measures, in deterring some of these illegal acts. However, where top management is dishonest and plays a major role in the fraud, the value of personnel security is largely nullified. Personnel security can prove effective only in a business environment conducive to ethical standards and behavior.

COMMUNICATION SECURITY

Financial institutions currently are able to purchase a microprocessor-based cryptographic unit for safeguarding their EFTS transactions. The device seeks to counter wiretap interceptions of customer PIN numbers. After more than two years of research, a West Coast company is said to have developed an inexpensive device for safeguarding the privacy of data transmissions. The device uses a new method of scrambling messages; unless one has the needed device and its proper code, the unscrambling of the message is said to be more difficult than with other encryption devices. Technology has also given rise to devices that identify authorized users based on such personal characteristics as their signatures, fingerprints, voiceprints, and handprints. Devices to analyze the shape of a user's hand can now be purchased for $300 per terminal, signature analysis devices are readily available for $1000 per terminal, and voice and fingerprint analysis devices can be purchased for between $5000 and $9000 per terminal.

Electronic espionage poses a potentially serious problem for the cashless society. The cost of devices for tapping the communication lines of an EFT system is dropping, while the value of the data being transmitted is increasing. According to intelligence sources, for example, Russian agents are said to be using advanced interceptive devices on microwave transmissions in the United States; the data they intercept are then fed to their high-speed computers, which, in turn, extract the sensitive data in the transmission. A former employee, with the aid of an intelligence terminal and his knowledge of his former employer's security system, extracted the firm's unannounced product designs. To counter these electronic security breaches, both the private and public sectors have increasingly turned to a system of passwords and encryption.

Passwords have been used since antiquity to identify authorized personnel. Increasingly, passwords are being used in EFTS to identify authorized users; before a user can gain access to the system, he must first give the correct password. In addition, a password may be used in conjunction with a security code; the password identifies the firm or department and the security code identifies the specific individual within that firm or department who has entered the system. Most passwords, however, do not allow a user access to the entire system. Passwords are also changed periodically (daily, weekly, or monthly) to ensure that unauthorized individuals will not access the system.

However, criminals have been known to gain access to secret passwords; the criminal then uses the password to masquerade as an authorized user. The more common method of obtaining unauthorized access to a password is through stolen or lost documents. Further, criminals have also been known to intercept a user's password or other identifiers by simply wiretapping the user's terminal. All cases involving actual or suspected thefts of a password should be immediately reported and investigated. Passwords can prove of value in curtailing unauthorized use of an EFT system, but they are open to misuse by both dishonest employees and outsiders.

In the nineteenth century, both stenography and cryptography gained wide use. The ancient Egyptians and Sumerians are said to have refined both of these techniques to conceal information they were transmitting. Stenography makes use of invisible inks, and cryptography translates intelligible data into a nonintelligible form. Of the two techniques, cryptography lends itself best to EFTS.

Cryptography was widely used by the military during the American Civil War. The use of the telegraph for transmitting important military messages led to the development of cipher systems. Subsequently, the teletypewriter give rise to automatic cryptography. Thomas Jefferson is said to have developed one of the most sophisticated nineteenth-century cipher systems. G. S. Vernam, one of the founding fathers of modern cryptography, also developed a sophisticated cipher system. It was a two-paper tape reader device; one tape contained the correct message, while the second tape contained misinformation. The misinformation was added to the correct message, and the enciphered message was then sent over telegraph lines. The receiver had a similar device and was thus able to subtract the misinformation from the enciphered message. This mixing of information with random misinformation produced one of the first secure cipher systems.

Through the use of encryption devices, the sender of the message transforms the information into secret form by enciphering the message. The enciphered message is in a nonintelligible form. A legitimate receiver deciphers the information simply by reversing the transformation previously performed on the original data so as to reveal the original message. Cryptoanalysis is the process by which an authorized user attempts to intercept the enciphered message and break its code. Encryption devices are readily available, and their cost is decreasing. Although encryption deters the external attacker, it is of limited value when dealing with the dishonest insider who abuses his position of trust to manipulate the system. Passwords and cryptography alone are of limited value; they must be employed in conjunction with other security arrangements.

SECURITY THREATS

A major financial consortium transfers funds between major commercial accounts in different banks via their shared EFT system. One of its employees transfers $50 million to a bank account that he controls. A financial institution sends its sensitive files to one of its major branches; the files are stored on reels of tape. A dishonest employee makes copies of the tapes and sells them to his employer's competitor. The employer is unaware that one of its key competitors now has a list of all its customer accounts, future marketing plans, and other confidential data.

Security threats to the cashless society come from several sources. The major threat, however, comes from system users and operators, operations support personnel, and system maintenance personnel. A dishonest user may engage in a number of illegal activities. He may make modifications to the hardware and terminal; he may also issue requests of the operating system which result in its misuse. If he has access to other users' information and programs, he may also remove or modify them. It is extremely difficult for an operating system to monitor the activities of all its users.

A system operator has major access privileges that provide an array of opportunities for misusing the system; the operator can exercise these from the comfort of a console to alter, destroy, and copy files without being detected. Similarly, operations support personnel enjoy numerous opportunities to misuse the system; for example, a tape librarian can substitute blank tapes for masters. System maintenance personnel can easily misuse the system because of their position and access privileges. There are ample cases of programmers who have modified the operating system to circumvent security measures. The vendor's programming system representative can also compromise the system by simply planting trapdoors and delivering bogus documentation. Telephone maintenance personnel and the vendor's customer engineers have also been known to misuse the system. Their technical know-how and knowledge of the system makes them a serious potential threat.

EFTS technology makes it easy to store, query, and manipulate vast amounts of data within a brief span of time. Misuse of EFTS data can imperil not only corporate well-being, but also that of the consumer. Privacy legislation and the potential for exposure to privacy lawsuits have led some financial institutions and businesses to enact stringent security safeguards. However, both the private and public sectors lag in the area of security. For many years, security was relegated to a secondary status; it was costly, and corporate public relation officers shied away from it. However, security must be brought to the forefront if the cashless society is to be made secure from criminal abuse.

8
WHITE-COLLAR CRIME
IN THE ELECTRONIC SOCIETY

Employees for a major electronic firm are alleged to have stolen an estimated $750,000 worth of semiconductor components. The theft is said to have taken no more than 20 minutes to carry out; the police fear that the thieves will have no difficulty in finding a buyer. In a separate case, two men are alleged to have attempted to exchange cocaine for more than $30,000 worth of computer memory chips. In a large eastern city, the employee of a major pharmaceutical company was charged with rigging his employer's computer to cover up the theft of $1 million worth of valuable drugs. The defendant is alleged to have sold the stolen drugs to a "fence."

White-collar crime is a serious and growing problem in America; white-collar felons steal more than $40 billion annually. These economic crimes take on an array of forms: securities frauds, bankruptcy frauds, consumer "rip-offs," bribery and kickback schemes, and numerous other frauds. The sophisticated white-collar felon poses a serious threat to the financial integrity of our society; increasingly, organized crime has also made its way into the white-collar crime area. It behooves us to analyze the potential impact the cashless society may have on these economic crimes.

DEFINING THE PROBLEM

White-collar crimes have been defined as illegal acts characterized by guile, deceit, and concealment; force or the occurrence of physical injury plays a secondary role. These economic crimes may be perpetrated against business, government, labor unions, and the general consuming public. The objective of these felons may be to obtain money, property, or services; occasionally, the white-collar felon may also seek to avoid the payment or loss of money or property. Often these crimes are committed by men and women who occupy positions of trust in business and government; corporations have also been known to commit numerous white-collar offenses.

Organized crime has also made deep inroads into the area of white-collar crime; long the province of the executive, professional, and clerk, white collar crime has increasingly become the province of the mobster as well. The gangster of the 1920s has given way to the sophisticated modern mobster, well-versed in the ways of the world of business; occasionally, organized crime figures work hand-in-hand with businessmen and professionals. One underworld informant, testifying before a Uinted States Senate Subcommittee, described this illicit relationship as follows:

> I am trying to show you some highlights of the involvement of organized crime and white-collar crime and their collusion; for . . . organized crime . . . could not function without the help of commercial banks and stock brokers in the United States and their counterparts overseas.

The Syndicate's influx into the legitimate business sector merits serious scrutiny. One Syndicate group, operating nationally, is said to control one of this nation's largest hotel chains; another group is alleged to own some of New York City's largest skyscrapers. A midwestern crime group is said to own real estate valued in excess of $100 million; a multibillion dollar conglomerate is said to be under organized crime control. The Syndicate has also made its way into the banking and financial sectors, and other key sectors of the economy. Several eastern banks are said to be fronts for powerful crime groups; several large retail chains are also alleged to be secretly controlled by powerful crime groups. Armed with the requisite business know-how and capital, organized crime has joined ranks with the white-collar felon in pillaging the economy.

Students of EFTS-related crimes have traditionally concentrated their efforts on crimes directly connected to EFTS. Security measures have been geared at protecting the cashless society from direct efforts to undermine it; scant attention has been paid to how EFTS can be employed to further white-collar crimes. For example, will EFTS facilitate bankruptcy frauds? What impact will EFTS have on Syndicate fencing and loanshark operations? These are questions that remain to be explored. Although EFTS will spawn new categories of crime, they may also augment the ability of sophisticated criminals to perpetrate numerous white-collar crimes, which may grow dramatically in both numbers and sophistication under an EFTS environment.

CATEGORIES OF WHITE-COLLAR CRIME

A dozen felons were charged by the authorities with trying to fence more than $3 million in stock stolen from a bank. Some of the securities were sold to banks and businessmen, who then proceeded to use them as collateral for loans in overseas banks. In a separate case, the police suspect that a loose-knit group of several hundred criminals, operating in several countries through corporate shells, have been involved in a multimillion dollar stock fraud scheme. One of the felons outlined the scheme as follows:

> I have been able to accomplish trades and purchases of securities totalling millions of dollars with no more than $100,000 cash. My margins, at times, exceeded 95 percent of the purchase price of the securities, requiring only five percent of my own funds; and many times that five percent was not even cash, but stolen securities.

Securities-Related Frauds

These are said to account for more than $4 billion in annual losses in the United States. Stolen securities are used as collateral for loans and other financial transactions; they are also used by dishonest businessmen to bolster the sagging net worth of their companies. One dishonest executive is said to have rented stolen securities from Syndicate members and used them to obtain a large loan from a bank. Syndicate-controlled brokerage firms have also been implicated in a number of securities-related crimes; dishonest bank and brokerage firm employees have also been known to divert valuable securities to organized crime figures. In an EFTS environment, where several hundred billions of dollars worth of securities may be transferred daily over the wires, the problem of securities fraud and theft is serious. Securities frauds could take on more complex and frightening forms.

Bribes and Kickbacks

These schemes are found in a wide range of business and government operations: sales, advertising, services, employment, contracts, and others. They are found in dealings between members of the private sector and also between businessmen and government officials. The objective of these illicit acts may be to obtain new business or retain existing business, cover up short deliveries or inferior goods and services, influence legislation, and numerous other activities. Bribes and kickbacks are said to account for more than $2 billion annually and affect every facet of our economy. One large manufacturing firm is alleged to have paid more than $200,000 in kickbacks to the purchasing agent of another firm, over a period of several years, so as to retain its business. The payments were made through several secret Swiss bank accounts. In another case, a bank official was indicted for accepting more than $500,000 in bribes from a criminal group that specialized in counterfeit securities.

Numerous techniques have been employed to funnel bribes and kickbacks. Sophisticated felons have been able to evade detection through complex financial schemes, often involving several banks and foreign countries. Bribes and kickbacks may become easier to funnel in an EFTS environment. Electronically and in minutes, they can be funneled into foreign secret bank accounts, leaving no paper trail behind for the authorities to follow.

Bankruptcy Frauds

These frauds (also known as "scams") are said to exceed $70 million annually. The basic strategy in a scam operation is to purchase merchandise on credit from numerous suppliers; the goods are then disposed for cash, and the proceeds are canceled. The felons then file for bankruptcy. Sophisticated criminals often establish a phony company; funds are deposited in a bank account to establish credit, and the creditors are often provided with doctored income statements. One criminal ring, in a sophisticated scam, bilked creditors out of more than $100,000. The funds were diverted into accounts controlled by the felons.

Detecting and prosecuting these frauds may prove difficult in the cashless society; EFTS lend themselves to scam operations. Corporate assets and earnings can be fabricated through the simple manipulation of a computer. With the assistance of dishonest EFTS employees, criminals can create the semblance of a healthy financial posture and dupe creditors into extending them large quantities of goods on credit.

Embezzlement and Pilferage

Dishonest employees steal more than $4 billion annually from their employers in the form of cash, goods, and services. For many corporations, thefts by employees constitute a major problem; 60 to 75 percent of all retail inventory shortages are accredited to thefts by employees. In some industries, up to 50 percent of a firm's employees may be involved in some form of theft. Those thefts can take various forms: overcharging customers and pocketing the difference, making fictitious advances to employees, overloading expense accounts, shipping merchandise to a friend's or relative's house, and many others. In a paperless system, embezzlement and pilferage schemes may prove more difficult for employers and the authorities to detect.

Consumer Frauds

More than 800 consumer frauds have been identified, to date, by the authorities; their numbers continue to grow. Con men are said to bilk consumers out of more than $20 billion annually. Among the better known of these schemes are charity frauds, work-at-home schemes, home and auto repair swindles, unscrupulous correspondence schools, degree mills, and many others. An EFTS environment will facilitate these frauds and make it more difficult for consumers to obtain restitution. In an EFTS environment, the consumer will lose his present ability to manipulate his finances. A consumer now can place a stop order with his bank on a check he has issued to a swindler; in an EFTS environment, where funds are transferred in minutes, he will lose this leverage. Since he will have no canceled check as proof of payment, suing the swindler for recovery may also prove difficult.

Illegal trade practices, frauds involving government programs and contracts, insurance swindles, and numerous other white-collar crimes may prove easier to perpetrate in a cashless environment. Felons will find it easier to move funds from one account to another. EFTS will also facilitate the laundering of ill-gotten money; funds from domestic bank accounts will be transferred to foreign accounts in a matter of minutes. The absence of a paper trail will make the detection and prosecution of these crimes difficult. Further, the vulnerability of EFTS to manipulation—the fabrication, alteration, and deletion of data—will enable sophisticated felons to create and manipulate millions of dollars at the touch of a button.

ORGANIZED CRIMINAL ACTIVITY

Organized crime is said to gross $50 billion annually from its illicit activities; its earnings exceed those of the auto industry. According to the Chamber of Commerce of the United States, in one city alone, mob-controlled businesses bring in more than $500 million annually. Unfortunately, organized criminal activity permeates every sector of our economy; the Syndicate controls vast political and economic resources. It constitutes a criminal confederation of conspiratorial groups engaged in daily illegal activity, working with one another when it proves expedient to do so. Their objective is economic and political power. Some of these criminal groups have numerous international contacts; many operate in several foreign countries. The impact of EFTS on their traditional criminal endeavors may prove profound.

Illegal Drugs

This illicit market represents a multibillion dollar annual operation for the Syndicate; it is well-organized and financed. Law enforcement sources place its worth at $10 billion annually. The drug trade, however, relies heavily on secret financial transactions; mob agents conduct these secret transactions in numerous foreign countries, and mob couriers carry the needed funds to consummate the drug buys. A paper-based payment system carries with it the danger of detection; a cashless society ensures that large sums of money can be paid in a matter of minutes, over an electronic network composed of thousands of miles of wires. It ensures anonymity for the sophisticated criminal, and little fear of detection by the authorities.

Gambling

These illicit activities are big business for the Syndicate; more than $20 billion is wagered annually with the underworld. Gambling operations encompass lotteries, off-track race horse betting, illegal gambling establishments, and betting on numerous sporting events. What impact EFTS will have on illegal gambling operations remains to be seen; however, it is doubtful that EFTS will stifle illegal gambling operations as some law enforcement sources believe. Rather, it may force these operations to adopt more sophisticated techniques to evade detection and prosecution.

Loansharking

These operations constitute a lucrative source of income for organized crime. Loansharks lend money at extortionate rates of interest, varying from as little as 250 to as much as 1000 percent annually. A client who borrows $20,000 from a loanshark, at a 20 percent weekly interest rate, may be expected to pile up $208,000 worth of interest in one year alone. Loansharking operations, according to the New York State Commission of Investigation, provide a "principal avenue by which crime syndicates have invaded the entire area of legitimate business." Loansharks have demonstrated an uncanny ability to adapt to the changing financial environment. High-level loansharks have established corporate fronts as covers for their activities; some have used financial institutions as vehicles for their illicit operations. The cashless society may make local and unsophisticated loansharks vulnerable to police detection and prosecution; however, sophisticated, high-level loanshark operations, servicing an affluent clientele, will escape prosecution by simply employing the corporate umbrella to disguise their operations.

Labor Racketeering

Labor unions have, traditionally, posed an attractive target for the Syndicate. With their pension funds—amounting to more than $100 billion—they are a tempting prey; according to federal prosecutors, union locals in 25 different sectors of business and industry are now said to be under the control of organized crime. Occasionally, businessmen openly call on the Syndicate to assist them with labor-related problems; for example, the executive of a multibillion dollar retail chain was charged with soliciting the assistance of the Syndicate to persuade striking labor leaders to scale down their demands.

Syndicate members have shown little reluctance to "dip their hands" into union treasuries. Mob figures have borrowed billions of dollars in union pension funds to finance mob-connected or mob-controlled businesses. Whether EFTS will discourage such activities remains dubious; the Syndicate has demonstrated an uncanny ability to adapt to sophisticated financial innovations. Rather, EFTS may prove a useful vehicle in the mob's stealing of union funds. EFTS may make it possible for them to funnel union funds into many of their diverse ventures without leaving a noticeable trail behind.

The cashless society will also give rise to new categories of crime: frauds that are related to its technology will make themselves felt. However, EFTS will also have an impact on present white-collar crime. The white-collar felon and his Syndicate counterpart will, when armed with EFTS technology, develop more sophisticated techniques to defraud their victims and evade prosecution. EFTS may result in more costly white-collar crimes and may make it more difficult for law enforcement to bring these felons to prosecution. The potential impact of EFTS on economic crimes merits close study.

9
CONSUMER AND CIVIL
LIABILITY ISSUES

The American Bankers Association plans to launch a pilot program designed to cut down the flow of canceled checks. Rather than returning a canceled check, participating banks will simply signal the sender electronically that a check has been received. The transaction signals will be sent between computers over a direct line; the test will include more than 40 financial institutions. Sponsors of the program hope that the system, if implemented, will save the banking industry in excess of $1 billion annually.

The Virginia legislature considered legislation that would have made banks in the state liable for their errors; the bill was defeated by a small margin. A Rhode Island pharmaceutical company filed a $12 million lawsuit against a computer systems developer, charging it with "negligence, misrepresentations, and breach of contract." In Maryland, a computer leasing firm filed a $627 million suit against several insurance firms for failing to pay on its insurance claims.

Computer-related litigation is increasing; it pits employer against employee, bank against customer, buyer against seller, and vendor against user, to name a few. In a cashless society—where key financial and personal data will be daily transmitted over a complex system of computers and communication wires—fraud, error, and the malfunctions of EFTS will give rise to a multitude of civil suits.

CONSUMER PROBLEMS

Numerous lawsuits may arise from two areas relating to consumers: first, the data collection process; and second, the credit transaction stage. EFTS will service millions of Americans; it will store voluminous data on each consumer. The data will come from an array of sources and will find their way into many EFTS computers. However, the potential for erroneous and fraudulent data reaching the system's data banks is one for serious concern;

the detriment that negative data can have on a consumer's credit rating, and also his standing in the community, cannot be dismissed.

Inaccurate data can be the outcome of one or more of the following:

- The consumer may have been mistaken for another.
- The information may come from biased sources.
- The data may be based on malicious gossip.
- A system employee may inadvertently computerize erroneous data.
- Felons may alter the data stored in the system.
- The data base may be incomplete.

Much of the data that credit bureaus, financial institutions, private investigators, and other private sources collect, often comes from court records, newspapers, trade journals, arrest records, and numerous other public documents; for example, if a Mr. Henry Smith is sued and a judgment against him is obtained, this information might make its way into the EFTS computers. The probability that the judgment may be entered under the wrong Henry Smith is not beyond the realm of possibility.

Occasionally, biased data may also make their way into a consumer's EFTS file. For example, a consumer may feel that a retailer cheated him; in retaliation, the consumer may renege on his payment. The consumer's failure to pay would find its way into the EFTS computers. Unfortunately, the record would not reflect the real reason the consumer failed to live up to his side of the bargain. The record might also incorporate biased data the angry retailer may have provided the credit bureau.

Derogatory information may also find its way into a consumer's EFTS file. For example, a businessman may have been denied life insurance because of a derogatory report that accredits one of his neighbors with statements that the businessman drinks heavily. The president of a large credit bureau best summarized the problem as follows:

> You go to a neighbor and establish rapport. . . . Then you ask, "What's your opinion of X's home life; how do you think of him as a family man?" This will usually elicit some hint. . . . Then you start digging. You press them as far as they go, and if they become recalcitrant, you go somewhere else.

Private investigators have also been known to fabricate consumer information; these data, too, may eventually make their way into the consumer's EFTS file. Malicious gossip—like biased data—may also make its way into a consumer's records.

Computer errors are common and not always easy to detect; purging a record of these errors can prove both costly and time consuming. In a cashless society, the probability that errors will be incorporated into a consumer's file should not be dismissed. As a result, a consumer may find that his credit standing, his ability to obtain insurance, and even his career, may have been seriously hampered by these errors. Few consumers possess the requisite sophistication to take legal steps to review and purge their records of erroneous data; in a cashless society, where the erroneous data might be stored in several EFTS systems, the task might prove even more difficult.

Computerized data stored in EFTS may be altered by a felon. Men and women in positions of power and leadership might find themselves the targets of blackmailers and political opponents. By simply altering an individual's EFTS file, the perpetrator could deal a prominent political figure a serious blow. Another potential problem is incomplete consumer data; this, too, may distort the credit standing of a consumer.

A consumer's credit rating is the outcome of several credit stages; each of these is regulated by law. These stages will be affected by the cashless society. The first stage is that of prenegotiations; during this phase, the consumer—through advertising or a felt need—seeks out the lender. The second stage is that of negotiations; during this phase the consumer and lender discuss the arrangements under which the consumer is to repay the borrowed funds. The consumer relies on written and oral representations made to him by the lending institution. The third stage is that of formalization; here the consumer and lending institution enter into a formal agreement. The performing stage constitutes the fourth stage of a credit transaction. Here the consumer makes his payments, as agreed, and is provided with written documentation that he has carried out his part of the agreement. The final stage is termination; at this stage the lending institutions move against a consumer who has failed to abide by their agreement. This last stage may take the form of repossession, foreclosure, or attachment. The cashless society will have an impact on all of these credit transaction stages.

Injured consumers can turn to either privacy or consumer laws for recourse. The law of privacy, already discussed in great detail in Chapter 4, will prove of some benefit when addressing consumer problems connected to fraud, error, and system malfunctions. These often result in invasions of privacy. However, privacy legislation does not address questions related to consumer credit transactions. For consumer injuries related to these, one must turn to consumer laws related to credit protection.

CONSUMER CREDIT PROTECTION LAWS

Consumer credit is regulated by an array of federal and state laws. At the state level, a bewildering variety of specialized statutes address issues related to consumer credit. Among these are the laws that regulate usury, small loan statutes, motor vehicle installment sales, revolving charge accounts, and installment loans. The federal government has also enacted numerous laws regarding the payment–credit system; the outcome of both state and federal laws, unfortunately, has been to create the appearance of confusion. In addition, some of these laws may prove difficult to apply in an EFTS society.

Uniform Commercial Code

First promulgated in 1948, the Code has been adopted by every state except Louisiana. It is the outgrowth of joint efforts by the National Conference on Commissioners on Uniform State Laws and the American Law Institute. These two sponsoring groups also constitute an editorial board, whose task it is to monitor developments in the areas affected by the Code. The Code consists of eight articles; these govern and regulate the majority of our present financial transactions. Article 4 of the Code is specifically concerned with the area of bank collections and deposits; it outlines uniform rules governing the interbank collection process and the bank–customer relationship in the collection and payment of items.

In a paper-based monetary system, a credit transfer is first initiated when the depositor instructs his bank to pay money to another; the bank proceeds to debit the depositor's account and credit that of the other party. The depositor's instructions are often in writing; occasionally, they may also be oral. The bank then proceeds to send the payee's bank a draft drawn on it or a correspondent bank; it may also effect the transfer through the Fed or Bank Wire. In an EFTS society, however, a depositor will be able to initiate a transfer by using a remote terminal. His instructions will be communicated to a processing center, which will then complete the transfer or switch the message to an appropriate processing center. The transfer of funds will be electronic. However, students of the Code fear that an EFT will cause problems for the Code. The consensus is that these problems will stem from two areas: differences in terminology and in concept.

The definitional problems are the more visible of the two; for example, the word "item" poses problems. The Code defines an item as "any instrument for the payment of money."[1] It is taken to mean a writing. The problem, however, is whether a writing includes magnetic tapes, disks, paper tapes, or punched cards employed in an EFT system. Some legal writers take the position that these instruments can be defined as writings for purposes of the Code, since they contain payment messages similar to those found on a check. Article 4 does provide for contractual deviations from its specific provisions; however, these deviations would only serve to undermine the uniformity of the Code. The Code's provisions now are understood and accepted by all states except Louisiana; marked deviations from it would only undermine its homogeneity.

Even ignoring the Code's definitional problems, it faces serious conceptual

[1] U.C.C. Sec. 4–104.

problems concerning EFTS. In a checking system, the bank–customer relationship is contractual in nature. The bank assumes the obligation to pay money according to instructions provided by the customer. If the bank fails to abide by these instructions, it is liable to the customer for any resulting losses suffered. For example, if a bank honors a forged check, this constitutes a breach of its contract with its customer.[2] A bank may also be found to have breached its agreement if it fails to honor a properly payable check.[3]

The Code, however, also imposes duties and obligations on the customer. He is expected to inspect his periodic bank statements and returned checks for alterations and forgeries; he must promptly notify his bank of any discrepancies he finds.[4] Failure to do so will exempt the bank from any liability to the customer. The Code also imposes a duty on the customer to draw his check properly. A customer who, through his negligence, substantially contributes to his own loss, is precluded from asserting defenses against a payor who pays in good faith and in accord with reasonable commercial standards.[5]

The customer, however, does have the right to expect that any transfers made by his bank will be performed correctly. Further, he has reasonable basis to expect that an error to which he did not contribute will be remedied and he will be compensated for losses he has suffered. The bank must, under the Code, act in good faith and exercise reasonable care in its dealings with its customers. The Code thus seeks to balance the rights of both the depositor and his bank.

EFTS, however, raise serious problems for the Code. The question of "signature verification"—so crucial to the Code—has no meaning when applied to a monetary system that employs "electronic blips" to conduct financial transfers. In addition, fraud and error take on different forms in EFTS. EFTS computers are vulnerable to both criminal attack and error by system employees. However, it may take months or even years before a customer finds that he has been defrauded or that his financial record is in error. His failure to give prompt notice may bar him from recovery under the Code. If a customer wants to negate a credit transfer now, he simply instructs his bank to stop payment; if the bank fails to heed his instructions, the bank and not the customer is liable for the loss. However, in an EFTS environment, where funds will be transferred electronically from one account to another in a matter of minutes, a stop payment order will have no meaning.

The Code directs both customer and bank to act with "ordinary care" and in "good faith." However, the standard for what is ordinary care may change in an EFTS environment; it may need to be redefined. As for the good faith standard, this, too, may need redefining in the cashless society. The Code defines good faith to mean "honesty in fact in the conduct or transac-

[2] Sec. 4–103.
[3] Sec. 4–402.
[4] Sec. 4–406.
[5] Sec. 3–406.

tion concerned."[6] In a complex EFT system, a customer might have a difficult time demonstrating his honesty if his bank did not act in good faith. For example, how does a customer prove that he never authorized a transaction in a system where signature verification plays no role? The Code also provides that a bank that wrongfully dishonors an item (check) will be liable to its depositor for all damages proximately caused by its action.[7] How does one prove that it was wrongful to dishonor "electronic blips"? To prove this may require a depositor to retain the costly assistance of experts. The Code's definition of a wrongful dishonoring may have to change under EFTS.

The advent of EFTS raises serious questions about the Code's future. Whether broadly framed Code standards, drawn for a paper-based system, will suffice for complex and intricate EFTS remains to be seen. The consensus among legal writers, however, appears to be that the Code will lose its effectiveness—unless steps are taken to remedy this—in the cashless society.

Garnishment

Garnishment is any legal or equitable procedure through which the earnings of an individual are required to be withheld for payment of a debt. Garnishment procedures are established by state law and vary from state to state. However, in an effort to discourage predatory extensions of credit, the Congress enacted the Consumer Protection Act (CPA).[8] The CPA places limits on the garnishment of a debtor's wages:

> The maximum part of the aggregate disposable earnings of an individual for any work week which is subject to garnishment may not exceed . . . 25 per centum of his disposable earnings for that week.

The CPA goes on to define earnings as

> compensation paid or payable for personal services, whether denominated as wages, salary, commission, bonus, or otherwise, and includes periodic payments pursuant to a pension or retirement program.

Under the CPA, up to 75 percent of a debtor's disposable earnings are protected from garnishments by creditors.

It is not clear, however, whether the CPA's exemptions extend also to income a debtor deposits in his bank account. Under our present check system, a debtor circumvents this problem by simply not depositing his check in his bank. However, this may not always be possible in a cashless society. In an EFTS society, an individual's wages will automatically be deposited in a

---

[6] Sec. 1–201 (19).
[7] Sec. 4–402.
[8] 18 U.S.C. 1671 et seq.

bank by his employer. Creditors will be able to evade the safeguards of the CPA by simply attaching the funds once they are deposited.

It has been suggested that the CPA be amended to extend its safeguards to EFTS bank accounts. However, even if this is done, the CPA's exemptions will prove difficult to apply because banks will not always find it easy to distinguish deposits of earnings or pension payments from payments from other sources. It may also prove difficult for a bank to know whether a debtor's wages were already garnished at their source, since privacy laws make it difficult to exchange personal or financial data about an individual. New garnishment procedures and safeguards—specifically designed for the cashless society—may have to be implemented to meet the needs of an EFTS society.

Assigning Liability

In November 1978, Congress passed the Electronic Fund Transfer Act (EFTA),[9] primarily because Congress felt that

> the use of electronic systems to transfer funds provides the potential for substantial benefits to consumers. However, due to the unique characteristics of such systems, the application of existing consumer protection legislation is unclear, leaving the rights and liabilities of consumers, financial institutions, and intermediaries in electronic fund transfers undefined.

The objective of the act is to

> provide a basic framework establishing the rights, liabilities, and responsibilities of participants in electronic fund transfer systems. The primary objective of [the EFTA] is the provision of individual consumer rights.

The act's scope is broad; it defines an "electronic fund transfer" to mean

> any transfer of funds, other than a transaction originated by check, draft, or similar paper instrument, which is initiated through an electronic terminal, telephonic instrument, or computer or magnetic tape so as to order, instruct, or authorize a financial institution to debit or credit an account. Such term includes, but is not limited to, point-of-sale transfers, automated teller machine transactions, direct deposits or withdrawals of funds, and transfers initiated by telephone.

An "account" is defined as including any "demand deposit, savings deposit, or other asset account." The EFTA empowers the Federal Reserve Board

---

[9] P.L. 95–630.

to prescribe regulations for the purpose of carrying out the objectives of the statute.

To safeguard the consumer from predatory financial practices, the EFTA requires that a financial institution disclose to a consumer—at the time he contracts for the EFT service—the terms and conditions of his account. The consumer must also be informed—in "understandable language"—what his liabilities are in instances involving an unauthorized EFT; he must also be given the name, address, and telephone number of the establishment he must contact in instances in which he suspects that an unauthorized transaction has been or may be effected. The bank must also notify a consumer, in writing, at least 21 days prior to the effective date of any change in any term or condition that would increase his service fees or liability. However, the bank need not give prior notice where the change is necessary to restore or maintain the security of its EFT system.

The EFTA also directs that a bank provide its customer with written documentation for each electronic fund transfer he initiates. The documentation should include the following:

- Amount involved.
- Date the transfer was initiated.
- Type of transfer.
- Identity of the consumer's account and that of the bank from which or to which funds were transferred.
- Identity of any third party to whom or for whom the funds were transferred.
- Location or identification of the electronic terminal involved.

In addition, the bank should provide its customers with a periodic statement which sets forth:

- The fees or charges assessed by the bank against the customer's account.
- Balances in the customer's account both at the beginning of the period in question and also at its close.
- A telephone number and address which the customer can contact to inform the bank of any errors in his account.

A customer who detects an error in the statement the bank has provided must promptly inform the bank either orally or in writing. The error must be described and the reasons for believing an error has occurred must be given. The bank has up to 10 business days to investigate the error and report its findings to the customer. However, a bank can take up to 45 days, if necessary, to conclude its investigation. If the bank determines that an error did, in fact, occur it must take prompt action to correct it within one business day. The EFTA provides for treble damages against any bank found attempting to cover its errors.

However, a customer who covers—through negligence or design—an unauthorized transfer of funds from an account will be liable for

> the amount of money or value of property or services obtained in such unauthorized electronic fund transfer prior to the time the financial institution is notified, or otherwise becomes aware of, circumstances which lead to the reasonable belief that an unauthorized electronic fund transfer involving the customer's account has been . . . affected.

Further, a customer who fails to report errors or losses within 60 days after receiving documentation from the bank cannot hold the bank liable for losses; nor is the bank liable to a customer who fails to report the theft or loss of an EFTS card within two business days.

However, a bank will be liable to a customer for any losses that result from its breach of the terms and conditions of their contract. The EFTA exempts a bank from liability for any losses caused by an act of God or other circumstances beyond its control; however, the bank must demonstrate it exercised reasonable care to prevent such an occurrence. The EFTA also provides criminal penalties for anyone convicted of knowingly and willfully using, attempting to use, or conspiring to use any counterfeit, fictitious, lost, stolen, or fraudulently obtained EFTS debit instrument for purposes of obtaining money, services, or property.

Some consumer advocates, however, charge that the EFTA favors the financial community over the consumer; that by giving the Fed—no friend of the consumer—regulatory powers over the act, it specifically ensures that the banking interests will prevail in the cashless society. In addition, the EFTA's criminal sanctions fail to address EFTS-related crimes that make no use of debit instruments; thus an array of EFTS crimes will not be covered by the act. Some consumer advocates go so far as to state that the EFTA is "old before its time." Whether the act will suffice to meet the needs of consumers in an EFTS environment remains to be seen.

SOFTWARE-RELATED PROBLEMS

The computer constitutes the workhorse of the cashless society; a typical computer facility consists of two major components: the hardware and software (programs). It is the software that controls and directs the operations of the hardware by defining the sequence of operations of the hardware. The dramatic innovations in computer technology have made EFTS a reality. However, these technological breakthroughs are often costly; investors are concerned with legal safeguards for their investments. There are ample legal protections for innovations in the hardware area. However, both investors and inventors are concerned with whether computer software can find similar legal safeguards.

Legal scholars have made numerous efforts to address this issue. Some have concluded that software may find protection under one or more of the following areas of law: (1) state trade secret laws; (2) federal copyright laws; and (3) federal patent laws. Whether these legal doctrines, however, provide the needed safeguards is a matter of dispute. Some concerned writers argue that they are adequate, others note that present laws need to be amended, and still others call for new legislation in this area. There is, however, genuine concern that present laws may not be totally adequate to safeguard software.

Trade Secrets

Trade secrets are any formulas, patterns, devices, or compilations of information that are used in one's business and give that individual (or corporation) an opportunity to obtain an advantage over competitors who do not know or use them. A trade secret is often associated with a device or process for continuous use in the operation of the business. It may take the form of a chemical formula, or a machine for the production of an article; it may also take the form of a code for determining discounts, rebates, or other concessions in a price list or catalogue. Trade secrets differ from other secret business data in that they are not simply information as to single or ephemeral events in the conduct of a business. For example, trade secret protections would not extend to such things as the salary of an employee, investments made or contemplated by a corporation, or the date fixed for the announcement of a new product.

There is no agreement as to what the proper subject matter of trade secret laws should be. Some legal scholars would extend the trade secret protections only to inventions, for example, only to secret processes. Others would extend these protections to any information that is valuable to its owner and involves an element of novelty. This would include such things as mailing lists. Some legal writers would go so far as to extend these safeguards to all abstract or general ideas in the commercial or industrial sector. For example, advertising plans would be included within the protection of the trade secret laws.

Those who advocate extending the trade secret safeguards to computer software argue that since programs are "novel, secret, valuable, and difficult to reacquire" they should be accorded the protection of the trade secret laws. Great effort and cost, they note, have gone into developing them. They also note that both equity and fairness mandate such safeguards; they argue that only the developer or owner of a program should reap its benefits. A wrongdoer should not be rewarded for copying a program. Proponents also argue that these protections ensure that a developer has an advantage over his competitors and is rewarded for his investment. Further, trade secret safeguards will not allow an employee who has misappropriated his employer's ideas to profit by his wrongdoing.

These proponents also note that the trade secret protections will eliminate much of the present waste. Thousands of programmers now duplicate each other's efforts daily. These proponents also find support in the Constitution; they note that the founding fathers made it clear that one of the objectives of government is to protect discoveries and "promote the Progress of Science."

Extending the full scope of the trade secret laws to computer software, however, has detractors as well. These argue that public disclosure promotes rather than hinders the flow of commerce; it avoids wasteful duplicative efforts. It allows the general public access to the fruits that would otherwise be monopolized by a handful; it results in lower market prices for a product. Disclosure, they note, only discourages monopolies; it permits the free marketplace forces to reign.

The courts, however, have taken a middle position; they note that it is simply not sufficient for an individual (or corporation) to label a process or information as secret. It must be proven to be so. The individual must demonstrate to the court's satisfaction that the process or information is not already public; the individual must also demonstrate the extent to which the process or information is known by the public at large or competitors in the marketplace.

There is a consensus that in instances where the computer software has been embodied in some physical form (for example, as a representation of a process of know-how associated with a process) it might be covered by the trade secret protections. However, the trade secret doctrine would not apply to purchasers of programs. Thus every time a program is sold, its user can study its design and copy it. The doctrine thus does not extend all its safeguards to computer software; the uniqueness of this technology makes it difficult to do so. Current trade secret laws have only limited application in the area of computer software.

Copyrights

Proponents of safeguards for computer programs have also turned their attention to the federal copyright laws. Unlike the state trade secret laws, which vary from locality to locality, the copyright laws are anchored in both the Constitution and statutory enactments of Congress. The Constitution empowers Congress to secure for "limited Times to Authors . . . the Exclusive Rights of their . . . Writings." However, whether a computer programmer can be considered an author and the program a writing for purposes of the copyright laws is in doubt. As is the case with the trade secret laws, those that oppose such protections argue that copyright laws are ill suited to protect computer programs. Others take the position that present copyright laws do suffice, and some note that the coyright laws, if amended, can provide effective protection for computer programs. The more conservative legal scholars, however, are strongly opposed to including such works within the ambit of the copyright laws; they view such efforts as unconstitutional.

The U.S. Supreme Court has defined authorship under the copyright laws to include the "originator or maker" of a writing. To be an author, one must have fashioned the work from his or her own independent efforts; the writing must reflect a sufficient degree of intellectual labor by the author. Many legal scholars, however, note that the initial stages of a computer program would have no difficulty in meeting the requirement of authorship; this would include flowcharts, source programs, assembly programs, and machine programs. Computer programs have been compared, by these writers, to coded writings; several courts have come to hold that coded material may be copyrighted.

The creation of a program, however—like any writing—requires intellectual labor. Proponents of copyright protections for programs see this as added evidence that programs, like writings, should be accorded copyright safeguards. They note that the courts, as well as amendments to the Copyright Act of 1909, have already extended the copyright protections to analogous technologies. A federal court faced with the question of whether copyright laws applied to sound recordings summarized it as follows:

> Technical advances, unknown and unanticipated in the time of our founding fathers, are the basis for the sound recording industry. The copyright clause must be interpreted broadly to provide protection for this method of fixing creative work in tangible form.[10]

Extension of the copyright laws to sound recordings offers strong support for extending these legal safeguards to computer programs.

Section 4 of the Copyright Act of 1909 provides that "works for which copyright may be secured under this title shall include all writings of an author." In 1971, the act was amended to bring sound recordings within the ambit of the copyright laws. The act was further modernized in 1976; these new changes went into effect on January 1, 1978. However, attempts to include computer programs within the ambit of the Copyright Act of 1976 fell short of their objective. Section 117 of the 1976 act retains the old act's reluctance to extend its protections to computer programs:

> [T]his title does not afford to the owner of copyright in a work any greater or lesser rights with respect to the use of the work in conjunction with automatic systems capable of storing, processing, retrieving, or transferring information, or in conjunction with any similar device, machine, or process.

---

[10] *Shoab* v. *Kleindienst,* 345 F. Supp. 590 (1972).

For over 15 years, the Copyright Office has compared computer programs in printout form to a writing. The printed program has been analogized by the Office to a "How to" book. However, programs in printout form are not normally marketable. Customers usually receive their programs on magnetic tapes or punched cards. Programs are not meant to be read by the user, but are meant only to enable him to control the computer. Many legal writers are reluctant to compare machine language programs to a writing; the majority of the programs now sold are in machine readable form.

It can be said, however, that the consensus among most legal experts is that the copyright laws—both old and new—should cover the printed or written programs. However, it is the machine readable program that poses a problem for the copyright laws; the majority opinion appears to be that these will not enjoy the protection of the copyright laws. Some legal writers disagree with this majority opinion; they not that the 1976 act should cover machine readable programs, unless such protection constitutes an unconstitutional act.

There is agreement, however, among many legal experts that the copying of a machine readable program would not constitute a copyright infringement under the pre-1976 act. However, some of these experts take the position that such infringements could be prosecuted under the new act. Proponents of copyright protections for programs would like to see the 1976 act fill the void in this area left by the old act. However, more powerful legal groups have traditionally opposed any extension of the copyright laws to machine readable programs; the more conservative legal scholars go as far as to argue that such activity would be unconstitutional.

To date, neither the courts nor the Congress has addressed a number of questions that surround the extension of copyright laws to computer programs. For example, how much creativity should be required to copyright programs? Further, who is the author of such programs—is it the programmer, the machine operator, or the compiler of the data? Computer programs do not yet enjoy the total safeguards accorded other writings.

Patent Law

The proponents of legal safeguards for computer programs have also looked to the federal patent laws.[11] The objective of the Patent Code is to ensure that the invention or discovery of an individual is not infringed upon—"making, using, or selling"—by another; these safeguards would extend for 17 years throughout the United States. The Code gives the inventor only a limited monopoly over an invention or discovery. Applications for a patent are filed with the Patent Office; rejections by that Office may be appealed by the inventor of the Patent Office Board of Appeals. An applicant can appeal an adverse decision by the Board to the Court of Customs and Patent

---

[11] 35 U.S.C. et seq.

Appeals; decisions by this court can be reviewed, on motion, by the U.S. Supreme Court.

To qualify for a patent, an invention or discovery must have been previously unknown. The Code specifically provides that

> A patent may not be obtained though the invention is not identically disclosed or described as set forth in . . . this title, if the differences between the subject matter sought to be patented and the prior art are such that the subject matter as a whole would have been obvious at the time the invention was made to a person having ordinary skills in the art to which said subject matter pertains.

Attempts to extend the patent laws to programs, however, have come under attack on the groups that they were either known or obvious at the time they were made. Programmers often duplicate each other's efforts; this only lends credence to those legal experts who oppose extending the patent laws to programs. They argue, with some justification, that unlike an invention or discovery a program lacks novelty; it cannot be said not to have been previously known. The Patent Code also requires that an inventor personally apply for the patent. However, in the case of a program it may sometimes be difficult to ascertain who the inventor is, thus making it difficult to comply with the Code.

The possibility of patenting computer programs has also met with strong opposition from the Patent Office. In addition, the President's Commission on the Patent System has recommended that patents not be granted for programs. Some legal writers have also noted their opposition on the ground that programs constitute mental steps, which are not covered by the patent laws. Further, there is no "one definition" for a program, it has been defined as being everything from a "set of directions" to a "package of ideas." The Patent Code requires that an invention or discovery be described in "full, clear, concise, and exact terms." This cannot be said to be true of the description of a program.

Several lower court decisions, however, have given the proponents of patentability for programs cause for some optimism; some of these decisions have extended the patent safeguards to analogous industries. However, the question of program patentability is far from resolved; it has powerful opponents in both government and industry. To date, neither the Congress nor the courts have fully addressed this question; unless they take active steps to resolve this dispute, the question of patentability for programs will continue to be an academic exercise.

COMPUTER-RELATED LIABILITIES

The cashless society's reliance on computers will create complex and novel legal problems. Human and mechanical errors and malfunctions will be daily occurrences usually difficult to detect and prove in a court of law. The privacy laws and bank-related federal and state statutes attempt to delineate the rights and duties of consumers and their financial institutions. They do not address those of computer users and hardware and software vendors. Disputes involving these other groups must be resolved by the laws of negligence, contracts, warranties, and products liability. These are the legal doctrines to which the other EFTS participants must turn.

Negligence

"Negligence" is the failure of an individual (or corporation) to exercise that degree of care, in a certain situation, which he is by law obligated to use to safeguard the rights and property of others. A negligent act need not be an intentional act; rather, it simply constitutes the breach of a legal duty, which could have been avoided had the individual exercised precautions. There are four key elements that must be proven by the injured party in any civil action for negligence: (1) there must be a duty or obligation, recognized by law, that requires an individual (or corporation) to conform to certain standards; (2) there must be a failure to conform to those standards; (3) there must be a close causal connection between the conduct and the resulting injury; (4) and the victim must have suffered an economic loss from the negligent act.

Computer-related negligence litigation will increase dramatically in the EFTS society. Much of the civil litigation in this area will stem from losses caused by computer mechanical breakdowns and system employee errors. Power losses, explosives, floodings, fires, and computer disfunctions may result in actions for negligence; errors by computer operators, programmers, tape librarians, and other employees within an EFT system will likewise result in civil suits. Some legal scholars add that civil suits may also arise from a failure to utilize a computer in a reasonably prudent manner, and also from failures to use due care in the use of a computer output. One legal scholar has given the following bleak picture regarding computer-related litigation: "The liability of manufacturers and suppliers to their customers has been expanding for half a century or more, and the . . . (future) will . . . witness (computer) . . . liability . . . extended far beyond anything which presently exists."

However, complex and sophisticated computer-related negligence suits may prove costly and difficult to litigate because of evidentiary problems. One lawyer, with many years of experience in this and related areas of litigation, has described the problem as follows: "After my involvement . . . in computer litigations and antitrust litigations, I am convinced that the cost of litigating computer cases will dwarf the cost of antitrust cases . . . even if you are successful in your . . . action, your loss is going to be tremendous."

The typical negligence suit, however, will frequently involve losses caused by human rather than mechanical error. For example, faulty programming, errors in mailing lists, accounting errors, and similar negligent acts will dominate much of the litigation in this area. Related negligence cases have already made their appearance in our courts. One of the more publicized cases involved a large credit company that operated its own computer. An error in the company's computer informed its collection division that the purchaser of an automobile had fallen behind on his payments. Despite the purchaser's protestations that he had made all his auto payments (which was accurate), the company's agents repossessed the car. The owner sued, and the court awarded him damages. The judge gave the following reasoning, which should serve as indicia of what EFTS may hold in store:

> In this computerized age, the law must require that men in the use of computerized data regard those with whom they deal as more important than a perforation on a (punched) card. Trust in the infallibility of a computer is hardly a defense.

In a related case, the plaintiff had contracted with the defendants to appraise the value of a building. In processing the data in their computers, the defendants made an error in their computations; the error resulted in plaintiff's building being undervalued for purposes of insurance. Subsequently the building burned down in a fire, and the plaintiff sued the defendants for its losses. The court ruled that the defendants had been negligent and were liable for their conduct, since that conduct was the cause of the economic loss suffered by the plaintiff.

Contract

A contract is an agreement between two or more parties, enforceable in a court of law. A contract may be either express or implied. In the former case, the parties to the contract reveal by their words and actions their intention to create an agreement which the law recognizes; in the latter case, the law imposes the agreement on the parties because of their actions or behavior. Contracts may fall into one of two categories:

1. *Unilateral contracts* are created when one of the parties to the agreement promises to do something in exchange for an act to be performed by the other party.
2. *Bilateral contracts* are those where mutual promises are exchanged by both parties to the transaction.

The essential elements of every contract are an *offer* and an *acceptance*. Threre can be no contract if there is no acceptance. In addition, one cannot contract to perform illegal acts.

Computer-related problems can often be resolved in advance by well-drawn contracts. The parties to a contract seek to remedy any potential dispute by outlining the rights and duties of both sides to the agreement. In the event of a computer malfunction or error, the parties can turn to their contract; it will have specified which of the parties is liable and for how much. However, a contract assigning damages made in advance of a breach will not be valid—according to legal experts—unless it meets the following two criteria: (1) the amount so fixed in the contract must be a reasonable forecast of just compensation; and (2) the harm that is caused by the breach must not be incapable or very difficult to estimate accurately. These criteria are followed and enforced by the courts; any computer-related contract that seeks to assign damages must consider and integrate them if it is to survive a court challenge. In addition, a contract must not be unconscionable (unfair); courts are reluctant to enforce what they perceive to be unconscionable contracts. For example, a salesman who induces a buyer to sign a contract through fraudulent representations cannot expect to a court to uphold the contract; a court will refuse to enforce it on the grounds that it is unconscionable.

In the cashless society, those who draft EFTS contracts should provide for both mechanical malfunctions and employee errors; they should also provide for natural disasters and other potential threats to the viability of an EFT system. Human errors can be addressed within contracts. However, a contract must not overwhelmingly favor one party over the other(s); such a contract can be attacked as being unconscionable. In addition, the contract should be specific as to damages, rights, duties, and obligations; it should be specific as to liability. Ill-drafted contracts will only result in prolonged litigation and defeat their objectives.

A contract can also include key exculpatory clauses; these relieve a party to the agreement from liability for specified computer breakdowns or calamities. For example, a clause may read as follows:

> A failure by either party to perform its obligations under this contract or a delay in performance as a result of an explosion, accident, fire, or mechanical breakdown, interruptions in the supply of power or materials, epidemic, industrial dispute or anything outside that party's control, will not constitute a breach of this contract.

However, an exclusionary clause cannot constitute a blanket exclusion from all liability. Courts are reluctant to enforce blanket exclusionary clauses on the grounds that they are unconscionable. Appropriate exclusionary clauses—drawn in conformity with the needs of all parties to the contract and the technology in question—provided they are not unfair, will be enforced by the courts. Exclusionary clauses should be considered when drafting computer-related contracts. Well-drafted contracts can go a long way in alleviating some of the litigation that may arise in an EFTS society.

Warranties

Warranties are collateral promises related to contracts; they may take the form of either an express or implied promise, representation, assurance, or undertaking on the part of a seller to his buyer. Traditionally, warranties on the sale of goods were governed by the Uniform Sales Act and its successor, the Uniform Commercial Code. It has been suggested that in those instances where a computer vendor misrepresents to a user the speed, memory capacity, or type of language used regarding the hardware or software of a computer, the user can find legal recourse under a warranty. However, the traditional approach of the Act and the Code may prove of little assistance to an injured user.

Both the Act and the Code were drafted to deal with situations involving only a seller and his immediate buyer. The distant buyer, who has had no direct dealings with the seller, is not covered by either the Act or Code. In addition, both statutes require that a buyer, if he is to recover under his warranty, give reasonable notice of the breach to the seller. A distant buyer, however, is in no position to do this. In addition, the Code defines "goods" as "all things which are movable at the time of identification to the contract for sale." Courts have proven reluctant to extend this definition to computer software. The Code also sanctions a disclaimer to defeat a warranty; a seller thus can defeat a warranty simply by inserting a disclaimer in his contract to limit his liability. However, the courts have demonstrated a marked shift away from the rigidity of these statutes. Users of computer hardware and softwear may be able to profit from this legal trend.

At the turn of the century, consumer advocates called attention to the rampant abuses involving the marketing of defective food and goods. These reformers noted that the injured buyer had difficulty proving negligence since the sales involved wholesalers and dealers and not the manufacturer. The buyer found it difficult to demonstrate that a retail dealer or wholesaler was negligent. These advocates called for making the manufacturer accountable. They noted that the manufacturer should be called to stand behind his product. The burden of the loss should be placed on the manufacturer, since he was best placed to distribute the loss. In the interest of life and safety, it was argued that the maker should be held strictly liable for any injuries his products caused to the buyer; it made little difference if the buyer was far removed from the seller. By placing his goods on the market, the seller represented to the entire world that they were suitable and safe for use.

The judicial shift surfaced in 1932, in the new classic case of *Baxter* v. *Ford Motor Company*.[12] A Washington court held that the manufacturer of an automobile, who represented that its windshields were shatterproof, was liable to a buyer who was injured by the shattered glass. The automobile maker had made no false statements to the buyer, nor had it been negligent, and the buyer had made his purchase through a dealer. This marked a radical departure from the traditional legal requirement that only a buyer who had dealt directly with the seller could recoup for his losses. A buyer now needed only to demonstrate that a representation had been made by the

---

[12] 12 P. 2d 409.

seller, that the object of that representation had been to reach a "class of buyers" (of which the injured party was one), and that the buyer relied, in part, on that representation in making his decision. After the Ford decision, a far removed buyer could bring suit against a manufacturer for injuries sustained. Several other court decisions upheld this marked judicial shift. In 1960, a New Jersey court handed out a landmark decision in the case of *Henningsen* v. *Bloomfield Motors, Inc.*[13] In this case, the court held both the automobile manufacturer and the dealer who sold the vehicle liable for injuries sustained by a relative of the buyer.

Courts to date have taken the position that an implied warranty exists as regards the safety of a wide assortment of products. A buyer need not show he had any direct dealings with the seller, nor need he demonstrate that the seller made any false or misdealing representations to induce him to make the purchase. He need only show that he made the purchase partly because of representations made by the seller regarding the quality of the product.

The express and implied warranty provisions of the Uniform Commercial Code will prove of little value to the user of computer hardware or software. However, numerous court decisions in related areas of the economy may be helpful in establishing that a seller may have breached his implied warranty to the user. Some computer sellers have sought to evade the implied warranty doctrine through disclaimers. For example, some sellers have sought to evade all warranties concerning the efficiency, speed, and accuracy of a computer by the following disclaimer:

> [Company X] makes no representations, warranties or guarantees, expressed or implied, including without limitation any warranties of merchantability or fitness for intended use other than the express representations, warranties and guarantees contained in this agreement.

Sellers frequently group these disclaimers with those for negligence. Courts, however, have demonstrated a reluctance to acknowledge warranty disclaimers if they appear to contravene public policy or are outright unfair.

Strict Product Liability

An outgrowth of the implied warranty doctrine, this legal doctrine holds both the manufacturer and distributor of a defective product that is inherently dangerous strictly liable for injuries suffered by a user. The user need only demonstrate that the seller is engaged in the business of selling such a product and that the product is expected to reach the user in the form in which it is sold. The fact that the user and seller have not contracted directly, or that the seller has taken all steps necessary to ensure the safety of the product, matters little; neither can serve as a defense for the seller. Public

[13] 161 A. 2d 69.

policy, the courts hold, dictates that the seller be strictly liable for any injuries the user suffers.

Civil litigation in an EFTS society may proceed under one of several legal doctrines. An array of privacy laws and consumer laws are available to safeguard the rights of the consuming public. Several legal doctrines are also available to computer users against vendors who sell unsafe or defective hardware or software. The problem, however, is not one of not enough laws, but rather one of applying a sophisticated technology to antiquated judicial apparatus.

Present procedural and evidentiary rules may make complex EFTS litigation extremely costly. The snail's pace of our judiciary may make it impossible to resolve EFTS-related disputes within an acceptable time frame. There are those who see our judges as scholars, struggling through the legal maze in quest of truth. Technology, however, may mark an end to this "sacerdotal myth" and may remind us that the objective of a legal system is to resolve disputes both justly and at an acceptable cost to the litigants.

10
THE CASHLESS ECONOMY

At the age of 62, and nearing retirement, an Oregon man was surprised to learn that the Social Security Administration computer had no record of any of the payments he had been making. "They ran it through the computer and told me I didn't have any Social Security coming," he said. A survey by an insurance group found that of those polled, 55 percent preferred dealing with people rather than computers in their daily business activities, even if it meant paying a higher service cost.

Federal Reserve figures show that the recent annual consumer debt exceeds $1 trillion. More than $300 billion of this debt is for consumer credit installments, more than $800 billion is for household mortgages, and more than $70 billion is for noninstallment credit. Consumer credit card charges alone account for more than $50 billion. The combined indebtedness for government, business, and consumers is said to exceed $4 trillion.

The impact of EFTS on our economy will be profound. Key economic data will be readily available to both government and business; key decision makers at all levels of government will draw on current EFTS data bases to improve the accuracy of their decisions. No sector of the economy will escape the scrutiny of EFTS, nor will geographic barriers deter the flow of EFTS data.

ECONOMIC FORECASTS

EFTS will have a profound and visible impact on society's everyday economic decision making. EFTS will accumulate an enormous data base on all facets of our economy; these economic data will be readily available to government officials, corporate managers, investors, economists, and others. Although not flawless, such data will nevertheless provide an accurate and timely picture of the various sectors of the economy. Proponents of EFTS note that our montary and fiscal policies should markedly improve in accuracy; corporate marketing plans should likewise improve. Consumer tastes and buying trends will be easier to identify from the voluminous EFTS data base. Productivity studies will, increasingly, become more accurate.

Our social scientists should also benefit from this abundance of economic and personal data. Political scientists will be able to document or discredit numerous long-held political theories; criminologists, studying patterns of economic crime, will have access to a wealth of readily available financial data. Urban planners may find relevant and detailed data regarding the geographic distribution of our population, and they may also be better able to project future urban needs.

Economic criminals may find it more difficult to evade police detection as investigators and prosecutors gain access to key EFTS financial data. A printout or magnetic tape may provide the police with a detailed outline of a defendant's criminal offenses. The laundering of money may also become more difficult, as the Internal Revenue Service (IRS) and the United States Customs Service (CS) refine their techniques. IRS and CS investigators and policymakers will be able to detect economic criminal trends with more success than they have had. The Federal Reserve, with access to current and in-depth EFTS data bases, will be able to augment the impact of its rules and regulations on the economy.

Voluminous EFTS data bases, however, are also fraught with potential political problems. They may enable small economic elites—whose power is based not in capital but in data—to wield indirect economic and political power through their ability to control the storage and dissemination of EFTS data. Through their control of society's economic data base, this small ruling circle can exert influence over our daily lives. A "data-based elite" can pose a serious threat to our very democratic system of government. Control can take a subtle and indirect form. EFTS data bases, unless properly safeguarded, can become the tools of economic and political manipulators.

However, detailed economic data can prove to be valuable in gauging the success of our economic policies. Such data can assist planners in identifying an array of economic ills; they can also prove to be an extremely useful barometer for measuring the success of numerous private and public economic programs.

AN INEXPENSIVE SYSTEM

The costs connected to the handling of cash, checks, credit cards, and other forms of currency are said to exceed $12 billion annually. To this must also be added the growing paper glut. The recording of billions of daily financial transactions not only drives up banking costs, but it also augments the volume of paper in circulation. In addition, billions of dollars are spent annually in the area of security, to ensure that present exchange mechanisms are protected from fraud, theft, and counterfeiting. Unfortunately, these rising costs are often passed on to the consumer; they further augment our inflationary spiral.

The cashless society may cut rising banking costs; it may lead to an inexpensive financial vehicle for transacting our daily business. In addition, the growing, and costly, private armies of guards and investigators—supported by an array of sophisticated electronic tools—may diminish in number under EFTS. The public now bears the annual cost of this industry. Banks will find little, if any, need for guard and armored car services in a cashless society. These savings may be passed on to the banks' clients.

COMPETITIVE BANKING

Banking has become increasingly competitive; the commercial banks find their markets under attack by the thrift institutions. Passage of the depository Institutions Deregulation and Monetary Control Act of 1980 (Act) marks the end of the balkanization of the financial industry. In the last several years, the compartmentalized structure of American banking has given way to fierce competition. The 1980 Act may augment banking competition. It expands the market of the thrifts by allowing them to make some consumer loans and offer credit cards and trust services. The Regulation Q prohibitions (the rule that limited the interest paid to passbook savers) have also been done away with by the Act. In addition, financial institutions are now able to pay interest on checking accounts.

The Act also overrides state usury laws. Many of these state statutes have been, in the past, called unrealistically low by the banking industry. The Act also enhances the jurisdiction of the Federal Reserve and lowers the reserve requirement for Fed member banks. Sponsors of the Act argue that those provisions will enhance competition in the banking area. Proponents of EFTS look on the Act as a positive influence on the growth of EFTS; the Act, they note, will give rise to a competitive EFTS. The consumer, they argue, will be the final winner.

EFTS will make it possible for both small and large banks to grow nationally, provided both have equal access to EFTS. The thrifts have already gained a foothold in the cashless society, as they have increasingly viewed EFTS as a vehicle for challenging the commercial banks, they have made serious inroads in the consumer services area. EFTS will also reduce many of the costs associated with the construction of banking facilities. EFTS may also make it possible for the larger thrifts to penetrate the international banking arena, long the domain of the giant commercial banks. The competition for customer deposits will increase under the cashless society; consumers will face an expanding and competitive banking market, from which they can only hope to benefit.

RETAIL OPERATIONS

Retailers also stand to gain from EFTS not only in terms of improved sales but also in terms of improved inventory control, consumer marketing, and security. EFTS retail terminals will increasingly authorize payments, verify accounts, and extend credit. They will also decrease the amount of time needed to culminate a transaction, and they will monitor inventory surpluses and scarcities. Retailers will be able to keep abreast of changing consumer trends. Further, traditional crime—a costly problem for many retailers—may decrease in the cashless society. The cost of crime, passed on to the consumer in terms of higher prices, should no longer prove a factor under EFTS.

Retailers will also be able to improve their collection procedures; with funds transferred electronically from a consumer's account to that of the retailer, collection problems will become a thing of the past. In addition, retailers will be able to assess a consumer's credit standing within a brief period of time, weeding out with greater accuracy the poor credit risks. Retailers will also incur fewer personnel-related costs as the number of employees they will need to run their operations decline under EFTS.

However, EFTS may also accentuate the growing competitive gap between the large and small retailers. The costly EFTS technology may prove to be beyond the buying range of many smaller retailers; further, unless prosecutors demonstrate greater vigor in the antitrust area, the small retailer may become an extinct species. EFTS poses a profound challenge and dilemma for the retail industry.

WALL STREET REVISITED

Securities investment advisors and brokers may also profit from the in-depth data base EFTS will make available to them. Securities market trends and investor buying patterns will become easier to discern in an EFTS society. EFTS will also enable the securities industry to provide its clients with current and detailed financial data regarding their investments.

Government regulators, however, will have to refine their investigative tools and techniques if they are to keep abreast of the impact of EFTS on the securities industry. Stock-related frauds may become more difficult to detect and prosecute; trading on inside information, now illegal, may become difficult to deter as data become more voluminous and their proliferation more difficult to contain. In addition, theft of data may become a chronic problem as corporate giants attempt to uncover their competitors' financial secrets.

SHIFTS IN MONETARY POLICY

Money is defined as an aggregate of currency, demand deposits, and other assets that can be readily converted into a payment medium. Efforts to control the supply of money in circulation have addressed the traditional monetary system. Regulatory measures have been enacted to specifically address our traditional concept of money. EFTS, however, may facilitate the conversion of additional categories of assets into monetary assets; they will change our traditional definition of money. They may also significantly affect the rate of growth of our money supply.

EFTS will also significantly decrease the amount of money held by the average individual. Money, as we know it, will lose its present form; paper currency will give way to electronic impulses. In addition, the level of economic activity may change as monetary transactions become less time consuming, less costly, and more convenient to conduct. New tools may be Lenders will find it easier to assess the credit-worthiness of a consumer

IMPACT ON CREDIT

The impact of EFTS on the ability of different credit grantors to compete effectively may affect the amount of credit available. Consumer lines of credit and credit cards have encouraged the growth of credit; they have also resulted in an increased demand for consumer goods. Consumer credit affects every facet of our economy. The impact of EFTS on lenders and borrowers will, as a result, have a profound impact on the economy.

Lenders will find it easier to assess the credit-worthiness of a consumer by simply tapping his EFTS files. An individual's credit history will be available to a lender in a brief span of time; lenders will also be able to assess, with greater accuracy, their lending policies. EFTS will also reduce the default and delinquency rate of borrowers; it will enable a lender to inform other lenders—rapidly and at small cost—of credit worthiness of a borrower.

There is little evidence to suggest that EFTS will spark a rapid growth of credit. However, although the more conservative elements within our economic sector fear that EFTS will result in a radical growth of credit, some consumer advocates take the position that EFTS will give rise to numerous forms of credit abuse. The availability of credit and tools to control its flow may have to be reassessed in an EFTS society.

CONSUMER IMPACT

EFTS may also benefit the consumer by providing an array of inexpensive financial services; in addition, consumers will benefit from a more competitive banking sector. As the thrifts compete with commercial banks for consumer deposits, the consumer stands only to benefit. In addition, the consumer will be provided with an array of novel banking services to choose from and will also have the advantage of banking from his office or home. However, consumers will increasingly lose control over their finances. They will lose the option to "stop payment" and also the convenience of the "float." Their finances will become an "open secret" and proving payment may become extremely difficult in a society where funds take the form of electronic blips.

No sector of the economy will escape the impact of EFTS; our traditional financial structures and regulatory agencies will have to adapt to this new technology. Our political liberties—already threatened by the advent of other technologies—will increasingly be tested and come under subtle attack in the cashless society. The impact of EFTS on our economic sector will be profound; we need to take steps that will ensure that while we facilitate our daily financial transactions through the use of EFTS, we do not evade our political values.

11
GOVERNMENT IN THE CASHLESS ERA

A computer-related error has cost the government of Australia more than $100 million in lost funds, and there is little hope of recovery. The loss grew out of a programming error that went undetected for many years, and resulted in large overpayments to pharmacists dispensing National Health prescriptions. When floods inundated a California community, millions of dollars in claims and payments were handled by a government computer. Payments for Medicaid, black lung benefits, welfare, and food stamps are no longer processed by an army of government social workers but rather by computers, which make key decisions that affect the lives of millions of Americans daily. Increasingly, funds and data are transferred electronically.

The role of government in the area of EFTS raises major social, economic, and political questions. It also gives rise to jurisdictional conflicts between agencies. For example, the U.S. Postal Service finds itself embroiled in a jurisdictional dispute with the Federal Communcations Commission over electronic message services. The USPS has threatened to bypass the FCC by routing the data through Canadian circuits. Civil libertarians have also entered the debate, warning that EFTS may erode our Constitutional safeguards; economists ask who will fund the development of EFTS. The government's role in the cashless society has sparked serious debate.

FREEDOM TO CHOOSE

Section eight of Article I of the Constitution empowers the Congress to regulate the commerce and also to "coin Money, regulate the Value thereof, and of foreign Coin." It also empowers Congress to "provide for the Punishment of counterfeiting the Securities and current coin of the United States." Few would dispute the power of government to dictate to its citizens the medium it seeks to employ as "money." Under our present payment mechanisms, freedom of choice has not been an issue of concern. However, in the area of EFTS, choice is an issue—one fraught with political and Constitutional implications.

EFTS have, from the first, faced the problem of acceptability. Many of the poorer and uneducated elements of our society do not trust financial institutions—which they view as representatives of the Establishment—nor do they grasp the intricacies of a paperless payment system. The poor in our society have traditionally felt uncomfortable dealing with Establishment institutions. Unfortunately too, they have frequently been victimized by some of these institutions; further, they have demonstrated little inclination to embrace a cashless payment system. The overwhelming majority of our poorer classes continue to use traditional modes of payment. Few of them make use of checking accounts or credit cards; for these millions of Americans, EFTS evoke little or no support. The dawn of the nation-state marked the shift to paper currency; however, large segments of the population continued to use silver and gold coins as an exchange mechanism.

The impact of EFTS on the uneducated also raises problems. Many of our citizens lack the requisite sophistication to grasp a complex and novel technology like EFTS; even our better educated elements occasionally have difficulty using ATMs, POSs, and telephone-billpaying systems. These systems were designed with middle-America in mind. EFTS also pose a problem for those who partake in the annual multibillion dollar underground economy. How will many of these Americans—both poor and affluent—who choose to employ only cash in their daily business transactions, react to a payment system that would record all their illegal financial transactions? Further, how would the more than 8 million illegal aliens who now reside in this country react to EFTS? Fearful that the government would employ this technology to locate them, they may refuse to partake; in addition, the illegal alien constituency is undereducated and thus ill prepared to grasp the complexities of EFTS.

EFTS also raise the question of whether our financial institutions will prove willing to invest large sums of capital to make EFTS available to the poor; with little to gain financially, they may choose to bypass the poor segments of our society and invest heavily in the affluent markets. Many inner city businesses have already migrated to the more affluent suburbs; might not the same happen with EFTS? Thus the low-income consumer who might be willing to partake in EFTS might find himself excluded. In addition, any hope of eventually educating the low-income consumer in the use of EFTS might fail to materialize with this exodus. In essence, if the poor are excluded from EFTS, we could witness the rise of two societies: one paper based, the other cashless. Participation in the cashless society would carry with it class connotations, and would serve to widen the already existing class distinctions in our society.

Some have suggested that the government should provide funds and tax incentives to those financial institutions that establish EFTS services for the lower income groups. The National Commission on Electronic Fund Transfers has suggested that we develop an alternative "EFTS payment system for low-income consumers that is more suited to their particular needs and wishes." The Commission pointed to Europe in support of its recommendations. In Europe, where many households are not able to afford accounts with depository institutions, governments have funded the postal Giro System to meet their needs; this system of noninterest-bearing accounts is used by many Europeans to conduct their daily financial transactions.

Freedom of choice, however, continues to remain a problem for EFTS. Consumer advocates fear that large financial institutions will eventually dominate EFTS—there are ample examples of this in other industries—and force a monopoly on the consuming public. Civil libertarians fear that EFTS will infringe on the citizen's right to govern his own finances as he chooses, free of duress and manipulation. Some minority leaders see EFTS as an Establishment tool, which will only further widen the gap between the "haves" and the "have-nots." The poor and undereducated continue to use our traditional payment mechanisms and demonstrate little interest in EFTS. If EFTS are to develop into a national payment mechanism, they must do so without infringing on the individual's freedom to choose.

GOVERNMENT OWNERSHIP

EFTS technology is costly and may prove beyond the ability of small businesses to afford; in addition, some minority businessmen noted that the advent of EFTS may make it even more difficult for them to compete effectively in the marketplace. It has been suggested that the federal government either fund or in some instances directly operate key EFTS facilities so as to make it possible for small businesses and minority-owned firms to compete effectively. Proponents of government ownership of EFTS note that the Constitution empowers the government to regulate commerce; thus government involvement or ownership of EFTS would be within its Constitutional mandate. They note that in Europe, governments often fund and support postal Giro Systems.

Proponents of government involvement in EFTS also point to the high risks and costs associated with the development of EFTS, and note that this provides an additional basis for some form of government financing. However, both the Fed and the FHLBB have indicated that they are unwilling to either operate or establish POS switching services. Efforts to fund a pilot EFTS message switching service by the Federal Home Loan Bank of San Francisco has already met with opposition from the Justice Department, which has taken the informal position that such development should be funded and developed primarily by the private sector. Further, opponents of government ownership of EFTS also have powerful friends in Congress; pressure for government not to become directly involved in EFTS has also come from this area. However, whether the private sector has both the ability and motivation to develop an EFTS society free of some government involvement remains doubtful.

It should be noted that government involvement in the ACH area is already an established fact. The Fed establishes rules and regulations for those ACHs that employ its facilities for their processing; the Fed, together with the originating and receiving depository institutions, plays a key role in the workings of ACHs. However, the Fed has refused to become directly involved in the development of pure EFTS. Further, some government officials argue that for the Fed to directly operate such systems would constitute a conflict of interest, since this would bring the Fed into direct competition with many of the same financial institutions it regulates. Government ownership and operation of EFTS have also met with opposition from some members of Congress who view this as a potential threat to the individual's civil liberties. Government access to millions of EFTS files, they note, raises the threat of an Orwellian society.

Proponents of government ownership of EFTS, however, note that the government does have a legitimate Constitutional interest in the nation's payment mechanisms. In addition, they argue that since most of the volume processed by ACHs originates with government agencies, the government does not have a vested interest in the development of EFTS. Further, they note that government involvement in EFTS will ensure that minority business owners will not be discriminated against.

There are those, however, who take a moderate position; they do not believe that government ownership of EFTS will resolve some of the potential problems that small and minority-owned businesses may face. Rather, this group fears that Washington's bureaucrats may create new risks and even greater problems. These moderates, however, also do not agree with those in the private sector who are opposed to any form of governmental involvement. Rather, they suggest that EFTS be regulated like any other public utility; this approach, they suggest, would encompass the best of both the private and public sectors. However, a cursory analysis of public utilities leaves some skeptical.

A government-owned and operated EFT system does carry with it the potential for political abuse; the privacy and civil liberties of the citizenry could be threatened by unscrupulous bureaucrats. However, some government involvement could also prove beneficial. Many ACHs rely on the Fed's assistance for their present operations. Government does have both a vested and Constitutional interest in the nation's payment system. Direct government involvement, however, in the private economic sector has traditionally brought with it red tape, inefficiency, and monopoly. The bureaucrat is not equipped to totally supplant the private sector in the area of EFTS; however, both government and the private sector have a role to play and a middle ground must be found.

THE REGULATORS

The Washington bureaucracy has been compared to a many-headed Hydra. It houses numerous agencies, and is manned by an army of faceless bureaucrats. Government agencies regulate every facet of the economy; EFTS have not escaped their interest. Dozens of these agencies will play and have played, with varying impact, a role in the development of the cashless society.

Federal Reserve System

Established by the 1913 Federal Reserve Act, the Fed is the nation's central banking system. The Fed's Board of Governors determines general monetary, credit, and operating policies for the system as a whole, and also formulates the Fed's rules and regulations; the Board also has jurisdiction over the admission of banks and trust companies into the Fed. In addition, the Board establishes security guidelines for Fed member banks. Members must also first obtain Board permission before they can establish branches in foreign countries. The Fed is further empowered to act as a clearinghouse and collection agency for its members, and as the fiscal agent of the federal government. The Fed has a key role to play in the development of EFTS, one that should not be underestimated given its key role in our economy.

Federal Home Loan Bank Board

Established in 1932 by the Federal Home Loan Bank Act, the FHLBB is an independent agency of the executive branch funded by member savings and loans. There are 12 regional Federal Home Loan Banks; their capital stock is owned entirely by member institutions. The FHLBB has already taken the position that it is willing to play a role in the development of EFTS.

Federal Deposit Insurance Corporation

The FDIC is an independent executive agency, with its management vested in a three-person Board of Directors; the Comptroller of the Currency is one of its directors. The FDIC is funded solely by member banks; among other things it insures the deposits of member institutions up to the statutory limit. Banks that engage in practices the FDIC deems to be unsafe and unsound may find their deposit insurance coverage terminated. The FDIC may also approve or disapprove an application by a member bank to establish and operate a new branch or to move its main office or a branch from one location to another. Security measures and procedures of member banks must also be in compliance with FDIC guidelines. The FDIC has demonstrated an interest in EFTS, and will certainly play a role in their establishment.

National Credit Union Administration

The NCUA is responsible for the chartering of federal credit unions. The NCUA also insures both federally-chartered and state-chartered credit unions; NCUA examiners conduct periodic checks to determine the solvency of member credit unions. The NCUA also assists its members in improving their operations. The larger credit unions have increasingly demonstrated an interest in EFTS; the NCUA, responsive to their needs, has demonstrated an interest in EFTS.

United States Postal Service

The USPS has increasingly demonstrated an interest in the electronic transfer of messages and is now experimenting with EMS. It has, however, met with some opposition from both the large communication firms and the FCC. The USPS now is operating an experimental EM system, Intelpost, between New York City, Washington, and London. Intelpost transmits messages electronically with the assistance of satellite communications. The USPS has also proposed the initiation of ECOM. However, the development of EMS has been hindered by the USPS's disputes with the powerful communications carriers—who fear that the USPS will supplant them in the electronic message delivery market—and also with the FCC, which fears the USPS will infringe on its jurisdiction.

Federal Communications Commission

Created by the Communications Act of 1934, the FCC is empowered to regulate interstate and foreign communications, including all wire, radio, telephone, telegraph, television, and satellite communications. The objective of the legislation was to ensure that the FCC would safeguard the public's interest in the communications area. Common carriers have increasingly come to see the computer communications industry as a lucrative market; however, participation by the carriers in the data processing industry has evoked an FCC response, which raises serious questions for the growth and development of EFTS.

The FCC has no regulatory powers over the data processing industry; however, the FCC does have powers to regulate common carriers and to ensure that they provide "adequate and efficient communications services at reasonable and nondiscriminatory rates and practices." The FCC has taken the position that computer-related services which are essentially communications fall under its regulatory powers. Thus a business that employs data processing as incidental to what appears to be a communication service would find itself subject to FCC regulations. An EFT system that sends its messages by wire or satellite communications could fall under FCC regulations. However, before the FCC could exert jurisdiction, it would have to demonstrate that the EFT system performs a "communication" as opposed to a "data processing" function. Since an EFT system must, by necessity, also perform some communication functions, it could fall under FCC regulations. The type of regulatory influence the FCC may choose to exert over EFTS remains to be seen. However, if the FCC does choose to treat EFTS as a communications common carrier, then it profoundly affects the direction the cashless society may take.

The role of the government in the development and establishment of EFTS continues to be a subject of dispute. Some powerful economic and political groups are opposed to any form of government involvement in EFTS; others seek some form of limited government involvement, with the major role to be played by the private sector. The form and direction EFTS takes may represent the outcome of an accommodation between the private and public sectors.

12
INTERNATIONAL OUTLOOK

A study of the American retailing industry found that by the late 1980s, retailers will be spending in excess of $1 billion for EFTS-related equipment. The current retail market base of 8000 payment terminals will grow to more than 140,000 such units by 1989; further, the study projects that large retail chains will install an additional 6000 POSs during this same period. In addition, it is projected that an added 24,000 ATMs will be installed, and retail transactions by 1989 should exceed $90 billion; many of these transactions will be handled by EFTS.

Scientists note that future satellite systems will be capable of multiple routing, space segment processing and switching, and other complex modes of data transmission; advanced crytographic techniques will be employed to ensure the security of this data transmission. In the United States, the EFTS revolution has taken on a national dimension; EFTS proponents also note that an international EFTS society may soon become a reality. Critics, however, are not as optimistic. They point out that for international EFTS to take shape, much will depend on energy supplies, the domestic and international regulatory climate, the decreasing price of EFTS-related technology, and, most important, the general economic and political climate both here and abroad. Rudimentary forms of EFTS are in use in many Western industrialized nations, but truly international EFTS must surmount serious political, social, and economic challenges. Whether this is possible remains to be seen.

EUROPE'S EFTS

Great Britain, France, and Scandinavia all use ATMs. Several other Western nations, as well as Israel and Japan, are also on the road to EFTS. Cash-dispensing machines have found a receptive climate in many of these nations; increasingly, the bank wires are being employed to transfer larger sums of money. In many of these countries, the direct deposit of payrolls has been customary for many years. Further, a number of European depository institutions have also established ACHs. The ACH movement gained its initial momentum in the late 1960s. The first British ACH which went into operation in 1968, now processes several hundred million payments each year.

European ACHs have been employed not only to process payroll credits and debit transfers but also for cash dispenser exchanges, guaranteed check payments, and check truncation. The Scandinavians employ their ACHs primarily in processing payroll credits, the French employ them mostly for their direct debit transactions, and the Belgians use them for check truncation. As in the United States, European governments are the major users of ACHs. In many European countries, governments have worked closely with the private sector in the development of EFTS. In some of these countries (for example, Belgium), central banks not only participate but also operate the ACHs for their depository institutions, wheras in other European countries, a service bureau or separate corporate entity is retained to operate them. In Sweden, however, ACH facilities usually are jointly owned by the financial institutions that partake in them; however, in West Germany, where banking systems are more highly decentralized and most consumer payments are handled by the postal Giro Service, ACHs are not as visible.

Access to European ACHs varies from country to country; in some countries, direct access is limited to the major clearing banks. In others, it's open to all depository institutions; for example, in Sweden both commercial banks and thrifts have equal access to the ACH. In Britain, however, before a corporate entity can send its tapes directly to an ACH a bank must sponsor the corporation and accept responsibility for any financial losses it may cause. European ACHs also handle the bulk of government assistance payments; many of these are in the form of direct deposits.

The highly centralized banking and political systems found in many European countries lend themselves to the development of ACHs. In addition, Europe's experience with the postal Giro Service has made its populace more receptive for a shift to EFTS. ACHs and ATMs are found in almost every European country; opposition to EFTS has not been as vocal or adamant as it has in the United States.

GIRO SERVICES

All industrialized societies make use of checks and drafts; what makes the European payment system unique is its widespread use of Giro services. In a checking system, the payor is the originator of the item, presenting it to the payee, who in turn deposits it at a depository institution. The depository then presents the check to the payor's bank for collection. If the funds in the payor's account are not sufficient to cover the transaction, the check is then returned to the payee's bank with a notice that the payor's account lacks sufficient funds to cover the transaction. In a Giro system, however, the transaction would not be initiated unless the payor first demonstrated that he had the requisite funds in his account. The payor instructs the postal Giro Service, usually in writing, to transfer a specified sum of money from his account to that of the payee; the service then proceeds to follow the payor's instructions.

Giro services are extremely popular in Europe, where they are available to a broad cross section of the population. Some European governments directly subsidize these services, making them inexpensive for low-income groups. Thus the majority of European consumers have postal Giro accounts, which they use to conduct most of their daily financial transactions; whereas in the United States a large number of low-income consumers have no depository accounts. An array of sophisticated Giro services are available, competing effectively with the commercial banks for the consumer market.

Given the success of the Giro services, European consumers are more favorably disposed toward national automated payment systems. In addition, Europe's highly centralized banking system facilitates such a transition, unlike the feud between the state and national banking interests that has retarded the growth of EFTS in the United States. European governments have also demonstrated a willingness to play a key role in the development of EFTS; the success of the Giro services has acclimated the consumer to a direct government role in the payment mechanisms employed daily.

FUTURE OF EFTS IN EUROPE

The majority of the European nations are democracies; many of them are highly industrialized, and have the requisite trained personnel to operate sophisticated EFTS. Automated payment systems are not alien to their citizens; in addition, the small geographic size of most European countries makes it unnecessary to spend large sums of money on the costly communications equipment needed to connect the diverse components of a sophisticated EFTS.

In addition, the numerous racial, religious, and ethnic rivalries that surface in the United States and retard key economic decisions are negligible in most European countries. Most European countries are free of the federalism that pits federal interest against those of the localities; there are no state branching or sharing laws regarding EFTS. In addition, there are no antitrust hurdles for European bankers to overcome. The absence of these artificial barriers facilitates the growth of EFTS in Europe.

Europeans, however, have also demonstrated many of the same anxieties that Americans have toward EFTS. They are concerned that EFTS will facilitate invasions of privacy; consumer advocates and civil libertarians, like their American counterparts, have indicated their concern that EFTS raises both consumer and constitutional issues. The growth of EFTS may also become a political issue between Europe's political Right and Left. A number of European countries have already enacted privacy legislation, among them Sweden, France, and West Germany. Critics, however, charge that the object of the legislation has been aimed at discouraging U.S. financial institutions from expanding to Europe rather than safeguarding the citizen's privacy.

Europeans are also increasingly concerned about computer-related crimes. Many European law enforcement officials openly acknowledge that they lack the investigatory training to detect and bring to prosecution many of the complex computer-related crimes. Litigating computer-related crimes will also prove to be a problem for the European legal system. Europe's legal edifice is no more prepared to deal with EFTS than is America's. However, the uniformity of laws within European countries eliminates some of the legal problems endemic to a federal system. European lawyers and prosecutors need not concern themselves with thousands of federal and state judicial decisions or with the myriad local and federal rules and regulations that make it difficult to establish a uniform law enforcement or prosecutorial policy toward EFTS in the United States.

The problem of security is also a major concern for Europeans, who have increasingly been plagued with terrorist attacks. European terrorists have also turned their attention to computer facilities; EFTS may present attractive targets for these groups. EFTS security will become a matter of serious concern in Europe. Sophisticated and well-armed groups of terrorists can pose a serious problem to the development of EFTS. Europe's EFTS are in the making; rudimentary systems have already taken shape in some countries. The requisite technology and trained personnel are available. However, the direction and structure EFTS will take depends, in large part, on how European governments and the financial community perceive the need for EFTS.

A REVIEW OF CANADA'S EXPERIENCE

Canadian financial institutions, like many of their American counterparts, are increasingly moving toward EFTS to handle many of their paper-based transactions. In a 1975 statement on EFTS by the then Finance Minister, the Canadian government acknowledged that EFTS could give rise to serious problems for Canadian consumers:

> The movement away from a paper-based system of payment will result in the eventual linking of a variety of institutions, financial, retail and government, and ultimately affect the day-to-day transactions of the individual consumer. It is important that this evolution be such as to protect the rights of individual Canadians, to enhance the competitive environment for deposit-taking institutions and the computer/communications service industry, and to ensure the development of an efficient and equitable payment system.

Canada's Department of Justice was directed to provide recommendations regarding these potential problems; of special concern to the Canadians were not only potential problems in the area of consumer rights but also privacy and computer crime. The Canadians have also been concerned about the ability of their legal system to adequately meet the needs of an EFTS society. Many of the aspects of EFTS that have perturbed American policymakers have also perturbed their Canadian counterparts; of special concern has been the potential for serious EFTS-related crimes.

In the early 1970s, Canada's financial institutions—principally the chartered banks—were facing many of the same problems that their American counterparts faced: paper-based financial transactions were growing both in value and cost. Computer technology, however, provided an answer; many of Canada's larger financial institutions were increasingly moving from manual to electronic methods for handling their daily financial transactions. On-line savings account services had made their appearance. A bank's customer could now go to any of its branches and make either deposits or withdrawals; the data were relayed back to the bank's central computer through a branch terminal. A bank's branches were now able to exchange data with one another in a matter of minutes. A customer no longer needed to restrict activities to one branch. Canadian banks during the 1970s also started recording many of their financial transactions on magnetic tapes, giving rise to Canada's ACH revolution. In addition, the Canadian government encouraged many of the large organizations to pay their employees by direct deposit to their accounts.

Canada, however, is a small country in population, dwarfed by its American neighbor. This has given rise to fears that Canada's EFTS will be dominated by American firms. The Canadians have shown special concern in the communication processing area; they have required that EFTS communication processing functions be under the control of Canadian rather than foreign firms. The Canadians are also concerned that if their EFTS fall under the control of the multinationals or the larger Canadian financial institutions, many of the country's small banks will be excluded from participating in the system; as a result, the government has instructed its Department of Commerce, the Bank of Canada, and the Receiver General for Canada to ensure that EFTS not be closed to the smaller financial institutions.

The Canadians have, from the first, feared that their EFTS revolution could fall under the sway of a small number of powerful domestic banking interests. Such a development would only further aggravate Canada's regional and linguistic animosities. As early as 1973, Canada's government sought to minimize such potential problems by declaring that it would oppose any efforts by the country's powerful economic interests to monopolize EFTS. In mid-1970, the Canadian Finance Ministry once again reiterated the government's position; it declared that EFTS should be:

- Equitable between deposit-taking institutions and among their customers.
- Efficient in terms of cost.
- Competitive with respect to the payment services offered.

However, the Canadian government has also been, and continues to be, concerned with the problem of EFTS-related crimes. The Department of Justice has noted its concern that EFTS crimes may be difficult to both detect and bring to prosecution. Canada's legal system shares many of the same flaws found in the United States. It is feared that evidentiary and procedural problems may hamper complex EFTS prosecutions; further, Canadian courts—like their American counterparts—have displayed a hesitancy to apply traditional criminal laws to computer-related crimes. The Canadians thus share many of our investigatory and prosecutorial difficulties in the area of EFTS; in addition, the Canadians are concerned that civil litigation involving complex EFTS cases may prove a problem. Unresolved copyright and patent problems also cloud Canada's EFTS. The Canadians share many of the same potential problems with their American cousins in the area of EFTS.

TRANSBORDER TRANSACTIONS

The development of truly international EFTS will depend largely on the politics of transborder data flow. Both Western and Third World countries have enacted an array of regulations to control the flow of computerized data in and out of their borders. In large measure, these policies have been dictated not so much by economic factors as by political considerations. The French, for example, were quick to act in this direction when they learned that American firms had more economic data on their country than did their own government. As early as 1973, the Swedes established a Data Inspection Board to regulate and license the communication of data. Increasingly, many countries are following the Swedish and French examples and are placing limits on the transmission of personal and corporate data out of their confines; in addition, some countries now require that computerized data be stored only in the country in which they are produced. These restrictions on the international flow of data can seriously impede the transborder flow of EFTS data.

Many of these transborder data flow restrictions often take the form of privacy laws. In 1978, five European countries took steps to safeguard personal and corporate data by enacting privacy protection laws. In West Germany, the Data Protection Act not only regulates the processing of personal information but also prohibits the export of such data for processing outside of Germany; all such data—unless authorized otherwise—would have to be processed within Germany and in accord with its laws. Denmark, Norway, Austria, and France have enacted similar laws. The French have even established a regulatory agency to control the export of data; under the French Data Processing Files and Freedom Act, the government can prohibit a firm from exporting data to another country for purposes of processing. More than 35 countries regulate the flow of transborder data; more than 30 other countries are in the process of enacting similar regulations. This could have a serious adverse impact on the establishment of international EFTS.

However, some of the Western countries that restrict the flow of transborder data do provide for some exceptions; for example, a firm that can demonstrate that the country of destination has similar stringent privacy safeguards will be allowed to export the data. However, although several European countries qualify for export purposes—since many of them have tough privacy laws that apply equally to both the private and public sectors—the United States may face difficulties. Privacy regulations in the United States are directed largely at the public sector; the private sector, save for some voluntary guidelines, has largely escaped regulation in this area. Thus U.S.-based firms might not be viewed as being able to guarantee the privacy of the European data they import for processing. The free flow of transborder data between the United States and Europe—with the exception of some private financial and personal data protected by federal banking laws—could face impediments.

The position of the U.S. government has been, and continues to be, that no country should place unnecessary restrictions on the flow of transborder data; the Organization for Economic Cooperation and Development (OECD) has outlined voluntary guidelines for the flow of transborder data. However, France and several other countries have noted their opposition. Some of these nations view the unrestricted flow of transborder data as favoring the larger American firms. Nationalism, pressures from the political parties of the Left, and also fears that small, indigenous data processing firms will not be able to compete effectively with the American giants have led some of these countries to embrace protectionist policies in the area of transborder flow of data; their future impact on the development of an international EFTS should not be ruled out.

EFTS AND THE THIRD WORLD

Massive amounts of financial and personal data are exported daily out of Third World countries for processing and storage in the computers of Western nations. Increasingly, the Third World finds itself dependent on foreign corporations for the processing of its social, economic, and political data. In an effort to stem this export of data and encourage the processing and storage of data within their borders, many Third World nations have taken steps to regulate the export of data.

The needed computer technological base of the Third World can be said to be in a state of infancy, and the telecommunications revolution is just beginning. In addition, these countries lack the trained professionals to man sophisticated computer systems. Many of these countries find that they must retain the services of foreign experts to operate their computers. Even affluent countries like Algeria find that they must wait several years before they can train the requisite personnel to man their data processing facilities; as a result, many of the Third World nations are finding that regulations alone will not break their dependency on foreign data processing firms. Whether the Third World will ever be able to catch up with the developed nations in the area of data processing remains doubtful; efforts to incorporate these nations within an international EFT system could be viewed by them as a form of "informal colonialism." EFTS may come to symbolize for some Third World countries an added dependence on the West.

The Third World finds itself rocked by internal political instability; coups, assassinations, and border wars occur daily. Further, these nations face serious economic problems. Large percentages of their populations live at the borderline of starvation. Many of these countries have also been plagued by epidemics and climatic changes. Feeding, healing, and clothing their citizenry must, by necessity, take precedence; few precious resources can be spared to develop the requisite EFTS technology and pool of trained personnel. Thus EFTS could come to be viewed by them as a Western tool to control their economies. These countries can be expected to continue to enact regulations to curtail the flow of their financial data to the West.

EFTS has taken roots in Europe, Canada, and Japan. These countries possess both the requisite technology and trained personnel to move into the cashless society. Japan, for example, has begun to implement a vast educational effort in the area of computer technology. However, the growing problem of costly energy, political instability in many developing nations, and the proliferation of regulations to restrict the flow of transborder data will have a serious impact on the growth of international EFTS. A world torn by political and economic instability is not conducive to the growth of an international cashless society.

13
UNRESOLVED ISSUES—
THE FUTURE OF EFTS

As EFTS technology becomes more widespread, some Congressional sources fear that law enforcement agencies will make efforts to gain access to its confidential computerized data; they argue that we need additional statutory safeguards. In Stockholm, the Royal Institute of Technology has conducted research in the computer analysis of photographs; the object of the research is to enable scientists to improve their studies of industrial pollution and better diagnose cancer. The U.S. Secret Service, charged with the task of safeguarding the lives of important government officials, fears that determined assassins can murder by computer. Computer systems used to control high-speed trains, airplanes, the flow of petrochemicals, and life-support systems in hospitals can be sabotaged or programmed to commit violent acts.

The advent of EFTS is tied to the dramatic developments in computer and communications technologies; the future of EFTS is, in large measure, tied to the developments in these technologies. EFTS, however, also evoke an array of social questions that continue to fuel the debate. EFTS are hostages of a larger and ongoing debate in our society: the debate over "technology at what cost?"

PENDING SOCIAL QUESTIONS

Traveling far above the earth, satellites will aim narrow beams of microwave energy at select earth targets. These scanning/spot-beam satellites will lower the cost of digital communications and make them feasible in the not too distant future. The technology to construct an inexpensive national—and perhaps even international—pure EFT system will soon be readily available. However, some key social questions remain unresolved.

Social Desirability

Although a rudimentary EFTS network has already taken root in America, Western Europe, and Japan, a sizable percentage of the populations of these countries has remained outside the confines of the EFTS debate, displaying little interest in EFTS. However, an educated, vocal, and organized minority has raised key questions regarding the social implications of EFTS. "What," they ask "is the value of having EFTS?" "Will EFTS mean that the larger financial institutions will have a greater hold on our daily financial transactions? Will it lead us to a totalitarian society?" In Europe, some of this opposition has taken a violent form. European groups opposed to computer technology have broken into the offices of computer service centers and have set fire to their tapes and magnetic cards. The Parisian offices of a major computer user have been attacked with rockets. More and more, computer technology finds itself the target of violent groups.

Proponents of the cashless society have long argued that EFTS will offer consumers convenience, security, and an inexpensive vehicle with which to conduct their daily financial transactions. However, questions that revolve around the social value of having EFTS have yet to be resolved. To date, the EFTS debate has remained, largely, the province of technologists and a handful of lawyers and businessmen. The question of social desirability has yet to be fully addressed.

Social Cost of Security

Physical and personal security measures have already been instituted in a number of both private and public computer facilities. Technologists and law enforcement sources note that these do not suffice, and added security measures will be needed to safeguard EFTS from criminal elements. However, this expanded security will also bring with it added invasions of privacy. In ensuring the privacy of millions of EFTS users, these security programs will infringe on the privacy of the army of operators, programmers, and others who will man the systems; EFTS employees will find themselves the target of an array of security measures. In ensuring the privacy of the user, society may find itself invading those of the men and women who will operate EFTS. To date, we have not fully addressed the social costs and implications of this facet of security.

End of Free Enterprise

The issue of government's role in EFTS has already been touched upon; however, the potential impact of government-subsidized EFTS has yet to be fully analyzed. Will a government-funded EFTS spell the end of what little free enterprise we have left? Will it lead to a further erosion of our precious few economic freedoms? These questions merit close scrutiny. Unfortunately, past government regulations have only increased rather than lowered the cost of services; we have too often witnessed powerful economic interests joining with government to establish monopolies and discourage competition.

Profit as a Goal

Traditionally, the objective of a payment mechanism has been to facilitate economic transactions. An EFT system, however, is more than merely a payment mechanism; it is also a private banking service. Proponents of EFTS view them in terms of expenditures and profits. Altruism plays no role in their banking. However, pure EFTS dominated solely by the profit motive may have a profound impact on the traditional role of government in a citizenry's payment mechanisms. It may lead to a departure from our traditional perspective of the role of government under the nation-state doctrine. A dramatic alteration in society's payment mechanisms must by necessity also have an impact on the individual's perception of those who govern. There are those who fear that a pure EFT system may lead to rule by a few powerful multinational corporations.

Increased Vulnerability

The Committee for the Liquidation or Deterrence of Computers (CLODO) —an underground European organization—is alleged to have carried out several terrorist attacks against French facilities. CLODO members have been quoted as saying "We are computer workers and therefore well placed to know the present and future dangers of computer systems. Computers are the favorite instruments of the powerful. They are used to classify, control and to repress." Attacks and bombings of computer centers have been documented in many Western nations. The computer may eventually supplant the corporate official as the target of terrorism. A pure EFT system may, in fact, augment society's vulnerability to attack by well-organized and highly motivated terrorist groups.

Historians are quick to point out that the invention of gunpowder enabled the kings of Europe to bring their feudal magnates under the state's central control. The nobility could no longer seek refuge in their castles; European kings could easily destroy their walls with this new technology. The computer—given the industrial world's increased dependence on it—may augment the West's vulnerability from terrorism. By destroying key EFTS facilities, political malcontent groups can easily deal a country a serious economic blow. In its efforts to secure itself from attack, a democratic nation might find itself using totalitarian solutions. A society that fears for its existence may easily embrace desperate solutions.

LEGISLATIVE IMPACT

Each year, federal and state bank examiners inspect the financial records of more than 23,000 financial institutions in America; they check for discrepancies in accounting procedures, loan policies, internal security measures, and compliance with government regulations. The examiners work in small teams of up to 40, and may spend as much as 10 weeks examining a bank's records. Many of the laws and regulations they enforce were designed specifically for a paper-based payment system. Some of these laws, however, could have a profound impact on EFTS.

Foreign Corrupt Practices Act (FCPA)[1]

In the mid-1970s, more than 600 major American corporations were reported to have been engaged in systematic foreign payoff and kickback schemes. In an effort to deter these corrupt practices, Congress passed the FPCA. The statute makes it illegal for an American corporation or any of its officers to offer, pay, or promise to give anything of value to any foreign official for purposes of

A. influencing any act or decision of such foreign official in his official capacity, including a decision to fail to perform his official function; or

B. inducing such foreign official to use his influence with a foreign government or instrumentality thereof to affect or influence any act or decision of such government or instrumentality.

The FPCA also makes it illegal for a corporation or any of its officers to offer, pay, or promise to give anything of value to a foreign political party or its officials for purposes of influencing their decisions. Anyone convicted

of violating the FPCA faces fines of up to $10,000 and/or imprisonment for up to five years.

The FCPA also empowers the Attorney General of the United States to take civil action and enjoin any individual, corporation, partnership, or sole proprietorship that violates its provisions. Prosecutors could apply the statute any time a telephone or other means of communication is employed in interstate or foreign commerce by a corporate entity or its officers in furtherance of a corrupt practice. Thus if a corporation or its officers employed EFTS in interstate or foreign commerce to funnel illegal payments to a foreign official or political party, they could face prosecution under the FCPA.

However, the government has shied away from FCPA prosecutions; moreover, the government has yet to clearly define the statute's parameters. Further, there have been no EFTS-related prosecutions under the FCPA. In addition, it should be noted that in a cashless society, where electronic blips would constitute illegal payoffs.

---

[1] P.L. 95–213.

Right to Financial Privacy Act (RFPA)[2]

Passed in 1978 by Congress, the RFPA seeks to limit the government's access to the financial records of bank customers:

> [N]o Government authority may have access to or obtain copies of the information contained in the financial records of any customer other than in the sealed records of the grand jury, unless such records have been used in the prosecution of a crime for which the grand jury issued an indictment or presentment.

In addition, a government agency may employ an administrative subpoena or summons to obtain the financial records of the target of an investigation only if:

(1) there is reason to believe that the records sought are relevant to time before the financial records are disclosed; (and)

(2) a copy of the subpeona or summons has been served upon the customer or mailed to his last known address.

The individual in question is empowered by the RFDA to file a motion in opposition to the government's request at a local federal district court. The RFPA's jurisdiction is broad and covers not only banks but also card issuers, industrial loan companies, trust companies, and credit unions. It provides for civil penalties against those financial institutions that fail to abide by its provisions.

The government, however, need not always employ a subpoena, summons, or search warrant to gain access to confidential financial records; the target of the probe may choose to authorize disclosure. However, before a financial institution complies with the voluntary disclosure, the customer must first provide it with a written statement which:

(1) authorizes such disclosure for a period of not in excess of three months;

(2) states that the customer may revoke such authorization at any time before the financial records are disclosed; (and)

(3) identifies the financial records which are to be disclosed.

In those instances where the government is unable to resort to a formal vehicle (a subpoena or search warrant) to gain access to a suspect's financial records, it may request them through a formal letter. However, it can do so only if:

[2] 12 U.S.C. 3401–3422.

- There is reason to believe that the records sought are relevant to a legitimate law enforcement inquiry.
- A copy of the request has been served upon the customer (suspect) or mailed to his last known address.

However, the suspect may, as in the case of a subpoena or search warrant, file a written opposition to the formal (request) letter at a local federal district court. In his opposition, the suspect must outline for the court the reasons why the government should not be allowed access to his financial records.

The RFPA has not handcuffed the government, as some of the statute's critics charge; the authorities need not always notify the suspect (and thus afford him the opportunity to file an opposition to their request) if they can demonstrate to a court that by giving such notice they may:

- Endanger the life or physical safety of another individual.
- Cause the target of the investigation to flee prosecution.
- Result in the destruction of or tampering with evidence.
- Result in the intimidation of potential witnesses.
- Otherwise seriously endanger or jeopardize an investigation or other official proceeding.

A government agency may not, however, transfer those financial records it has seized to a sister agency unless the latter first certifies, in writing, that these documents are relevant to a legitmate law enforcement inquiry it is conducting. The RFPA also provides the following for civil penalties against any government or private official found violating its provisions:

1. A fine of $100 without regard to the volume of records involved.
2. Payment of any actual damages sustained by the customer as a result of the disclosure.
3. Such punitive damages as the court may allow, where the violation is found to have been willful or intentional.
4. In the case of any successful action to enforce liability under this section, the costs of the action together with reasonable attorney's fees as determined by the court.

The RFPA, however, has been attacked by both civil libertarians and law enforcement sources. Civil libertarians charge that its civil sanctions are far from sufficient to deter the authorities and financial institutions from violating its provisions; the authorities, however, argue that the RFPA makes it difficult, if not impossible, for them to conduct a confidential investigation. Its requirement that the authorities first inform a suspect of the documents they seek to seize makes it difficult, they argue, to build a viable criminal case. A sophisticated felon, they note, can derail a government investigation by simply filing an opposition to the government's request for documents. The opposition, even if frivolous, could tie up the government in litigation for months. However, whether these fears are justified remains to be seen.

Added Legislative Efforts

Legislators at both the state and federal levels have enacted and introduced a number of statutes to address potential EFTS problems. Colorado, Maryland, Montana, Tennessee, and a number of other states have already enacted EFTS legislation. At the federal level, a number of EFTS-related bills have made their way to the Congress. The federal Depository Institutions and Monetary Control Act, passed in early 1980, authorizes the establishment of remote service units and the automatic transfer of funds. A proposed federal EFTS privacy bill, if enacted, would safeguard the privacy of EFTS users by prohibiting service providers and their employees from disclosing the "existence, location, date, time, contents, . . . or any item involved in an electronic fund transfer." To gain access to such records government investigators would have to demonstrate that

> such acquisition or interception may provide evidence of a criminal offense which involved murder, kidnapping, robbery, extortion, forgery, bribery, embezzlement, fraud, racketeering . . . or any other crime which threatens serious physical injury to an individual or will result in serious damage to property and is punishable by imprisonment for more than one year.

Efforts are also at hand to reform the communication laws, and legislation has been introduced in Congress to reduce the present paper glut. The problem, however, is not one of sparsity of laws and regulations; nor is it a technical problem that confronts EFTS. The cashless society is fraught with social, political, and economic issues that have yet to be resolved. Whether our society will be able to successfully address many of these issues may determine the outcome of America's journey to the cashless society.

CONCLUSION

In Europe, computer facilities have increasingly become the targets of terrorists; in Charlotte, North Carolina, an Army officer has given a sworn affidavit that she witnessed computer records being intentionally erased so that Army volunteers who failed the entrance exams could take them again. FBI agents, armed with a search warrant, seized computer printouts and a terminal log sheet from an expensive private school. The computer terminal at the school is alleged to have been used to penetrate at least 20 Canadian computer systems.

The computer and communications revolutions have made the cashless society a reality; rudimentary EFTS have taken root in several countries. Scientists are now working on the development of a new generation of supercomputers. However, the concern for privacy continues; in addition, consumer advocates fear—with some justification—that EFTS may give rise to new forms of consumer-related abuses. Civil libertarians have also entered the debate, and there are fears that EFTS may augment the potential for police abuses.

The cashless society will also have an impact on the socioeconomic fiber; the lower economic groups may find themselves barred from access to EFTS. There are also serious social concerns for the individual's freedom of choice. Millions of Americans are satisfied with our traditional payment mechanisms; pressuring them to embrace EFTS may raise questions of a political and constitutional nature. In addition, many of the smaller financial institutions fear that EFTS will fall under the control of the banking giants; further, questions have been raised regarding the funding of EFTS. The role of government in the cashless society is also in question; some have suggested that the government treat EFTS as a public utility. The role of government in the cashless society continues to evoke controversy.

There is also concern with the issue of crime in the cashless society. Our present law enforcement apparatus consists of more than 40,000 police agencies. Many of these employ fewer than 10 full-time personnel. Further, the majority lack resources and training and are ill-prepared to bring to successful prosecution complex EFTS crimes. Our prosecutorial apparatus fares no better; the majority of our prosecutorial offices lack the requisite tools to prosecute sophisticated cashless crimes. In addition, EFTS may give rise to new and more sophisticated forms of white-collar crime; it may also provide organized crime with new targets of opportunity. Extortion and bribery may take on new forms.

In addition, our judiciary may be unable to deal with EFTS. Many of our federal and local courts—especially those in large urban centers—are inundated wtih litigation; costly and complex litigation will only worsen the present backlog. For example, more than 180,000 civil and criminal cases make their way annually before our federal courts, another 20,000 reach the appellate level, and the present federal case backlog exceeds 196,000 civil and criminal cases. EFTS litigation will only aggravate this situation; further, complex EFTS cases will call for an army of technical experts. The cost of such complex litigation in the cashless society may reach prohibitive levels, well beyond the reach of many individuals and small businessmen.

The regulatory maze will also seriously hamper EFTS; indeed, many of the regulators have already turned their attention to EFTS. Rivalries and jurisdictional disputes have taken root; the FCC and the USPS are locked in combat over the electronic transfer of data. In efforts to comply with hundreds of thousands of rules and regulations—and the numbers grow daily—EFTS face a difficult future; as a result, EFTS services may become increasingly costly. Our branching and antitrust laws—often at odds with one another—further complicate the area of regulation. The regulators may, in the final analysis, deal EFTS a costly blow.

At the international level, the political and economic instability in both the Third World and the West can only delay the rapid growth of EFTS. America's declining global economic and political power is not conducive to the growth of EFTS. Further, many of the Third World countries, fearful that the West may employ EFTS as vehicles for economic domination, have enacted laws that hamper the transborder flow of data; in addition, the Third World is concerned more with feeding its people than with supplying them with a new payment mechanism. The developing countries also lack the requisite resources and personnel to build and staff indigenous EFTS.

The growth of EFTS, in the final analysis, is tied to America's technological know-how and the ability of political and economic institutions to meet the challenges of a rapidly changing world. The domestic problems of privacy, consumer abuse, and crime—given the requisite will and commitment—can be contained. We have the technology to both construct EFTS and limit related abuses. EFTS constitute a test of not only the technology but also the democracy of the United States. Can the country adapt to profound technological change? The future of the cashless society will depend, in some measure, on the ability of American society to survive politically.

GLOSSARY OF EFTS TERMS

ACH	Automated Clearing House
APD	Automatic Payroll Deposit
APEX	Automated Payments Exchange
ATM	Automated Teller Machine
CBCT	Consumer Bank Communications Terminal
CDM	Cash Dispensing Machine
DDA	Demand Deposit Account
DDP	Direct Deposit of Payroll
Debit Card	Bank card used to access a customer's personal accounts
DPD	Direct Pay Deposit
ECR	Electronic Cash Register
EDP	Electronic Data Processing
EFTS	Electronic Funds Transfer Systems
MAPS	Monetary and Payment Systems Planning Committee
MICR	Magnetic Ink Character Recognition
MINTS	Mutual Institutions National Transfer System
NACHA	National Automated Clearing House Association
NETS	Nebraska Electronic Transfer System
Network	Telecommunications System
NOW	Negotiable Order of Withdrawal
Off-line	Pertaining to equipment or devices not under control of the central processing unit
On-line	Pertaining to a user's ability to interact with a computer
POS	Point-of-Sale terminal
SPC	Switching Process Center
SWIFT	Society for Worldwide Interbank Financial Telecommunication
Switch	Central processing point which receives, processes and forwards messages based on a defined address
TMS	Transmatic Money Service
Truncation	Replacement or funds transfer document by electronic data

APPENDIX A
ENACTED STATE COMPUTER CRIME LEGISLATION*

Jurisdiction	Bill	Effective Date	Penalty	Comments
Arizona	H.B. 2212	October 1, 1978	Felony—5 years first degree, 1½ years second degree. Fine imposed at court's discretion.	Defines types of computer crimes and specifies if first or second degree
California	H.B. S.66	January 1, 1980	16-month to 3-year prison sentence, $2500–$5000 fine, or both.	Make it a crime to directly or indirectly use a computer, computer system, or network for a crime
Colorado	H.B. 1110	July 1, 1979	Damages less than $50—Class 3 misdemeanor. Damages more than 50 but less than $200—Class 2 misdemeanor. Damages more than $200 but less than $10,000—Class 4 felony. Damages $10,000 or more—Class 3 felony.	Defines the specifics of a computer system (modeled after the Florida bill)
Florida	H.B. 1305	August 1, 1978	Damages greater than $200 but less than $1000—third degree felony. Damages in excess of $1000—second degree felony. Stiff imprisonment terms: 1–5 years.	

| Illinois | H.B. 1027 | September 11, 1979 | Services obtained, $1000 or less Class A misdemeanor. Services obtained more than $1000 Class 4 felony. | Makes it illegal to alter computer programs without consent of owner. |
| Michigan | H.B. 4112 | March, 1980 | If the violation involves $100, the person is guilty of a misdemeanor. If the violation involves more than $100, the person is guilty of a felony, punishable by imprisonment for not more than 10 years, or a fine of not more than $5000 or both. | Prohibits computer fraud; also addresses crimes connected to access of computers |

* These are the first computer crime bills enacted at the state level.

APPENDIX B
LOCAL JURISDICTIONS
WITH BRANCHING LAWS

Permitted Statewide	No Branching Laws	Prohibit Any Branching	Permit Some Branching
Alaska	Wyoming	Colorado	Alabama
Arizona		Florida	Arkansas
California		Illinois	Georgia
Connecticut		Kansas	Hawaii
Delaware		Minnesota	Indiana
District of Columbia		Missouri	Iowa
Idaho		Montana	Kentucky
Maine		Nebraska	Louisiana
Maryland		Oklahoma	Massachusetts
New Jersey		Texas	Michigan
Nevada		West Virginia	Mississippi
North Carolina			New Hampshire
Oregon			New Mexico
Puerto Rico			New York
Rhode Island			North Dakota
South Carolina			Ohio
South Dakota			Pennsylvania
Vermont			Tennessee
Washington			Utah
			Virginia
			Wisconsin

APPENDIX C
BRANCHING REQUIREMENTS
OF STATE STATUTES

State branching laws differ in their branching requirements. The more common branching statutes provide for the following:

- Alabama, Arkansas, Indiana, Massachusetts, Tennessee, and Utah have statutes that allow branching within the city and county the main bank office is located in.
- Mississippi allows branching within a radius of 100 miles from the main bank office.
- Pennsylvania, Iowa, and Virginia have statutes that allow branching within a city, county, or a county contiguous to the county the main bank office is in.
- Wisconsin allows branching within a county or a county contiguous to the county the main bank office is in.
- New Jersey allows branching outside the state of the parent bank.
- New York allows statewide branching for all banks.

APPENDIX D
FEDERAL COMPUTER SYSTEMS PROTECTION ACT

Draft of Bill as originally introduced by Senator Abraham D. Ribicoff in the 96th Congress (January 25, 1979):

A BILL

To amend title 18, United States Code, to make a crime the use for fraudulent or other illegal purposes, of any computer owned or operated by the United States, certain financial institutions, and entities affecting interstate commerce.

Be it enacted by the Senate and House of Representatives of the United States of America in Congress assembled, That this Act may be cited as the *Federal Computer Systems Protection Act of 1979.*

SEC.2 The Congress finds that—

(1) computer-related crime is a growing problem in the Government and in the private sector;

(2) such crime occurs at great cost to the public since losses for each incident of computer crime tend to be far greater than the losses associated with each incident of other white collar crime;

(3) the opportunities for computer-related crimes in Federal programs, in financial institutions, and in other entities which operate in interstate commerce through the introduction of fraudulent records into a computer system, unauthorized use of computer facilities, alteration or destruction of computerized information files, and stealing of financial instruments, data, or other assets, are great:

(4) computer-related crime directed at institutions operating in interstate commerce has a direct effect on interstate commerce; and

(5) the prosecution of persons engaged in computer-related crime is difficult under current Federal criminal statutes.

SEC. 3. (a) Chapter 47 of title 18, United States Code, is amended by adding at the end thereof the following new section:

"§ 102.8. Computer fraud and abuse

"(a) Whoever knowingly and willfully, directly or indirectly accesses, causes to be accessed or attempts to access any computer, computer system, computer network, or any part thereof which, in whole or in part, operates in interstate commerce or is owned by, under contract to, or in conjunction with, any financial institution, the United States Government or any branch, department, or agency thereof, or any entity operating in or affecting interstate commerce, for the purpose of—

"(1) devising or executing any scheme or artifice to defraud, or

"(2) obtaining money, property, or services, for themselves or another, by means of false or fraudulent pretenses, representations or promises, shall be fined a sum not more than two and one-half times the amount of the fraud or theft, or imprisoned not more than fifteen years, or both.

"(b) Whoever intentionally and without authorization, directly or indirectly accesses, alters, damages, destroys, or attempts to damage or destroy any computer, computer system, or computer network described in subsection (a), or any computer software, program or data contained in such computer, computer system or computer network, shall be fined not more than $50,000 or imprisoned not more than fifteen years, or both.

"(c) For purposes of this section, the term—

"(1) 'access' means to approach, instruct, communicate with, store data in, retrieve data from, or otherwise make use of any resources of, a computer, computer system, or computer network;

"(2) 'computer' means an electronic device which performs logical, arithmetic, and memory functions by the manipulations of electronic or magnetic impulses, and includes all input, output, processing, storage, software, or communication facilities which are connected or related to such a device in a system or network;

"(3) 'computer system' means a set of related, connected or unconnected, computer equipment, devices, and software;

"(4) 'computer network' means the interconnection of communication systems with a computer through remote terminals, or a complex consisting of two or more interconnected computers;

"(5) 'property' includes, but is not limited to, financial instruments, information, including electronically processed or produced data, and computer software and programs in either machine or human readable form, and any other tangible or intangible item of value;

"(6) 'services' includes, but is not limited to, computer time, data processing, and storage functions;

"(7) 'financial instrument' means any check, draft, money order, certificate of deposit, letter of credit, bill of exchange, credit card, or marketable security, or any electronic data processing representation thereof;

"(8) 'computer program' means an instruction or statement or a series of instructions or statements, in a form acceptable to a computer, which permits the functioning of a computer system in a manner designed to provide appropriate products from such computer system;

"(9) 'computer software' means a set of computer programs, procedures, and associated documentation concerned with the operation of a computer system;

"(10) 'financial institution' means—

"(A) a bank with deposits insured by the Federal Deposit Insurance Corporation;

"(B) a member of the Federal Reserve including any Federal Reserve bank;

"(C) an institution with accounts insured by the Federal Savings and Loan Insurance Corporation;

"(D) a credit union with accounts insured by the National Credit Union Administration;

"(E) a member of the Federal home loan bank systems and any home loan bank;

"(F) a member or business insured by the Securities Investor Protection Corporation; and

"(G) a broker-dealer registered with the Securities and Exchange Commission pursuant to section 15 of the Securities and Exchange Act of 1934."

(c) The table of sections of chapter 47 of title 18, United States Code, is amended by adding at the end thereof the following:
"1028, Computer fraud."

APPENDIX E
TRADE GROUPS
WITH INTERESTS IN EFTS

American Bankers Association
Washington, D.C.

American Business Communications Association
317B David Kingly Hall
Urbana, Illinois   61801

American Federation of Information
    Processing Societies, Inc.
1815 North Lynn Street
Arlington, Virginia   22209

American Finance Association
100 Trinity Place
New York, New York   10006

American Finance Association
Graduate School of Business Administration
100 Trinity Place
New York, New York   10006

American Institute of Industrial Engineers
25 Technology Park
Norcross, Georgia   30092

American Insurance Association
85 John Street
New York, New York   10038

American Savings & Loan League
Washington Building
15th Street, N.W.
Washington, D.C.   20005

American Society for Industrial Security
2000 K Street, N.W.
Washington, D.C.   20006

American Society for Information Science
1155 16th Street, N.W.
Washington, D.C.   20006

Association for Computing Machinery
1133 Avenue of the Americas
New York, New York   10036

Association for Systems Management
24587 Bangley Road
Cleveland, Ohio   44138

Association for Time Sharing Users
75 Manhattan Drive
Boulder, Colorado   80303

Association of Bank Holding Companies
730 15th Street, N.W.
Washington, D.C.   20005

Association of Computer Programmers
        and Analysts
Box 95
Kensington, Maryland   20795

Association of Data Processing
        Service Organization
210 Summit Avenue
Montvale, N.J.   07645

Bank Administration Institute
303 South Northwest Highway
Park Ridge, Illinois   60068

Carratu Limited
Oak House, Cross Street Sales
Greater Manchester, M33 IFU
England

Computer and Automated Systems
        Association of SME
Box 930, 20501 Ford Road
Dearborn, Michigan   48128

Computer and Business Equipment
    Manufacturers Assn.
1828 L Street, N.W.
Washington, D.C.   20036

Computer and Communications
    Industry Association
1500 Wilson Boulevard
Arlington, Virginia   22209

Computer Law Association
1666 K Street, N.W., Suite 800
Washington, D.C.   20006

Computer Law Service
28 State Street, Suite 2220
Boston, Massachusetts   02109

Conference of State Bank Supervisors
1015 18th Street, N.W.
Washington, D.C.   20006

Data Processing Management Association
505 Busse Highway
Park Ridge, Illinois   60068

Federal Bar Association
1815 H Street, N.W.
Washington, D.C.   20006

Independent Bankers Association of America
P.O. Box 267
Sauk Centre, Minnesota   56378

Information Industry Association
4720 Montgomery Lane
Washington, D.C.   20014

Institute for Certified Computer
    Professionals
35 East Wacke Dr.
Chicago, Illinois   60690

Insurance Institute of America
Providence and Sugartown Roads
Malvert, Pennsylvania   19355

Insurance Security Association
Fireman's Fund-American Insurance Company
San Francisco, California   94118

Interbank Card Association
110 East 59th Street
New York, New York   10038

International Communications Association
Box 836
Bellaire, Texas   77401

International EDP Auditors Association
7024 Edgebrook Lane
Hanover Park, Illinois   60103

International Word Processing Association
Maryland Road
Willow Grove, Pennsylvania   19090

National Association of Bank Directors
1800 K Street, N.W.
Washington, D.C.   20006

National Association of Bank Servicers
2280 South High Street
Columbus, Ohio   43207

National Association of Federal Credit Unions
1156 15th Street, N.W.
Washington, D.C.   20005

National Association of State
    Credit Union Supervisors
1001 Connecticut Avenue, N.W., Suite 800
Washington, D.C.   20036

National Association of State
    Loan and Credit Offices
1432 Philadelphia National Bank Building
Philadelphia, Pennsylvania   19107

National Association of State
    Savings and Loan Supervisors
1001 Connecticut Avenue, N.W.
Washington, D.C.   20036

National Insurance Association
2400 South Michigan Avenue
Chicago, Illinois   60616

National Savings and Loan League
1100 15th Street, N.W.
Washington, D.C.   20005

APPENDIX F
RECOMMENDED SECURITY CHECKLIST FOR EFTS SYSTEMS

RECOMMENDED PHYSICAL SAFEGUARDS

1. Damage from fire
   a. Computer is housed in a structure constructed of fire-resistant and noncombustible materials
   b. Computer room is separated from adjacent areas by noncombustible fire-resistant partitions, walls, and doors
   c. Paper and other combustible supplies are stored outside the computer area
   d. File tapes and disks are stored outside the computer area
   e. Raised flooring is made of noncombustible material
   f. Ceilings and support hardware are noncombustible
   g. Operators are trained in firefighting techniques
   h. Curtains, rugs, furniture, and drapes are noncombustible
   i. Smoke detectors are installed:
      (1) in ceiling
      (2) under raised floor
      (3) in air-return ducts
      (4) Smoke detectors are properly engineered to function in the computer room
      (5) Smoke detection systems are tested on a scheduled basis; testing also includes:
         (a) regularly scheduled fire drills
         (b) cleaning under raised floor regularly
         (c) checking for adequate supply of firefighting water
   k. You have battery-powered emergency lighting throughout the computer area
2. Damage from water exposure
   a. Computers are excluded from areas below grade
   b. Adequate drainage under the raised floor
   c. Drains are installed on floor above to divert water accumulation away from all hardware

    d. All electrical junction boxes are under the raised flooring held off the slab to prevent water overflow from adjacent areas

    e. Exterior windows and doors are watertight

3. Natural disaster exposure
    a. Building is structurally sound:
       (1) to resist wind storms and hurricanes
       (2) to resist flood damage
       (3) to resist earthquakes
    b. Building and equipment are properly grounded for lightning protection
    c. Building is on solid foundation
    d. Building is remote from any earthquake faults

4. Access control
    a. Is installation a likely target for criminals
    b. Are there guards on all entrances which lead to a computer area
    c. Firm has system for positive identification of employees
    d. Access to the computer area is restricted to selected personnel
    e. Keys and locks are changed at regular intervals or after termination of an employee
    f. Dismissed employees of computer environment are removed immediately, their admission badges picked up, and the necessary guard personnel notified
    g. Personnel are trained to challenge improperly identified visitors
    h. All exterior windows are covered with expanded metal grilles if near street level
    i. In areas where the crime rate is high there is bulletproof glass
    j. An individual cannot gain access with the knowledge of a security guard or another employee
    k. The central computer facility is staffed by at least two appropriately cleared personnel at all times
    l. The computer room is screened so that it is not visible from the street
    m. All remote terminals are uniquely identified

RECOMMENDED SOFTWARE SECURITY

1. Physical security
    a. The essential programs, software systems, and associated documentation in your Program Library are located in a locked vault or secured area
    b. Firm has provided backup files at a secondary location for both the programs and the associated documentation

2. Access restrictions
    a. Firm has restricted access to the essential programs and software systems on a need-to-know basis in the prime and backup areas

    b. Performs periodic checks to validate the security software utilities and tables of access codes
3. Remote terminals
    a. Firm employs keyword or password protection
    b. Firm changes keywords and passwords annually
    c. Firm employs software scrambling techniques during a transmission of vital data
    d. Firm employs hardware cryptographic devices during transmission of vital data

RECOMMENDED SERVICE PERSONNEL CHECKS

1. In-house
    a. Firm controls access to vital areas for custodial, electrical, and other in-house maintenance personnel
    b. Firm provides special escorts for maintenance personnel who are not appropriately cleared
2. Vendor
    a. Firm has a list of each vendor's authorized service and systems support personnel
    b. Firm insists on positive identification
    c. Firm supervises their activities to ensure that they don't compromise EFTS security

SAFEGUARDING FILES

1. On-line and off-line program files
    a. Duplicate files are stored in a separate building from the originals
    b. Programs are stored in low fire hazard containers
    c. There is a current inventory of such files
    d. Program changes are controlled and recorded
    e. Changes are made only to a reproduced version of the original program file with the original left intact
    f. Firm maintains a record of items withdrawn from production file area
    g. Firm maintains a backup of source data for programs under development

RECOMMENDED INTERNAL AUDIT CONTROLS

1. An overall audit control philosophy does exist relating to computer systems concerned with assets
2. Computer usage and production controls are employed

3.   User input is controlled to ensure receipt of all input data
4.   Output is monitored to ensure compliance with standards
5.   Error reporting and follow-up procedures do exist
6.   Quality control does exist to verify proper execution of reports
7.   Program changes are controlled
8.   All options of all programs are tested
9.   Conversions are controlled to ensure continuity
10. The installation does ensure separation of duties
11. The installation is adequately protected against intrusion
12. A backup does exist for programs and files
13. A backup does exist for hardware
14. The auditor does get involved during the system design phase

TIME-RESOURCE SHARING SAFEGUARDS

1.   Remote terminals are available only to selected individuals
2.   Access to terminal is controlled by
     1.   Locked doors
     2.   Posted guards
     3.   Other restraints
3.   The location of the terminal is such that each user's privacy is ensured
4.   Passwords are utilized to identify a specific terminal and a specific user
5.   The interval at which passwords are changed is appropriate to the security requirements
6.   The password is combined with physical keys or access badges
7.   The system software restricts a given individual to specific data files only
8.   The right to add, delete, or modify files is limited by software controls
9.   Access to the keyword and lockword files is restricted
10. The system maintains accurate records of all activity against each data file
11. Scramblers and other cryptographic techniques are utilized when appropriate
12. The time-resource sharing security system is monitored and reviewed
13. Program debugging of the security system is closely monitored and controlled

CONTINGENCY PLAN SAFEGUARDS

1. Backup facilities
   a.   Firm has a backup computer available
   b.   Firm has access to another computer
   c.   Firm has an implementation plan for use of backup installation
   d.   Firm has a regular maintenance schedule
   e.   Firm monitors it for compliance

2. Firm has a written contingency plan covering
    a. Who is responsible for each functional area
    b. A detailed notification procedure clearly specifying (who calls whom):
        (1) management
        (2) emergency crews
        (3) users
        (4) backup sites
        (5) service personnel
        (6) facilities personnel
    c. The responsibility for retaining source documents and/or data files for each application
    d. Identification of backup installations
    e. Destruction or safeguarding of confidential material in the central computer facility in the event the facility must be evacuated

APPENDIX G
AFFIDAVIT OF
PASSWORD RECEIPT*

I, *(print name of employee)* , acknowledge personal receipt of the system password(s), and I fully understand that I am responsible for the password(s) protection. I will comply with all instructions provided me, and will not divulge the password(s) or other confidential related data to any unauthorized person. I further understand that I will report any problem I may encounter in the use of the password(s) or any misuse of the password(s) by other persons.

_____   _____

SYSTEM   INSTITUTION

DATE: _____   _____

                                             SIGNATURE OF EMPLOYEE

Subscribed and sworn to before me this _____ day of _____, 19____.

_____

                                          Notary Public

* Sample affidavit to be used in safeguarding passwords employed in a computer operation. The affidavit could deter some misuses of passwords by EFTS employees.

APPENDIX H
SAMPLE COMPUTER
SECURITY QUESTIONNAIRE*

COMPUTER FACILITY SECURITY

1. Is there a designated systems security officer?
2. Is the facility open to public view?
3. Does person, or group, responsible for security perform unscheduled security reviews?
4. Does the facility have adequate doors?
    a. Do the doors have adequate locks?
    b. Are the doors locked when not in use?
5. Are vendor maintenance personnel permitted in the facility when installation personnel are not present?
6. Are building maintenance or cleaning personnel permitted in the facility when installation personnel are not present?
7. Are facility entrance keys or access control devices changed or recoded on either regular or unscheduled basis?
8. Are facility entry authorization and access mechanisms immediately revoked for terminated or suspended employees?
9. Does a written emergency plan exist?
10. Is the emergency plan tested (real or simulated) on a regular basis?
11. Are security devices operable in the event of a power failure?
12. Are external facility windows protected against intruder entry and water damage in event of breakage?
13. Are external tape library windows protected against intruder entry or breakage?
14. Does the facility have alarm systems which are operable when the facility is closed?
15. Are incoming letters and packages checked for bombs or incendiary devices prior to delivery to the computer room?

* Based on sample computer security questionnaire employed by the city of New York.

16. Are security awareness meetings held on a regular basis for facility personnel?
17. Are all supervisory personnel aware of the potential security vulnerabilities of areas under their control?
18. Are all facility doors and windows equipped with nonremovable hinge-pins?
19. Are analysts, programmers, and data entry personnel prohibited from entering computer room?
20. Are analysts, programmers, and data entry personnel required to log in when entering computer room?
21. Do facility personnel wear identification?
22. Are visitors identified and authorized prior to entering?
23. Are all visitors and service personnel required to sign an entry log?
24. Do VIP visitors bypass any of identification, authorization, or sign-in procedures?
25. Are facility water cooling systems adequately protected against unauthorized entry or tampering?

SYSTEM OPERATIONS SECURITY

1. Are batch data deliveries logged?
2. Are console reports reviewed regularly by supervisory personnel?
3. Do operators maintain trouble logs?
4. Are trouble logs reviewed regularly by supervisory personnel?
5. Are equipment use meters logged and reviewed by supervisory personnel?
6. Are all exceptions to standard operating procedures promptly investigated and corrective measures taken?
7. Are catalogued procedures and operational programs protected by access and modification protection software?
8. Are modifications to operational programs and catalogued procedures reviewed by qualified supervisory personnel?
9. Does security officer review operations logs and environmental control charts?
10. Are operators or supervisors permitted to run shifts by themselves?

LIBRARY SECURITY

1. Is the media library in a fireproof room?
2. Is the media library room separate from the computer room?

3. Do any pipes pass through the library room?
4. Does the library have glass windows?
5. Does the library have emergency lighting?
6. Does the library have fire detection equipment?
7. Does the library have fire suppression equipment?
8. Is one person responsible for the library?
9. Are all media withdrawn and returned by a librarian?
10. If so, is the library locked?
11. Are confidential media maintained in a separate area?
12. Are borrowed media logged in and out?
13. Does a written list of authorized borrowers exist?
14. Is there an inventory of media?
15. Is the library accessible to the general public?
16. Is the library accessible to employees?
17. Is there a tape retention plan?
18. Is there a documented and implemented procedure for following up overdue returns of borrowed material?
19. Does a formal control procedure exist for the processing and storage of noninstallation tapes?
20. Does your facility own or have access to degaussing equipment?
21. Are confidential tapes overwritten or degaussed prior to reuse by another application?
22. Do you permit processing of nonstandard label tapes?
23. Are data in confidential files enciphered?
24. Do you have a tape cleaner?
25. Do you periodically clean your tapes?
26. Do you periodically recertify your tapes and disks?

DATA SECURITY

1. Are confidential printouts adequately protected from unauthorized disclosure?
2. Are terminals that access confidential data adequately protected?
3. Are media containing confidential data adequately protected until disposition or destruction?
4. Are confidential trash and unusable negotiable instruments adequately protected until disposition or destruction?
5. Does user department perform destruction of its confidential trash and usable negotiable instruments?

6. Does the facility have a paper shredder available to it?
7. Is the destruction of confidential trash adequately controlled?

SECURITY MEASURES AGAINST FIRE AND WATER DAMAGES

1. Does facility have a fire detection system?
2. Have fire detection systems been tested within past six months?
3. Does fire control system automatically close down air conditioning and ventilation systems if activated?
4. Does facility have an adequate number of portable fire extinguishers?
5. Does facility have fire suppression equipment other than portable fire extinguishers?
6. Is there a written fire emergency plan?
7. Does fire emergency plan include evacuation and system shutdown procedures?
8. Are fire drills regularly held to test and evaluate fire emergency plan effectiveness?
9. Is all trash removed promptly from the facility?
10. Are fire exits kept clear and tested regularly?
11. Is smoking permitted in computer room?
12. Is smoking permitted in tape library?
13. Is tape storage area fire protected?
14. Is there a fire and water resistant media storage vault in data center?
15. Is the media storage vault secured to floor or wall?
16. Do water or steam pipes pass through the facility?
17. Has facility ever experienced water leakage from walls or ceiling?
18. Are waterproof covers available for equipment and data files?
19. Is installation subject to flooding?
20. Have written emergency plans for flooding or water damage been prepared?
21. Are there underfloor water detectors?

APPENDIX I
FIRST COUNT OF THE EQUITY FUNDING CORPORATION INDICTMENT*

UNITED STATES DISTRICT COURT
FOR THE CENTRAL DISTRICT OF CALIFORNIA
MARCH 1973 GRAND JURY

UNITED STATES OF AMERICA Plaintiff, v. STANLEY GOLDBLUM, SAMUEL B. LOWELL, JEROME H. EVANS, FRED LEVIN, MICHAEL E. SULTAN, JAMES CYRUS SMITH, JR., ARTHUR STANLEY LEWIS, DAVID JACK CAPO, LLOYD DOUGLAS EDENS, LAWRENCE GREY COLLINS, JAMES HOWARD BANKS, WILLIAM MERCADO, DONALD MCCLELLAN, WILLIAM EDWARD SYMONDS, LESTER MICHAEL KELLER, ALAN LEWIS GREEN, JULIAN S. H. WEINER, MARVIN AL LICHTIG, SOLOMON BLOCK, GARY STANLEY BECKERMAN, MARK CHARLES LEWIS, RICHARD GARDENIER, Defendants.	*No.* *CD* INDICTMENT [18 U.S.C. §371: Conspiracy; 15 U.S.C. §§77q(a), 77x: Fraud in Sale of Securities, False Statement in Registration Statement; 15 U.S.C. §§78j(b), 78l, 78m, 78ff; 17 CFR §240.10b-5, Regs. 12B, 13A: Fraud in Sale of Securities, False Statement in Documents Required to be Filed with Securities and Exchange Commission; 18 U.S.C. §1341: Mail Fraud; 18 U.S.C. §1014: False Statement to Bank; 18 U.S.C. §2314: Interstate Transportation of Securities Taken by Fraud; 18 U.S.C. §2511: Interception of Communications]

---

* Called the biggest fraud in American history, it illustrates the ease with which computers can be employed in sophisticated business frauds.

The Grand Jury charges:

COUNT ONE

[18 U.S.C. §371]

1. Beginning on or about January 15, 1965, and continuing to on or about April 1, 1973, in the Central District of California and elsewhere, defendants STANLEY GOLDBLUM, SAMUEL B. LOWELL, JEROME H. EVANS, FRED LEVIN, MICHAEL E. SULTAN, JAMES CYRUS SMITH, JR., ARTHUR STANLEY LEWIS, DAVID JACK CAPO, LLOYD DOUGLAS EDENS, LAWRENCE GREY COLLINS, JAMES HOWARD BANKS, WILLIAM MERCADO, DONALD MC CLELLAN, WILLIAM EDWARD SYMONDS, LESTER MICHAEL KELLER, ALAN LEWIS GREEN, MARVIN AL LICHTIG, JULIAN S. H. WEINER, SOLOMON BLOCK, GARY STANLEY BECKERMAN, MARK CHARLES LEWIS, RICHARD GARDENIER and unindicted co-conspirators William Gootnick, Ronald Secrist, Francis D. Majerus, Aaron Venouziou and Wolfson Weiner Ratoff and Lapin, and divers other persons known and unknown to the Grand Jury, wilfully and knowingly agreed, confederated, combined and conspired together to commit offenses against the United States, to wit, to violate Title 15, United States Code, Sections 77g(a), 77x, 78j(b), 78l, 78m, 78ff, Title 17, Code of Federal Regulations, Section 240.10b-5, Regulation 12B and Regulation 13A, and Title 18, United States Code, Sections 1014, 1341, 2314, and 2511, all as further described below:

A. It was a part of said conspiracy that said defendants and co-conspirators wilfully and knowingly would, in the offer and sale of securities of Equity Funding Corporation of America (hereinafter in this Count the term "EFCA" is used, unless the context requires otherwise, to refer to Equity Funding Corporation of America and its subsidiaries), by the use of the means and instruments of transportation and communication in interstate commerce and by the use of the mails, directly and indirectly, (a) employ devices, schemes and artifices to defraud; (b) obtain money and property by means of untrue statements of material facts and omissions to state material facts necessary in order to make the statements made, in the light of the circumstances under which they were made, not misleading; and (c) engage in transactions, practices and courses of business which operated and would operate as a fraud and deceit upon the purchasers of said securities of EFCA, and upon any and all persons to whom the said defendants and unindicted co-conspirators would offer to sell said securities of EFCA, in violation of Title 15, United States Code, Sections 77q(a) and 77x.

B. It was a further part of said conspiracy that said defendants and unindicted co-conspirators wilfully and knowingly, directly and indirectly, by the use of the means and instrumentalities of interstate commerce, of the mails, and of the facilities of national securities exchanges would use and employ manipulative and deceptive devices and contrivances in connection with the sale of securities of EFCA as defined in Rule 10b-5 (17 CFR 240.10b-5), prescribed by the Securities and Exchange Commission as necessary and appropriate in the public interest and for the protection of investors, in violation of Title 15, United States Code, Sections 78j(b) and 78ff.

C. It was a further part of said conspiracy that said defendants and unindicted co-conspirators wilfully would make untrue statements of material fact in registration statements filed with the Securities and Exchange Commission and would omit to state material facts required to be stated in registration statements filed with the Securities and Exchange Commission and necessary to make the statements therein not misleading, in violation of Title 15, United States Code, Section 77x.

D. It was a further part of said conspiracy that said defendants and unindicted co-conspirators wilfully and knowingly would make statements which were false and misleading with respect to material facts in applications, reports and other documents required to be filed and filed with the American Stock Exchange, the New York Stock Exchange, the Pacific Coast Stock Exchange and the Securities and Exchange Commission, in violation of Title 15, United States Code, Sections 78l, 78m, 78ff and Title 17, Code of Federal Regulations, Regulations 12B and 13A, promulgated under Title 15, United States Code, Chapter 2B.

E. It was further a part of said conspiracy that said defendants and unindicted co-conspirators, having wilfully and knowingly devised and intended to devise schemes and artifices to defraud, and for obtaining money and property by means of false and fraudulent pretenses, representations, and promises, would, for the purpose of executing said schemes and artifices and attempting to do so, knowingly cause to be delivered by mail by the United States Post Office, according to the direction thereon, certain letters, packages and other matter, in violation of Title 18, United States Code, Section 1341.

F. It was a further part of said conspiracy that said defendants and unindicted co-conspirators knowingly would make materially false statements and reports for the purpose of influencing the action of banks, the deposits of which were then insured by the Federal Deposit Insurance Corporation, upon commitments and loans and upon the change and extension of commitments and loans by renewal, deferment of action and otherwise, in violation of Title 18, United States Code, Section 1014.

G. It was a further part of said conspiracy that said defendants and unindicted co-conspirators with unlawful and fraudulent intent would transport and cause to be transported in interstate commerce falsely made, forged and counterfeited securities, knowing the securities to have been falsely made, forged and counterfeited, in violation of Title 18, United States Code, Section 2314.

H. It was a further part of said conspiracy that said defendants and unindicted co-conspirators would cause to be transported in interstate commerce securities of a value in excess of $5,000, knowing the securities to have been stolen, converted and taken by fraud, in violation of Title 18, United States Code, Section 2314.

1. It was a further part of said conspiracy that said defendants and unindicted co-conspirators wilfully would endeavor to intercept, and procure others to intercept and endeavor to intercept wire communications, and wilfully would use and endeavor to use, and procure others to use and endeavor to use an electronic device to intercept oral communications made and had on the premises of a business the operations of which then affected interstate commerce, in violation of Title 18, United States Code, Section 2511.

2. The foregoing objects of the conspiracy were to be accomplished, in substance, through acts, transactions and practices which would, directly and indirectly, fraudulently overstate the income and assets and misrepresent the growth and general business and financial condition of EFCA. Said acts, transactions and practices would enable the defendants to continue EFCA's normal business operations, to fraudulently increase the market price of EFCA stock, to acquire assets and companies of EFCA with falsely valued EFCA stock and other consideration, to borrow money on behalf of EFCA, to realize incomes from EFCA salaries, commissions, bonuses, fees and expense allowances and to sell fraudulently valued EFCA stock owned by them, all the while concealing from other EFCA shareholders, the general business community, regulatory agencies and the public the true business and financial condition of EFCA. More specifically:

A. Defendant STANLEY GOLDBLUM, President of EFCA, would set periodic standards for growth in income, assets and earnings of EFCA, which growth he did not expect to be achieved, and which growth was not achieved, through the conduct of legitimate business operations, and he would direct defendants JEROME H. EVANS, SAMUEL B. LOWELL and FRED LEVIN, officers of EFCA and of its subsidiaries, to ensure that the books, records and financial reports of EFCA and its subsidiaries, including, but not limited to, Equity Funding Life Insurance Company (EFLIC), would reflect the growth in income assets and earnings set forth in the standards. Upon receiving defendant STANLEY GOLDBLUM's directions, defendants JEROME H. EVANS, SAMUEL B. LOWELL and FRED LEVIN would make and would arrange with other employees of EFCA and of its subsidiaries, including, but not limited to, defendants MICHAEL E. SULTAN, JAMES CYRUS SMITH, JR., DAVID JACK CAPO, ARTHUR STANLEY LEWIS and LLOYD DOUGLAS EDENS, to make false and fictitious entries to various types of accounts, including, but not limited to, receivables from purchasers of Equity Funding programs, notes receivable, receivables on the residual right to receive commissions on the sale of contractual plans, investments, insurance premium income, insurance commission income and securities commission income.

B. In order to conceal the true condition of EFCA's business operations and to obtain funds necessary to continue EFCA's operations defendants STANLEY GOLDBLUM, SAMUEL B. LOWELL and FRED LEVIN would arrange for advances and loans of money, including, but not limited to, bank loans negotiated and maintained through the submission to banks of false financial information, and defendants STANLEY GOLDBLUM and SAMUEL B. LOWELL would further arrange for certain of those obligations not to be properly recognized and reflected on the books, records and financial statements of EFCA.

C. In order to promote and to conceal the activities of EFCA, including, but not limited to, the insertion of fictitious and inflated assets and the non-disclosure of certain liabilities on the books, records and financial statements of EFCA and in order to conceal the activities of defendants STANLEY GOLDBLUM and SAMUEL B. LOWELL, defendants STANLEY GOLDBLUM and SAMUEL B. LOWELL would arrange for the use of corporations registered in jurisdictions outside the United States, including, but not limited to, Equity Funding Capital Corporation, N. V., a Netherlands Antilles Corporation; Bishops' Bank and Trust Company, a Bahamian Corporation; Equity Immobilaire Industriale, S.p.A., an Italian Corporation; Compania de Estudios y Asuntos, a Panamanian Corporation; and Etablissement Grandson, a Liechtenstein Corporation; which corporations directly and indirectly entered into various transactions at the direction of said defendants STANLEY GOLDBLUM and SAMUEL B. LOWELL.

D. In order to follow the directions and meet the standards concerning the income, assets and earnings which EFLIC was expected to have, and to contribute to the income, assets and earnings of EFCA, defendant FRED LEVIN would give directions to defendants JAMES CYRUS SMITH, JR., ARTHUR STANLEY LEWIS and LLOYD DOUGLAS EDENS to insert on the books and records of EFLIC the necessary amounts of fictitious business. Defendants ARTHUR STANLEY LEWIS and LLOYD DOUGLAS EDENS would arrange with defendants LESTER MICHAEL KELLER and ALAN LEWIS GREEN and unindicted co-conspirator Aaron Venouziou to write computer programs for the creation of fictitious insurance policies and related fictitious financial information, and to have said policies and financial information generated in the form of computer print-out and tape listings. Defendant LLOYD DOUGLAS EDENS would arrange with defendant WILLIAM EDWARD SYMONDS to make entries on computer records in order that genuine policies which had lapsed would appear to be in force. Defendant LLOYD DOUGLAS EDENS would further prepare false financial statements purporting to reflect the financial condition of EFLIC and would arrange for false financial statements and other financial information to be sent in interstate commerce and through the mails to persons and corporations with whom EFLIC did business and to various state agencies responsible for regulating insurance companies.

E. For the purpose of generating income and providing operating capital through the use of fictitious insurance policies, defendants FRED LEVIN, JAMES CYRUS SMITH, JR., and ARTHUR STANLEY LEWIS would negotiate and enter into reinsurance agreements with other insurance companies who would thereby agree to pay commissions for the privilege of reinsuring portions of EFLIC's insurance business, not knowing that such business, or any portion thereof, was fictitious. Defendants LESTER MICHAEL KELLER and ALAN LEWIS GREEN would arrange for computer print-out and tape listings containing fictitious insurance policies to be sent in interstate commerce and through the mails to various reinsuring companies. Defendants JAMES CYRUS SMITH, JR., ARTHUR STANLEY LEWIS, WILLIAM EDWARD SYMONDS, LESTER MICHAEL KELLER, and ALAN LEWIS GREEN would arrange for the reinsuring companies to send in interstate commerce and through the mails checks and money to EFLIC representing commissions on insurance policies sent by EFLIC to the reinsuring companies. In order to fulfill the terms of the reinsurance agreements, to maintain the confidence and goodwill of the reinsuring companies and thereby to guarantee the continued reinsurance of fictitious insurance and reduce the danger of its disclosure, defendants ARTHUR STANLEY LEWIS, WILLIAM EDWARD SYMONDS and LESTER MICHAEL KELLER would arrange for lists of insurance reserve rates and values to be sent in interstate commerce and through the mails to the reinsuring companies; and defendants FRED LEVIN, JAMES CYRUS SMITH, JR., and LAWRENCE GREY COLLINS would arrange for correspondence regarding questions arising out of the interpretation and administration of the reinsurance agreements to be sent in interstate commerce and through the mails to the reinsuring companies.

F. In order to conceal the fact that monies were not being received on genuine business, and in order to provide further operating capital:

(1) Defendants FRED LEVIN and JAMES CYRUS SMITH, JR., would arrange with defendant JAMES HOWARD BANKS for the submission of death claims on fictitious insurance policies to be sent in interstate commerce and through the mails to the reinsuring companies and for the reinsuring companies to send in interstate commerce and through the mails checks and money to EFLIC representing death benefit payments on the basis of death claims.

(2) Defendants STANLEY GOLDBLUM, FRED LEVIN, MICHAEL E. SULTAN, JAMES CYRUS SMITH, JR., ARTHUR STANLEY LEWIS and LLOYD DOUGLAS EDENS would arrange for the development and sale, through use of the mails, of single premium annuities bearing the letterheads of Equity Funding Life Insurance Company, Bankers National Life Insurance Company, Equity Funding Life Insurance Company of New York and Northern Life Insurance Company all of which were subsidiaries of EFCA; and said defendants would further arrange that the sale of said annuities and the liabilities attributable thereto would not be properly reflected on the books, records and financial statements of the respective life insurance companies, or of EFCA.

G. In order to conceal the fictitious nature of the life insurance policies and to assist in the submission of fictitious death claims, defendant LAWRENCE GREY COLLINS would establish procedures for, and, with the aid of defendants WILLIAM EDWARD SYMONDS, MARK CHARLES LEWIS and RICHARD GARDENIER, oversee the manufacturing of fictitious insurance files and of fictitious death claim files which would correspond with the fictitious insurance policies placed on EFLIC's books and reinsured with reinsuring companies. Defendants MICHAEL E. SULTAN, JAMES CYRUS SMITH, JR., ARTHUR STANLEY LEWIS, DAVID JACK CAPO, LLOYD DOUGLAS EDENS, JAMES HOWARD BANKS, LESTER MICHAEL KELLER and ALAN LEWIS GREEN and unindicted co-conspirators Ronald Secrist and Francis D. Majerus would participate in the creation of the fictitious files.

H. In order to support EFLIC's assertions concerning its assets and to conceal its true business and financial condition from auditors and state examiners, defendants STANLEY GOLDBLUM, FRED LEVIN, JAMES CYRUS SMITH, JR., MICHAEL E. SULTAN, ARTHUR STANLEY LEWIS and LLOYD DOUGLAS EDENS would arrange through defendant GARY STANLEY BECKERMAN for the printing of counterfeit bonds which were to be listed as assets of EFLIC and which would be sent in interstate commerce to Chicago, Illinois. Said defendants would also arrange through defendant GARY STANLEY BECKERMAN for the printing of counterfeit bank documents and stationery to lend support to the purported genuineness of the counterfeit bonds. Defendant STANLEY GOLDBLUM, with the assistance of defendant MICHAEL E. SULTAN, would arrange to purchase certificates of deposit with EFCA funds, which certificates of deposit would be shown to auditors and state examiners and falsely represented to them to be assets of EFLIC and to have been purchased with funds of EFLIC. Defendants JAMES CYRUS SMITH, JR., ARTHUR STANLEY LEWIS and LLOYD DOUGLAS EDENS would arrange with unindicted co-conspirator William Gootnick to make alterations in computer records. To further guard against the disclosure of true business and financial information, and for the purpose of determining the course and direction of examinations conducted by certain state insurance examiners who were on EFCA's business premises, defendants STANLEY GOLDBLUM, FRED LEVIN, JAMES HOWARD BANKS and LAWRENCE GREY COLLINS would make arrangements to install, and defendants JAMES HOWARD BANKS and LAWRENCE GREY COLLINS would assist in installing, electronic surveillance equipment designed to intercept the private wire and oral conversation of said examiners.

I. In order to conceal the false and fictitious nature of various entries on the books and records of EFCA, defendant MICHAEL E. SULTAN would arrange through defendant GARY STANLEY BECKERMAN for the printing of certain counterfeit bank documents, including counterfeit confirmations of purchase and counterfeit debit memoranda. Defendants STANLEY GOLDBLUM, SAMUEL B. LOWELL and MICHAEL E. SULTAN would sign confirmations, contracts and letters falsely authenticating the amounts of various assets and accounts. Defendant SAMUEL B. LOWELL would give instructions, and adhering to those instructions, defendants WILLIAM MERCADO, DAVID JACK CAPO, ARTHUR STANLEY LEWIS and ALAN LEWIS GREEN would arrange to manipulate computer records containing detailed listings of the items in the account relating to receivables from purchases of Equity Funding programs so as to make the size of the account appear greater than it was; defendants DAVID JACK CAPO and DONALD MCCLELLAN would, with the cooperation of various employees of EFCA, including, among others, defendants FRED LEVIN, MICHAEL E. SULTAN, JAMES CYRUS SMITH, JR., ARTHUR STANLEY LEWIS, LLOYD DOUGLAS EDENS, LAWRENCE GREY COLLINS, JAMES HOWARD BANKS, WILLIAM EDWARD SYMONDS, ALAN LEWIS GREEN, GARY STANLEY BECKERMAN and RICHARD GARDENIER and unindicted co-conspirators Ronald Secrist and William Gootnick, obtain and devise names and addresses of individuals to whom fictitious investor confirmations, related to fictitious items in the said asset account could be sent; defendants DAVID JACK CAPO and DONALD MCCLELLAN would then arrange with the aforesaid defendants and unindicted co-conspirators to have the confirmations mailed to the addresses provided, to have them executed, and to have them returned via the mails to certain auditors in accordance with customary audit procedures, thereby making it appear as though the said fictitious items were genuine and reducing the possibility that the fraudulent nature of EFCA's books, records and financial statements would be exposed.

J. In order to facilitate EFCA's use of false and fraudulent financial data, defendants JULIAN S. H. WEINER, MARVIN AL LICHTIG and SOLOMON BLOCK and unindicted co-conspirator Wolfson Weiner Ratoff and Lapin, an independent certified public accounting firm whose responsibility it was to audit the books and records of EFCA, would conduct and cause to be conducted incomplete and insufficient audits and would accept and cause to be accepted substantial portions or all of the fictitious and inflated entries to asset and income accounts; said defendants and said unindicted co-conspirator would aid and assist in the preparation of false EFCA financial statements, and would cause said statements to be certified to have been audited in accordance with generally accepted auditing standards and to be an accurate representation of EFCA's financial position in accordance with generally accepted accounting principles.

K. For use in connection with the sale of EFCA securities and for the purpose of maintaining investor confidence in EFCA so as to induce both institutions and the general investing public to purchase and retain shares of EFCA common stock, thereby keeping the price of the stock at artificially inflated levels, defendants STANLEY GOLDBLUM, JEROME H. EVANS, SAMUEL B. LOWELL, FRED LEVIN, MICHAEL E. SULTAN, JAMES CYRUS SMITH, JR., DAVID JACK CAPO, LLOYD DOUGLAS EDENS, LAWRENCE GREY COLLINS, JAMES HOWARD BANKS, WILLIAM MERCADO, DONALD MCCLELLAN, WILLIAM EDWARD SYMONDS, LESTER MICHAEL KELLER, ALAN LEWIS GREEN, JULIAN S. H. WEINER, MARVIN AL LICHTIG, SOLOMON BLOCK, GARY STANLEY BECKERMAN, MARK CHARLES LEWIS and RICHARD GARDENIER would knowingly make and cause to be made false and fraudulent oral representations and statements and would arrange for the preparation, the filing with the Securities and Exchange Commission, and the distribution by mail and by other means to, among others, the American Stock Exchange, the New York Stock Exchange, the Pacific Coast Stock Exchange, banks and other financial institutions, financial analysts, stock brokerage houses, stockholders, prospective stockholders and other prospective investors in EFCA securities, of annual, semi-annual and quarterly reports, registration statements, prospectuses, proxy statements and other financial statements, some of which bore certifications of unindicted co-conspirator Wolfson Weiner Ratoff and Lapin, as well as press releases, which materials, as the defendants then and there well knew, would contain false, fraudulent and misleading promises, representations and statements of material fact, and would omit and conceal material facts.

(1)   Among the false statements which the said defendants would knowingly make were the following:

(a)   That on December 31, 1964, EFCA had an asset, Loans Receivable from Clients for Premium Loans, in the amount of $6,682,075.61.

(b)   That on December 31, 1965, EFCA had an asset, Loans Receivable from Clients for Premium Loans, in the amount of $9,210,597.

(c)   That on December 31, 1966, EFCA had an asset, Loans Receivable from Clients for Premium Loans, in the amount of $13,776,971.

(d)   That on December 31, 1967, EFCA had an asset, Loans Receivable from Clients for Premium Loans, in the amount of $19,512,475.

(e)   That on December 31, 1968, EFCA had an asset, Funded Loans and Accounts Receivable, in the amount of $35,476,037.

(f)   That on December 31, 1968, approximately $19,911,408 in funded loans and accounts receivable were held by EFCA itself or one of its subsidiaries while the remainder of the asset was pledged in connection with loans.

(g)   That on December 31, 1969, EFCA had an asset, Funded Loans and Accounts Receivable, in the amount of $51,188,119.

(h)   That during 1969 EFCA had a total gross income from consolidated operations of $45,571,643, of which $19,954,887 was attributable to securities sales commissions and $15,247,569 was attributable to insurance sales commission; and that during the same year EFCA had earnings from consolidated operations before income tax of approximately $12,590,278.

(i)   That on December 31, 1970, EFCA had an asset, Funded Loans and Accounts receivable, in the amount of $63,324,413.

(j)   That during 1970 EFCA had a total gross income from consolidated operations of $60,912,874 of which $15,931,895 was attributable to securities sales commissions and $17,638,207 was attributable to insurance sales commissions; and that during the same year, EFCA had earnings from consolidated operations before income taxes of $10,751,366.

(k)   That during 1970, 11,139 Equity Funding Programs had been sold, and that on December 31, 1970, 31,892 Equity Funding Programs were in effect.

(l)   That during 1970, EFLIC placed in force $834,102,704 in face value of direct, paid-for new life insurance policies.

(m)   That on December 31, 1971, EFCA had an asset, Funded Loans and Accounts Receivable, in the amount of $88,616,000.

(n)   That during 1971, EFCA had total revenues of $130,951,000, of which $14,824,000 was attributable to securities sales commissions and $62,482,000 was attributable to insurance premiums and commissions; and that during the same year EFCA had earnings before income taxes of $26,636,000.

(o)   That on December 31, 1971, EFCA had an asset, Contracts, Notes and Loans Receivable, of $34,162,000.

(p)   That on December 31, 1971, approximately $61,682,000 in funded loans and accounts receivable were held by EFCA while the remainder of the asset was pledged in connection with loans.

(q)   That during 1971, 13,813 Equity Funding Programs had been sold, and that on December 31, 1971, 41,121 Equity Funding Programs were in effect.

(r)   That during 1971, the insurance subsidiaries of EFCA placed in force $1,780,270,704 in face value of paid-for new life insurance policies.

(s)   That during the calendar year 1971, EFLIC acquired and sold a total of approximately $78,700,000 worth of debentures and collected a total of approximately $372,109.42 interest thereon.

(t)   That as of June 30, 1972, EFCA had notes receivable from Equity Funding Program participants of approximately $103,525,000.

(2) Among the material facts which the said defendants would knowingly conceal and omit to disclose and would knowingly cause to be concealed and to be omitted from disclosure were:

(a)   That during the calendar year 1968, EFCA incurred liabilities in the form of short-term notes and commercial paper placed through Dishy, Easton & Co., with various lenders in the amount of approximately $4,600,000 (some of which were payable in Swiss Francs) which remained outstanding at the end of 1968 and which were not disclosed on the books or financial statements of EFCA for 1968.

(b)   That during the calendar year 1969, EFCA incurred liabilities in the form of short-term notes and commercial paper placed through Dishy, Easton & Co., with various lenders in the amount of approximately $15,000,000 (all of which were payable in Swiss Francs) which remained outstanding at the end of 1969 and which were not disclosed on the books and financial statements of EFCA for 1969.

(c)   That during the calendar year 1970, there was inserted in the books and accounts of EFCA, and included in the financial statements of EFCA as part of Contracts and Notes Receivable, a note receivable from Etablissement Grandson, and that Etablissement Grandson was a shell corporation which did not owe EFCA the amount stated, and was without the ability or the intention to make any payments on the note.

(d)   That during the calendar year 1970, certain rights to receive future commissions were purportedly sold by EFCA to Compania de Estudios y Asuntos in return for the promise of Compania de Estudios y Asuntos to pay $13,500,000, and that Compania de Estudios y Asuntos was a shell corporation which was without the ability or the intention to guarantee the payment of any sum of money.

(e)   That of the $39,593,000 purportedly held by EFCA as Cash and Short-Term Investment, on December 31, 1971, approximately $20,000,000 was fictitious and that documents purporting to support the existence of the $20,000,000 had been counterfeited.

(f)   That of the $24,566,791.46 of bonds purportedly owned as assets by EFLIC on December 31, 1972, more than $23,000,000 were fictitious and that both bonds and certain documents purporting to support the legitimate existence of the bonds has been counterfeited.

(3) In making use of the aforesaid false and fraudulent financial information, defendant STANLEY GOLDBLUM, through the use of the mails and by other means, would contact and would cause to be contacted various financial institutions, including Bache & Co., New York Securities Company and Smith, Barney & Co., for the purpose of arranging groups of underwriters who would be used as conduits for the sale pursuant to prospectus, through use of the mails and by other means, of EFCA securities to the investing public, and the distribution, through the use of the mails and by other means, of prospectuses containing false and fraudulent financial information concerning EFCA.

(4) In making further use of the aforesaid false and fraudulent financial information, defendants STANLEY GOLDBLUM and FRED LEVIN, through the use of the mails and by other means, would contact and would cause to be contacted representatives of various corporations for the purpose of selling and exchanging stock of EFCA in return for the stock and assets of said corporations, and, for the purpose of inducing agreement to said sales and exchanges, said defendants would arrange for the distribution, by

mail and other means, of false and fraudulent financial information concerning EFCA to the officers, directors and stockholders of said corporations. Defendants STANLEY GOLDBLUM and FRED LEVIN would conclude acquisition arrangements with various corporations and would, through the use of the mails and by other means, cause stockholders of said corporations to exchange, by mail and other means, certificates of stock representing their ownership of the acquired corporations in return for certificates of stock in EFCA.

(5) In making further use of the aforesaid false and fraudulent financial information, various of the defendants, including STANLEY GOLDBLUM, SAMUEL B. LOWELL, JEROME H. EVANS, FRED LEVIN, MICHAEL E. SULTAN, JAMES CYRUS SMITH, JR., ARTHUR STANLEY LEWIS, DAVID JACK CAPO, LLOYD DOUGLAS EDENS, LAWRENCE GREY COLLINS, JAMES HOWARD BANKS, WILLIAM MERCADO, DONALD MCCLELLAN, WILLIAM EDWARD SYMONDS, MARVIN AL LICHTIG and GARY STANLEY BECKERMAN, would sell EFCA securities which they owned and held for their own benefit, well knowing of the false and fraudulent financial information concerning EFCA which had been publicly circulated and which they had assisted in generating and circulating, and without making public disclosure of what they knew to be the false and fictitious nature of said financial information.

3. To effect the objects of said conspiracy, the defendants and unindicted co-conspirators committed diverse overt acts among which are the following:

(1) On or about January 15, 1965, in the Central District of California, defendant STANLEY GOLDBLUM had the first of several conversations with defendant JEROME H. EVANS in which he told defendant JEROME H. EVANS to make fictitious entries in certain receivable and income accounts of EFCA.

(2) On or about March 8, 1965, in the Central District of California, defendant STANLEY GOLDBLUM signed one in a series of Annual Reports of EFCA, which were to be distributed to EFCA stockholders and others and which contained inflated figures for certain receivable and income accounts and for earnings per share.

(3) On or about September 30, 1966, in the Central District of California, defendants STANLEY GOLDBLUM and JEROME H. EVANS signed an application to list shares of EFCA common stock for trading on the American Stock Exchange.

(4) On or about March 15, 1968, in the Central District of California, defendants JULIAN S. H. WEINER and MARVIN AL LICHTIG, of the accounting firm of Wolfson, Weiner and Company, issued an unqualified CPA certification of the 1967 EFCA financial statements.

(5) On or about January 16, 1969, defendant STANLEY GOLDBLUM sold approximately five thousand (5,000) shares of EFCA common stock owned by him, which was one of many sales of shares of EFCA common stock owned by him.

(6) On or about January 20, 1969, defendant JEROME H. EVANS sold approximately two thousand two hundred (2,200) shares of EFCA common stock owned by him.

(7) On or about January 27, 1969, in the Central District of California, defendant JEROME H. EVANS sent a letter concerning Custodial Collateral Notes to Charles L. Hamilton at New England Merchants National Bank.

(8) On or about February 10, 1969, in the Central District of California, defendant STANLEY GOLDBLUM signed on behalf of EFCA a note for $4,535,195, which was one of a series of notes placed for EFCA through Dishy, Easton, & Company.

(9) On or about February 22, 1969, in the Central District of California, defendant STANLEY GOLDBLUM had a conversation with defendant FRED LEVIN, in which he instructed defendant FRED LEVIN that publicly held companies do not lose money.

(10) On or about March 13, 1969, in the Central District of California, defendants STANLEY GOLDBLUM, JULIAN S. H. WIENER and MARVIN AL LICHTIG had a conversation in which defendant STANLEY GOLDBLUM explained that he wanted to have certain items which he called "reciprocals" included within the EFCA account known as Funded Loans and Accounts Receivable.

(11) On or about March 21, 1969, in the Central District of California, defendants JULIAN S. H. WEINER and MARVIN AL LICHTIG and unindicted co-conspirator Wolfson Weiner Ratoff and Lapin issued an unqualified CPA certification of the 1968 EFCA financial statements.

(12) On or about September 19, 1969, in the Central District of California, defendant SAMUEL B. LOWELL had a conversation with defendant FRED LEVIN in which defendant SAMUEL B. LOWELL explained that the funded loans and accounts receivable asset account was inflated and that certain liabilities which should have been disclosed on EFCA's financial statements had not been disclosed.

(13) On or about November 30, 1969, in the Central District of California, defendant DAVID JACK CAPO, at the instruction of defendant SAMUEL B. LOWELL, made the first in a series of journal entries to an EFCA account known as Client Contractual Receivable.

(14) On or about December 15, 1969, in the Central District of California, defendants FRED LEVIN, JAMES CYRUS SMITH, JR., ARTHUR STANLEY LEWIS, LLOYD DOUGLAS EDENS and LAWRENCE GREY COLLINS had a conversation in which they dicussed placing in force, and reinsuring, life insurance policies which were not in force.

(15) On or about December 15, 1969, in the Central District of California, defendant WILLIAM MERCADO supervised the preparation of a computer print-out of funded loan receivable accounts containing a total for the accounts which was intentionally inflated.

(16) On or about February 12, 1970, in the Central District of Cali-

fornia, defendant JULIAN S. H. WEINER had a conversation with defendant SOLOMON BLOCK in which they discussed the accounting treatment which was to be given EFCA's client contractual receivable account.

(17) On or about March 24, 1970, in the Central District of California, defendants JULIAN S. H. WEINER and SOLOMON BLOCK, and unindicted co-conspirator Wolfson Weiner Ratoff and Lapin issued an unqualified CPA certification on the 1969 EFCA financial statements.

(18) On or about March 31, 1970, in the Central District of California, defendant SAMUEL B. LOWELL had a conversation with defendant MICHAEL E. SULTAN in which defendant SAMUEL B. LOWELL explained that because EFCA's legitimate earnings for the first quarter of 1970 were insufficient, defendant MICHAEL E. SULTAN would be required to make certain journal entries to increase the income reflected on EFCA's books.

(19) On or about May 5, 1970, in the Central District of California, defendant STANLEY GOLDBLUM had a conversation with Herbert Glaser, H. O. Van Petten, Norman Sanoff and Julius Lefkowitz in which they discussed the purchase by EFCA of Liberty Savings and Loan Association.

(20) On or about May 19, 1970, defendant STANLEY GOLDBLUM signed an agreement for the purported sale to Compania de Estudios y Asuntos of the rights to certain net trail commissions.

(21) On or about June 18, 1970, in the Central District of California, defendant MICHAEL E. SULTAN made a journal entry recording notes payable to Loeb, Rhoades & Company and a note receivable from Etablissement Grandson.

(22) On or about June 29, 1970, in the Central District of California, defendants STANLEY GOLDBLUM and FRED LEVIN had a conversation with Rodney Loeb, Ronald Cameron and James McElvany in which they discussed the purchase by EFCA of Independent Securities Corporation.

(23) On or about August 10, 1970, in the Central District of California, defendants FRED LEVIN, JAMES CYRUS SMITH, JR., ARTHUR STANLEY LEWIS, LLOYD DOUGLAS EDENS and LAWRENCE GREY COLLINS had a meeting in which they discussed the manner and method of creating and reinsuring fictitious insurance policies.

(24) On or about August 20, 1970, defendants STANLEY GOLDBLUM and MARVIN AL LICHTIG signed an application to list shares of EFCA common stock for trading on the New York Stock Exchange.

(25) On or about September 15, 1970, in the Central District of California, defendants STANLEY GOLDBLUM and FRED LEVIN had a conversation in which they discussed the creation and reinsurance of fictitious insurance policies.

(26) On or about October 14, 1970, defendants STANLEY GOLDBLUM and SAMUEL B. LOWELL gave instructions for two million dollars to be sent to Account Number 001-1-821-774 at Banque Cifico-Leumi in Geneva, Switzerland for the account of Etablissement Grandson.

(27) On or about November 2, 1970, in the Central District of Cali-

fornia, defendant LESTER MICHAEL KELLER, at the direction of defendant ARTHUR STANLEY LEWIS, wrote a computer program for the creation of fictitious insurance policies having a total face amount of approximately $430,000,000 and a total yearly premium of approximately $5,500,000.

(28) On or about December 4, 1970, in the Central District of California, defendant ARTHUR STANLEY LEWIS sent a memorandum to defendants LESTER MICHAEL KELLER and JAMES CYRUS SMITH, JR., concerning the relationship between EFLIC's fictitious insurance business and its reinsurance commitment.

(29) On or about December 16, 1970, in the Central District of California, defendant SAMUEL B. LOWELL had a conversation with defendant WILLIAM MERCADO during which they discussed the preparation of a computer print-out of funded loan receivable accounts which would contain an intentionally inflated total.

(30) On or about January 20, 1971, in the Central District of California, defendants JAMES CYRUS SMITH, JR., ARTHUR STANLEY LEWIS, LLOYD DOUGLAS EDENS and LAWRENCE GREY COLLINS and unindicted co-conspirators Francis D. Majerus and Ronald Secrist filled out and signed forms and used the forms to create fictitious insurance policy files.

(31) On or about March 1, 1971, in the Central District of California, defendants SAMUEL B. LOWELL, FRED LEVIN, JAWES CYRUS SMITH, JR., ARTHUR STANLEY LEWIS, and LLOYD DOUGLAS EDENS signed a 1970 Annual Statement of EFLIC which was to be filed and was filed with the Department of Insurance of the State of California.

(32) On or about March 15, 1971, in the Central District of California, defendants STANLEY GOLDBLUM and FRED LEVIN had a meeting with John Brundage of Bankers National Life Insurance Company in which they discussed the purchase by EFCA of Bankers National Life Insurance Company.

(33) On or about March 24, 1971, in the Central District of California, defendant JAMES CYRUS SMITH, JR., had a conversation with defendant JAMES HOWARD BANKS in which he explained that fictitious insurance policies had been reinsured and that defendant JAMES HOWARD BANKS would be expected to make death claims on various of the fictitious insurance policies.

(34) On or about April 1, 1971, in the Central District of California, defendant SAMUEL B. LOWELL had a conversation with Roger Coe, manager of Bishops' Bank and Trust Company, Ltd., in which defendant SAMUEL B. LOWELL said that defendant STANLEY GOLDBLUM had given instructions for Roger Coe to cease attempting to confirm a certain $2,000,000 receivable which was on the books of Bishops' Bank.

(35) On or about May 19, 1971, in the Central District of California, defendant JAMES HOWARD BANKS made the first in a series of death claims on fictitious EFLIC insurance policies by mailing to Phoenix Mutual Life Insurance Company a letter enclosing documents relating to the death of Fenton Taylor, insured under fictitious EFLIC policy number 7101481.

(36) On or about July 20, 1971, in the Central District of California,

defendant RICHARD GARDENIER supervised and helped to prepare fictitious insurance files and defendants JAMES CYRUS SMITH, JR., ARTHUR STANLEY LEWIS, DANIEL JACK CAPO, LLOYD DOUGLAS EDENS, and LAWRENCE GREY COLLINS completed the documents in the fictitious files and forged signatures on them.

(37) On or about September 30, 1971, in the Central District of California, defendants SAMUEL B. LOWELL and FRED LEVIN had a conversation in which defendant SAMUEL LOWELL asked how much income EFLIC could reflect on its books in order to reduce the amount of fictitious business which would need to be inserted on EFCA's books.

(38) On or about November 30, 1971, in the Central District of California, defendants FRED LEVIN, MICHAEL E. SULTAN, JAMES CYRUS SMITH, JR., ARTHUR STANLEY LEWIS and LLOYD DOUGLAS EDENS had a meeting during which they discussed the transfer of funds from EFCA to EFLIC and the counterfeiting of various documents reflecting fictitious purchases of commercial paper.

(39) On or about December 6, 1971, in the Central District of California, defendants STANLEY GOLDBLUM, SAMUEL B. LOWELL, FRED LEVIN and MARVIN AL LICHTIG signed a registration statement for the sale of $38,500,000 in EFCA convertible debentures, which registration statement was to be filed and was filed with the Securities and Exchange Commission.

(40) On or about December 9, 1971, in the Central District of California, defendant SAMUEL B. LOWELL had a telephone conversation with Hugh C. Brewer of First National City Bank concerning a proposed $75,000,000 loan to EFCA.

(41) On or about December 10, 1971, in the Central District of California, defendant STANLEY GOLDBLUM had a conversation with defendant MICHAEL E. SULTAN in which he told defendant MICHAEL E. SULTAN to proceed with the counterfeiting of documents relating to fictitious purchases of commercial paper.

(42) On or about December 18, 1971, in the Central District of California, defendants SAMUEL B. LOWELL and MICHAEL E. SULTAN had a conversation concerning the absence of assets in EFLIC and the necessity to transfer funds to EFLIC to conceal the absence of assets.

(43) On or about December 21, 1971, in the Central District of California, defendants ARTHUR STANLEY LEWIS and DAVID JACK CAPO had conversation in which they discussed creation of a computer print-out listing which would contain fictitious funded loan accounts.

(44) On or about December 23, 1971, in the Central District of California, defendants MICHAEL E. SULTAN, LLOYD DOUGLAS EDENS and GARY STANLEY BECKERMAN had a conversation in which they discussed the counterfeiting of documents relating to fictitious purchases of commercial paper.

(45) On or about December 23, 1971, in the Central District of California, defendants ARTHUR STANLEY LEWIS and ALAN LEWIS GREEN had a conversation in which they discussed creating a computer print-out listing which would contain fictitious funded loan accounts.

(46) On or about January 3, 1972, in the Central District of California, defendant LESTER MICHAEL KELLER arranged to be sent through the mails to Kentucky Central Life Insurance Company, a letter enclosing a computer tape listing of EFLIC's 1971 reinsurance cession for Kentucky Central.

(47) On or about January 14, 1972, in the Central District of California, defendant WILLIAM EDWARD SYMONDS, upon instructions of defendants ARTHUR STANLEY LEWIS and LLOYD DOUGLAS EDENS, began manipulating computer records so as falsely to show five thousand lapsed policies to be in force.

(48) On or about February 15, 1972, in the Central District of California, defendants FRED LEVIN and JAMES CYRUS SMITH, JR., had the first in a series of conversations during which they discussed the amount of fictitious insurance business which would have to be created in 1972.

(49) On or about March 1, 1972, in the Central District of California, defendants MICHAEL E. SULTAN and SOLOMON BLOCK had a conversation during which they discussed the making of an intentional mistake in the calculation of EFCA's 1971 earnings per share.

(50) On or about March 10, 1972, in the Central District of California, defendants WILLIAM EDWARD SYMONDS and RICHARD GARDENIER had a conversation during which they discussed the creation of fictitious insurance files.

(51) On or about March 15, 1972, in the Central District of California, defendants STANLEY GOLDBLUM, SAMUEL B. LOWELL and MICHAEL E. SULTAN had a conversation during which they discussed the making of fictitious entries to EFCA's Funded Loans and Accounts Receivable account and commission income accounts.

(52) On or about April 4, 1972, in the Central District of California, defendant MARVIN AL LICHTIG signed an EFCA annual report on Form 10-K which was to be filed and was filed with the Securities and Exchange Commission and which contained EFCA's 1971 financial statements.

(53) On or about April 11, 1972, in the Central District of California, defendant SAMUEL B. LOWELL had a meeting with L. E. Holloway of Wells Fargo Bank during which they discussed a $75,000,000 credit agreement and defendant SAMUEL B. LOWELL delivered to the said L. E. Holloway various EFCA Annual Reports.

(54) On or about June 15, 1972, in the Central District of California, defendants SAMUEL B. LOWELL, MICHAEL E. SULTAN and JULIAN S. H. WEINER had a conversation during which they discussed the making of a payment on a note receivable from Etablissement Grandson.

(55) On or about June 29, 1972, in the Central District of California, defendant JAMES CYRUS SMITH, JR., sent a letter to Dan Di Sipio which set forth the terms of a reinsurance agreement between EFCA and Pennsylvania Life Insurance Company and which gave instructions on the manner in which certain checks were to be made out.

(56) On or about July 14, 1972, in the Central District of California, defendants JAMES CYRUS SMITH, JR., ARTHUR STANLEY LEWIS, DAVID JACK

CAPO, LAWRENCE GREY COLLINS, LLOYD DOUGLAS EDENS, JAMES HOWARD BANKS, MARK CHARLES LEWIS and RICHARD GARDENIER helped to prepare fictitious hard copy insurance documents and forged signatures on the documents.

(57) On or about July 28, 1972, in the Central District of California, defendant ALAN LEWIS GREEN sent a computer tape listing of EFLIC's second quarter 1972 reinsurance cession to Ranger National Life Insurance Company.

(58) On or about September 1, 1972, in the Central District of California, defendants STANLEY GOLDBLUM and FRED LEVIN had a conversation in which they discussed the sale of single premium annuities.

(59) On or about October 26, 1972, in the Central District of California, defendants STANLEY GOLDBLUM, FRED LEVIN, MICHAEL E. SULTAN, JAMES CYRUS SMITH, JR., ARTHUR S. LEWIS and LLOYD DOUGLAS EDENS had a conversation in which they discussed the printing of counterfeit bonds.

(60) On or about December 18, 1972, in the Central District of California, defendant STANLEY GOLDBLUM had a telephone conversation with defendant FRED LEVIN in which they discussed the renting of an office in Chicago, Illinois, to be used as a mail drop in connection with the use of counterfeit bank documents.

(61) On or about December 20, 1972, in the Central District of California, on the instruction of defendant STANLEY GOLDBLUM, defendant GARY STANLEY BECKERMAN ordered stationery bearing the letterhead of the American National Bank and Trust Company of Chicago.

(62) On or about December 27, 1972, in the Central District of California, defendants DAVID JACK CAPO and DONALD MCCLELLAN compiled addresses of various persons to whom funded loan confirmations could be sent.

(63) On or about January 5, 1973, in the Central District of California, defendant SAMUEL B. LOWELL had a conversation with unindicted co-conspirator William Gootnick concerning the company's fictitious life insurance business.

(64) On or about January 8, 1973, in the Central District of California, defendant JAMES HOWARD BANKS had a conversation with defendant JAMES CYRUS SMITH, JR., in which they discussed the amount of money to be derived in 1973 from making death claims on fictitious life insurance policies.

(65) On or about January 15, 1973, in the Central District of California, defendant MICHAEL E. SULTAN made entries on counterfeit bank documents relating to fictitious purchases of commercial paper.

(66) On or about January 15, 1973, in the Central District of California, defendants FRED LEVIN, JAMES CYRUS SMITH, JR., MICHAEL E. SULTAN, LLOYD DOUGLAS EDENS and GARY STANLEY BECKERMAN met at EFCA's printing plant and commenced the printing of counterfeit bonds.

(67) On or about February 27, 1973, in the Central District of California, defendants LESTER MICHAEL KELLER and ALAN LEWIS GREEN in-

structed unindicted co-conspirator Aaron Venouziou on writing computer programs for fictitious insurance business.

(68) On or about March 12, 1973, in the Central District of California, defendants STANLEY GOLDBLUM, FRED LEVIN, MICHAEL E. SULTAN, JAMES CYRUS SMITH, JR., ARTHUR STANLEY LEWIS, LLOYD DOUGLAS EDENS and JAMES HOWARD BANKS had a conversation in which they discussed disposition of the counterfeit bonds.

(69) On or about March 14, 1973, in the Central District of California, defendant WILLIAM EDWARD SYMONDS sent computer print-out listings of insurance reserve rates and values to Kentucky Central Life Insurance Company and Great Southern Life Insurance Company.

(70) On or about March 14, 1973, in the Central District of California, defendant STANLEY GOLDBLUM had a conversation with defendant JAMES HOWARD BANKS in which they discussed the electronic surveillance of state insurance examiners who were working on EFCA's business premises.

(71) On or about March 14, 1973, in the Central District of California, defendants LAWRENCE GREY COLLINS and JAMES HOWARD BANKS together with Steven Michael Goodman and Lorn Aiken made the first of a series of installations of electronic surveillance equipment in an office where state insurance examiners were working on EFCA's business premises.

(72) On or about March 22, 1973, in the Central District of California, unindicted co-conspirator William Gootnick on the instructions of defendants JAMES CYRUS SMITH, JR., ARTHUR STANLEY LEWIS, LLOYD DOUGLAS EDENS, LAWRENCE GREY COLLINS and JAMES HOWARD BANKS, supervised the writing of computer programs designed to conceal the existence of EFLIC's fictitious insurance business from auditors and state insurance examiners.

(73) On or about March 23, 1973, in the Central District of California, defendants LAWRENCE GREY COLLINS, WILLIAM EDWARD SYMONDS and MARK CHARLES LEWIS, at the instructions of the defendant JAMES CYRUS SMITH, JR., removed all documents relating to the creation of insurance files from 341 North Maple Drive, Beverly Hills, California.

(74) On or about March 26, 1973, defendants STANLEY GOLDBLUM SAMUEL B. LOWELL, FRED LEVIN, MICHAEL E. SULTAN, JAMES CYRUS SMITH, JR., ARTHUR STANLEY LEWIS, LLOYD DOUGLAS EDENS, LAWRENCE GREY COLLINS, JAMES HOWARD BANKS and DONALD MC CLELLAN sold shares of EFCA stock which they owned.

(75) On or about March 27, 1973, in the Central District of California, defendants LAWRENCE GREY COLLINS and JAMES HOWARD BANKS, together with Steven Michael Goodman and Lorn Aiken, tried to install electronic surveillance equipment designed to intercept telephone conversations of state insurance examiners.

(76) On or about March 30, 1973, in the Central District of California, defendant MARVIN AL LICHTIG had a conversation with defendant FRED LEVIN during which defendant MARVIN AL LICHTIG asked whether defendant FRED LEVIN wanted any documents destroyed.

APPENDIX J
RIGHT TO FINANCIAL PRIVACY ACT

§ 3401. DEFINITIONS

For the purpose of this title, the term—

(1) "financial institution" means any office of a bank, savings bank, card issuer as defined in section 103 of the Consumers Protection Act (15 U.S.C. 1602(n)) [15 USCS § 1602(n)], industrial loan company, trust company, savings and loan, building and loan, or homestead association (including cooperative banks), credit union, or consumer finance institution, located in any State or territory of the United States, the District of Columbia, Puerto Rico, Guam, American Samoa, or the Virgin Islands;

(2) "financial record" means an original of, a copy of, or information

known to have been derived from, any record held by a financial institution pertaining to a customer's relationship with the financial institution;

(3) "Government authority" means any agency or department of the United States, or any officer, employee, or agent thereof;

(4) "person" means an individual or a partnership of five or fewer individuals;

(5) "customer" means any person or authorized representative of that person who utilized or is utilizing any service of a financial institution, or for whom a financial institution is acting or has acted as a fiduciary, in relation to an account maintained in the person's name;

(6) "supervisory agency" means, wtih respect to any particular financial institution any of the following which has statutory authority to examine the financial condition or business operations of that institution—

(A) the Federal Deposit Insurance Corporation;

(B) the Federal Savings and Loan Insurance Corporation;

(C) the Federal Home Loan Bank Board;

(D) the National Credit Union Administration;

(E) the Board of Governors of the Federal Reserve System;

(F) the Comptroller of the Currency;

(G) the Securities and Exchange Commission;

(H) the Secretary of the Treasury, with respect to the Bank Secrecy Act and the Currency and Foreign Transactions Reporting Act (Public Law 91–508, title I and II); or

(I) any State banking or securities department or agency; and

(7) "law enforcement inquiry" means a lawful investigation or official proceeding inquiring into a violation of, or failure to comply with, any criminal or civil statute or any regulation, rule, or order issued pursuant thereto.

12 U.S.C. 3401–3422.

§ 3402. CONFIDENTIALITY OF RECORDS; GOVERNMENT AUTHORITIES

Except as provided by section 1103(c) or (d), 1113, or 1114 [12 USCS § 3403(c) or (d), 3413, or 3414], no Government authority may have access to or obtain copies of, or the information contained in the financial records of any customer from a financial institution unless the financial records are reasonably described and—

(1) such customer has authorized such disclosure with section 1104 [12 USCS §3404];

(2) such financial records are disclosed in response to an administrative subpoena or summons which meets the requirements of section 1105 [12 USCS § 3405];

(3) such financial records are disclosed in response to a search warrant which meets the requirements of section 1106 [12 USCS § 3406];

(4) such financial records are disclosed in response to a judicial subpoena which meets the requirements of section 1107 [12 USCS § 3407]; or

(5) such financial records are disclosed in response to a formal written request which meets the requirements of section 1108 [12 USCS § 3408].

§ 3403. CONFIDENTIALITY OF RECORDS; FINANCIAL INSTITUTIONS

(a) No financial institution, or officer, employees, or agent of a financial institution, may provide to any Government authority access to or copies of, or the information contained in, the financial records of any customer except in accordance with the provisions of this title.

(b) A financial institution shall not release the financial records of a customer until the Government authority seeking such records certifies in writing to the financial institution that it has complied with the applicable provisions of this title.

(c) Nothing in this title shall preclude any financial institution, or any officer, employee, or agent of a financial institution, from notifying a Government authority that such institution, or officer, employee, or agent has information which may be relevant to a possible violation of any statute or regulation.

(d)(1) Nothing in this title shall preclude a financial institution, as an incident to perfecting a security interest, proving a claim in bankruptcy, or otherwise collecting on a debt owing either to the financial institution itself or in its role as a fiduciary, from providing copies of any financial record to any court or Government authority.

(2) Nothing in this title shall preclude a financial institution, as an incident to processing an application for assistance to a customer in the form of a Government loan, loan guaranty, or loan insurance agreement, or as an incident to processing a default on, or administering, a Government guaranteed or insured loan, from initiating contact with an appropriate Government authority for the purpose of providing any financial record necessary to permit such authority to carry out its responsibilities under a loan, loan guaranty, or loan insurance agreement.

§ 3404. CUSTOMER AUTHORIZATIONS

(a) A customer may authorize disclosure under section 1102(1) [12 USCS § 3402 (1)] if he furnishes to the financial institution and to the Government authority seeking to obtain such disclosure a signed and dated statement which—

(1) authorizes such disclosure for a period not in excess of three months;

(2) states that the customer may revoke such authorization at any time before the financial records are disclosed;

(3) identifies the financial records which are authorized to be disclosed;

(4) specifies the purposes for which, and the Government authority to which, such records may be disclosed; and

(5) states the customer's rights under this title.

(b) No such authorization shall be required as a condition of doing business with any financial institution.

(c) The customer has the right, unless the Government authority obtains a court order as provided in section 1109 [12 USCS § 3409], to obtain a copy of the record which the financial institution shall keep of all instances in which the customer's record is disclosed to a Government authority pursuant to this section, including the identity of the Government authority to which such disclosure is made.

(d) All financial institutions shall promptly notify all of their customers of their rights under this title. The Board of Governors of the Federal Reserve System shall prepare a statement of customers' rights under this title. Any financial institution that provides its customers a statement of customers' rights prepared by the Board shall be deemed to be in compliance with this subsection.

§ 3405. ADMINISTRATIVE SUBPOENA AND SUMMONS

A Government authority may obtain financial records under section 1102(2) [12 USCS § 3402(2)] pursuant to an administrative subpoena or summons otherwise authorized by law only if—

(1) there is reason to believe that the records sought are relevant to a legitimate law enforcement inquiry;

(2) a copy of the subpoena or summons has been served upon the customer or mailed to his last known address on or before the date on which the subpoena or summons was served on the financial institution together with the following notice which shall state with reasonable specificity the nature of the law enforcement inquiry:

"Records or information concerning your transactions held by the financial institution named in the attached subpoena or summons are being sought by this (agency or department) in accordance with the Right to Financial Privacy Act of 1978 [12 USCS §§ 3401 et. seq.] for the following purpose: If you desire that such records or information not be made available, you must:

"1. Fill out the accompanying motion paper and sworn statement or write one of your own, stating that you are the customer whose records are being requested by the Government and either giving the reasons you believe that the records are not relevant to the legitimate law enforcement inquiry stated in this notice or any other legal basis for objecting to the release of the records.

"2. File the motion and statement by mailing or delivering them to the clerk of any one of the following United States district courts:

"3. Serve the Government authority requesting the records by mailing or delivering a copy of your motion and statement to

"4. Be prepared to come to court and present your position in further detail.

"5. You do not need to have a lawyer, although you may wish to employ one to represent you and protect your rights.

If you do not follow the above procedures, upon the expiration of ten days from the date of service or fourteen days from the date of mailing of this notice, the records or information requested therein will be made available. These records may be transferred to other Government authorities for legitimate law enforcement inquiries, in which event you will be notified after the transfer."; and

(3) ten days have expired from the date of service of the notice or fourteen days have expired from the date of mailing the notice to the customer and within such time period the customer has not filed a sworn statement and motion to quash in an appropriate court, or the customer challenge provisions of section 1110 [12 USCS § 3410] have been complied with.

§ 3406. SEARCH WARRANTS

(a) A government authority may obtain financial records under section 1102 (3) [12 USCS § 3402(3)] only if it obtains a search warrant pursuant to the Federal Rules of Criminal Procedure.

(b) No later than ninety days after the Government authority serves the search warrant, it shall mail to the customer's last known address a copy of the search warrant together with the following notice:

"Records or information concerning your transactions held by the financial institution named in the attached search warrant were obtained by this (agency or department) on (date) for the following purpose: _____. You may have the rights under the Right to Financial Privacy Act [12 USCS §§ 3401 et. seq.].".

(c) Upon application of the Government authority, a court may grant a delay in the mailing of the notice required in subsection (b), which delay shall not exceed one hundred and eighty days following the service of the warrant, if the court makes the findings required in section 1109(a) [12 USCS §3409(a)]. If the court so finds, it shall enter an ex parte order granting the requested delay and an order prohibiting the financial institution from disclosing that records have been obtained or that a search warrant for such records has been executed. Additional delays of up to ninety days may be granted by the court upon application, but only in accordance with this subsection. Upon expiration of the period of delay of notification of the customer, the following notice shall be mailed to the customer along with a copy of the search warrant:

"Records or information concerning your transactions held by the financial institution named in the attached search warrant were obtained by this (agency or department) on (date). Notification was delayed beyond the statutory ninety-day delay period pursuant to a determination by the court that such notice would seriously jeopardize an investigation concerning _____. You may have rights under the Right to Financial Privacy Act of 1978 [12 USCS §§ 3401 et seq.]."

§ 3407. JUDICIAL SUBPOENA

A Government authority may obtain financial records under section 1102 (4) [12 USCS § 3402(4)] pursuant to judicial subpoena only if—

(1) such subpoena is authorized by law and there is reason to believe that the records sought are relevant to a legitimate law enforcement inquiry;

(2) a copy of the subpoena has been served upon the customer or mailed to his last known address on or before the date on which the subpoena was served on the financial institution together with the following notice which shall state with reasonable specificity the nature of the law enforcement inquiry:

"Records or information concerning your transactions which are held by the financial institution named in the attached subpoena are being sought by this (agency or department or authority) in accordance with the Right to Financial Privacy Act of 1978 [12 USCS §§ 3401 et seq.] for the following purpose: If you desire that such records or information not be made available, you must:

"1. Fill out the accompanying motion paper and sworn statement or write one of your own, stating that you are the customer whose records are being requested by the Government and either giving the reasons you believe that the records are not relevant to the legitimate law enforcement inquiry stated in this notice or any other legal basis for objecting to the release of the records.

"2. File the motion and statement by mailing or delivering them to the clerk of the _____ Court.

"3. Serve the Government authority requesting the records by mailing or delivering a copy of your motion and statement to

"4. Be prepared to come to court and present your position in further detail.

"5. You do not need to have a lawyer, although you may wish to employ one to represent you and protect your rights.

If you do not follow the above procedures, upon the expiration of ten days from the date of service or fourteen days from the date of mailing of this notice, the records or information requested therein will be made available. These records may be transferred to other government authorities for legitimate law enforcement inquiries, in which event you will be notified after the transfer;" and

(3) ten days have expired from the date of service or fourteen days from the date of mailing of the notice to the customer and within such time period the customer has not filed a sworn statement and motion to quash in an appropriate court, or the customer challenge provisions of section 1110 [12 USCS § 3410] have been complied with.

§ 3408. FORMAL WRITTEN REQUEST

A Government authority may request financial records under section 1102 (5) [12 USCS § 3402(5)] pursuant to a formal written request only if—

(1) no administrative summons or subpoena authority reasonably appears to be available to that Government authority to obtain financial records for the purpose for which records are sought;

(2) the request is authorized by regulations promulgated by the head of the agency or department;

(3) there is reason to believe that the records sought are relevant to a legitimate law enforcement inquiry; and

(4)(A) a copy of the request has been served upon the customer or mailed to his last known address on or before the date on which the request was made to the financial institution together with the following notice which shall state with reasonable specificity the nature of the law enforcement inquiry:

"Records or information concerning your transactions held by the financial institution named in the attached request are being sought by this (agency or department) in accordance with the Right to Financial Privacy Act of 1978 [12 USCS §§ 3401 et seq.] for the following purpose:

"If you desire that such records or information not be made available, you must:

"1. Fill out the accompanying motion paper and sworn statement or write one of your own, stating that you are the customer whose records are being requested by the Government and either giving the reasons you believe that the records are not relevant to the legitimate law enforcement inquiry stated in this notice or any other legal basis for objecting to the release of the records.

"2. File the motion and statement by mailing or delivering them to the clerk of any one of the following United States District Courts:

"3. Serve the Government authority requesting the records by mailing or delivering a copy of your motion and statement to

"4. Be prepared to come to court and present your position in further detail.

"5. You do not need to have a lawyer, although you may wish to employ one to represent you and protect your rights.

If you do not follow the above procedures, upon the expiration of ten days from the date of service or fourteen days from the date of mailing of this notice, the records or information requested therein may be made available. These records may be transferred to other Government authorities for legitimate law enforcement inquiries, in which event you will be notified after the transfer;" and

(B) ten days have expired from the date of service or fourteen days from the date of mailing of the notice by the customer and within such time period the customer has not filed a sworn statement and an application to enjoin the Government authority in an appropriate court, or the customer challenge provisions of section 1110 [12 USCS § 3410] have been complied with.

§ 3409. DELAYED NOTICE; PRESERVATION OF RECORDS

(a) Upon application of the Government authority, the customer notice required under section 1104(c), 1105(2), 1106(c), 1107(2), 1108(4), or 1112(b) [12 USCS § 3404(c), 3405(2), 3406(c), 3407(2), 3408(4), or 3412(b)] may be delayed by order of an appropriate court if the presiding judge or magistrate finds that—

(1) the investigation being conducted is within the lawful jurisdiction of the Government authority seeking the financial records;

(2) there is reason to believe that the records being sought are relevant to a legitimate law enforcement inquiry; and

(3) there is reason to believe that such notice will result in—

(A) endangering life or physical safety of any person;

(B) fight from prosecution;

(C) destruction of or tampering with evidence;

(D) intimidation of potential witnesses; or

(E) otherwise seriously jeopardizing an investigation or official proceeding or unduly delaying a trial or ongoing official proceeding to the same extent as the circumstances in the preceding sub-

An application for delay must be made with reasonable specificity.

(b)(1) If the court makes the findings required in paragraphs (1), (2), and (3) of subsection (a), it shall enter an ex parte order granting the requested delay for a period not to exceed ninety days and an order prohibiting the financial institution from disclosing that records have been obtained or that a request for records has been made, except that, if the records have been sought by a Government authority exercising financial controls over foreign accounts in the United States under section 5(b) of the Trading with the Enemy Act (50 U.S.C. App. 5(b)) [50 USCS Appx. § 5(b)], the International Emergency Economic Powers Act (title

II, Public Law 95-223) [50 USCS §§ 1701 et seq.], or section 5 of the United Nations Participation Act (22 U.S.C. 287c) [5 USCS § 287c], and the court finds that there is reason to believe that such notice may endanger the lives or physical safety of a customer or group of customers, or any person or group of persons associated with a customer, the court may specify that the delay be indefinite.

(2) Extensions of the delay of notice provided in paragraph (1) of up to ninety days each may be granted by the court upon application, but only in accordance with this subsection.

(3) Upon expiration of the period of delay of notification under paragraph (1) or (2), the customer shall be served with or mailed a copy of the process or request together with the following notice which shall state with reasonable specificity the nature of the law enforcement inquiry:

"Records or information concerning your transactions which are held by the financial institution named in the attached process or request were supplied to or requested by the Government authority named in the process or request on (date). Notification was withheld pursuant to a determination by the (title of court so ordering) under the Right to Financial Privacy Act of 1978 [12 USCS §§ 3401 et seq.] that such notice might (state reason) _____. The purpose of the investigation or official proceeding was _____.".

(c) When access to financial records is obtained pursuant to section 1114(b) [12 USCS § 3414(b)] (emergency access), the Government authority shall, unless a court has authorized delay of notice pursuant to subsections (a) and (b), as soon as practicable after such records are obtained serve upon the customer, or mail by registered or certified mail to his last known address, a copy of the request to the financial institution together with the following notice which shall state with reasonable specificity the nature of the law enforcement inquiry:

"Records concerning your tranactions held by the financial institution named in the attached request were obtained by (agency or department) under the Right to Financial Privacy Act of 1978 [12 USCS §§ 3401 et seq.] on (date) for the following purpose: _____ Emergency access to such records was obtained on the grounds that (state grounds).".

(d) Any memorandum, affidavit, or other paper filed in connection with a request for delay in notification shall be preserved by the court. Upon petition by the customer to whom such records pertain, the court may order disclosure of such papers to the petitioner unless the court makes the findings required in subsection (a).

§ 3410. CUSTOMER CHALLENGE PROVISIONS

(a) Within ten days of service or within fourteen days of mailing of a subpoena, summons, or formal written request, a customer may file a motion to quash an administrative summons or judicial subpoena, or an application to enjoin a Government authority from obtaining financial records pursuant to a formal written request, with copies served upon the Government authority. A motion to quash a judicial subpoena shall be filed in the court which issued the subpoena. A motion to quash an administrative summons or an application to enjoin a Government authority from obtaining records pursuant to a formal written request shall be filed in the appropriate United States district court. Such motion or application shall contain an affidavit or sworn statement—

(1) stating that the applicant is a customer of the financial institution from which financial records pertaining to him have been sought; and

(2) stating the applicant's reasons for believing that the financial records sought are not relevant to the legitimate law enforcement inquiry stated by the Government authority in its notice, or that there has not been substantial compliance with the provisions of this title.

Service shall be made under this section upon a Government authority by delivering or mailing by registered or certified mail a copy of the papers to the person, office, or department specified in the notice which the customer has received pursuant to this title. For the purposes of this section, "delivery" has the meaning stated in rule 5(b) of the Federal Rules of Civil Procedure.

(b) If the court finds that the customer has complied with subsection (a), it shall order the Government authority to file a sworn response, which may be filed in camera if the Government includes in its response the reasons which make in camera review appropriate. If the court is unable to determine the motion or application on the basis of the parties' initial allegations and response, the court may conduct such additional proceedings as it deems appropriate. All such proceedings shall be completed and the motion or application decided within seven calendar days of the filing of the Government's response.

(c) If the court finds that the applicant is not the customer to whom the financial records sought by the Government authority pertain, or that there is a demonstrable reason to believe that the law enforcement inquiry is legitimate and a reasonable belief that the records sought are relevant to that inquiry, it shall deny the motion or application, and, in the case of an administrative summons or court order other than a search warrant, order such process enforced. If the court finds that the applicant is the customer to whom the records sought by the Government authority pertain, and there is not a demonstrable reason to believe that the law enforcement inquiry is legitimate and a reasonable belief that the records sought are relevant to that inquiry, or that there has not been substantial compliance with the provisions of this title, it shall order the process quashed or shall enjoin the Government authority's formal written request.

(d) A court ruling denying a motion or application under this section shall not be deemed a final order and no interlocutory appeal may be taken therefrom by the customer. An appeal of a ruling denying a motion or application under this section may be taken by the customer (1) within such period of time as provided by law as part of any appeal from a final order in any legal proceeding initiated against him arising out of or based upon the financial records, or (2) within thirty days after a notification that no legal proceeding is contemplated against him. The Government authority obtaining the financial records shall promptly notify a customer when a determination has been made that no legal proceeding against him is contemplated. After one hundred and eighty days from the denial of the motion or application, if the Government authority obtaining the records has not initiated such a proceeding, a supervisory official of the Government authority shall certify to the appropriate court that no such determination has been made. The court may require that such certifications be made, at reasonable intervals thereafter, until either notification to the customer has occurred or a legal proceeding is initiated as described in clause (A).

(e) The challenge procedures of this title constitute the sole judicial remedy available to a customer to oppose disclosure of financial records pursuant to this title.

(f) Nothing in this title shall enlarge or restrict any rights of a financial institution to challenge requests for records made by a Government authority under existing law. Nothing in this title shall entitle a customer to assert the rights of a financial institution.

§ 3411. DUTY OF FINANCIAL INSTITUTIONS

Upon receipt of a request for financial records made by a Government authority under section 1105 or 1107 [12 USCS § 3405 or 3407], the financial institution shall, unless otherwise provided by law, proceed to assemble the records requested and must be prepared to deliver the records to the Government authority upon receipt of the certificate required under section 1103(b) [12 USCS § 3403(b)].

§ 3412. USE OF INFORMATION

(a) Financial records originally obtained pursuant to this title shall not be transferred to another agency or department unless the transferring agency or department certifies in writing that there is reason to believe that the records are relevant to a legitimate law enforcement inquiry within the jurisdiction of the receiving agency or department.

(b) When financial records subject to this title are transferred pursuant to subsection (a), the transferring agency or department shall, within fourteen days, send to the customer a copy of the certification made pursuant to subsection (a) and the following notice, which shall state the nature of the law enforcement inquiry with reasonable specificity: "Copies of, or information contained in, your financial records lawfully in possession of _____ have been furnished to _____ pursuant to the Right of Financial Privacy Act

of 1978 [12 USCS §§ 3401 et seq.] for the following purpose: _____.
If you believe that this transfer has not been made to further a legitimate
law enforcement inquiry, you may have legal rights under the Financial Privacy Act of 1978 [12 USCS §§ 3401 et seq.] or the Privacy Act of 1974 [5
USCS §§ 552a, 552a note]."
(c) Notwithstanding subsection (b), notice to the customer may be delayed
if the transferring agency or department has obtained a court order delaying
notice pursuant to section 1109(a) and (b) [12 USCS § 3409(a), (b)] and
that order is still in effect, or if the receiving agency or department obtains a
court order authorizing a delay in notice pursuant to section 1109(a) and
(b) [12 USCS § 3409(a), (b)]. Upon the expiration of any such period of
delay, the transferring agency or department shall serve to the customer the
notice specified in subsection (b) above and the agency or department that
obtained the court order authorizing a delay in notice pursuant to section
1109(a) and (b) [12 USCS § 3409(a), (b)] shall serve to the customer the
notice specified in section 1109(b) [12 USCS § 3409(b)].
(d) Nothing in this title prohibits any supervisory agency from exchanging
examination reports or other information with another supervisory agency.
Nothing in this title prohibits the transfer of a customer's financial records
needed by counsel for a Government authority to defend an action brought
by the customer. Nothing in this title shall authorize the withholding of information by any officer or employee of a supervisory agency from a duly
authorized committee or subcommittee of the Congress.

§ 3413. EXCEPTIONS

(a) Nothing in this title prohibits the disclosure of any financial records or
information which is not identified with or identifiable as being derived from
the financial records of a particular customer.
(b) Nothing in this title prohibits examination by or disclosure to any supervisory agency of financial records or information in the exercise of its supervisory, regulatory, or monetary functions with respect to a financial institution.
(c) Nothing in this title prohibits the disclosure of financial records in accordance with procedures authorized by the Internal Revenue Code [26 USCS
§§ 1 et seq.].
(d) Nothing in this title shall authorize the withholding of financial records
or information required to be reported in accordance with any Federal
statute or rule promulgated thereunder.
(e) Nothing in this title shall apply when financial records are sought by a
Government authority under the Federal Rules of Civil or Criminal Procedure
or comparable rules of other courts in connection with litigation to which
the Government authority and the customer are parties.
(f) Nothing in this title shall apply when financial records are sought by a

Government authority pursuant to an administrative subpoena issued by an administrative law judge in an adjudicatory proceeding subject to section 554 of title 5, United States Code [5 USCS § 554], and to which the Government authority and the customer are parties.

(g) The notice requirements of this title and sections 1110 and 1112 [12 USCS §§ 3410, 3412] shall not apply when a Government authority by a means described in section 1102 [12 USCS § 3402] and for a legitimate law enforcement inquiry is seeking only the name, address, account number, and type of account of any customer or ascertainable group of customers associated (1) with a financial transaction or class of financial transactions, or (2) with a foreign country or subdivision thereof in the case of a Government authority exercising financial controls over foreign accounts in the United States under section 5(b) of the Trading with the Enemy Act (50 U.S.C.App. 5(b)) [50 USCS Appx. § 5(b)]; the International Emergency Economic Powers Act (title II, Public Law 95-223) [50 USCS §§ 1701 et seq.]; or section 5 of the United Nations Participation Act (22 U.S.C. 287(c)) [22 USCS § 287c].

(h)(1) Nothing in this title (except sections 1103, 1117 and 1118 [12 USCS §§ 3403, 3417, 3418]) shall apply when financial records are sought by a Government authority—

   (A) in connection with a lawful proceeding, investigation, examination, or inspection directed at the financial institution in possession of such records or at a legal entity which is not a customer; or

   (B) in connection with the authority's consideration or administration of assistance to the customer in the form of a Government loan, loan guaranty, or loan insurance program.

(2) When financial records are sought pursuant to this subsection, the Government authority shall submit to the financial institution the certificate required by section 1103(b) [12 USCS § 3403(b)]. For access pursuant to paragraph (1)(B), no further certification shall be required for subsequent access by the certifying Government authority during the term of the loan, loan guaranty, or loan insurance agreement.

(3) After the effective date of this title [see 12 USCS § 375(b) note], whenever a customer applies for participation in a Government loan, loan guaranty, or loan insurance program, the Government authority administering such program shall give the customer written notice of the authority's access rights under this subsection. No further notification shall be required for subsequent access by that authority during the term of the loan, loan guaranty or loan insurance agreement.

(4) Financial records obtained pursuant to this subsection may be used only for the purpose for which they were originally obtained, and may be transferred to another agency or department only when the transfer is to facilitate a lawful proceeding, investigation, examination, or inspection directed at the financial institution in possession of such records, or at a legal entity which is not a customer, except that—

(A) nothing in this paragraph prohibits the use or transfer of a customer's financial records needed by counsel representing a Government authority in a civil action arising from a Government loan, loan guaranty, or loan insurance agreement; and

(B) nothing in this paragraph prohibits a Government authority providing assistance to a customer in the form of a loan, loan guaranty, or loan insurance agreement from using or transferring financial records necessary to process, service or foreclose a loan, or to collect on an indebtedness to the Government resulting from a customer's default.

(5) Notification that financial records obtained pursuant to this subsection may relate to a potential civil, criminal, or regulatory violation by a customer may be given to an agency or department with jurisdiction over that violation, and such agency or department may then seek access to the records pursuant to the provisions of this title.

(6) Each financial institution shall keep a notation of each disclosure made pursuant to paragraph (1)(B) of this subsection, including the date of such disclosure and the Government authority to which it was made. The customer shall be entitled to inspect this information.

(i) Nothing in this title (except sections 1115 and 1120 [12 USCS §§ 3415, 3420]) shall apply to any subpoena or court order issued in connection with proceedings before a grand jury.

(j) This title shall not apply when financial records are sought by the General Accounting Office pursuant to an authorized proceeding, investigation, examination or audit directed at a government authority.

§ 3414. SPECIAL PROCEDURES

(a)(1) Nothing in this title (except sections 1115, 1117, 1118, and 1121 [12 USCS §§ 3415, 3417, 3418, 3421]) shall apply to the production and disclosure of financial records pursuant to requests from—

(A) a Government authority authorized to conduct foreign counter- or foreign positive-intelligence activities for purposes of conducting such activities; or

(B) the Secret Service for the purpose of conducting its protective functions (18 U.S.C. 3056; 3 U.S.C. 202, Public Law 90-331, as amended [3 USCS § 202; 18 USCS § 3056 and 3056 note]).

(2) In the instances specified in paragraph (1), the Government authority shall submit to the financial institution the certificate required in section 1103(b) [12 USCS § 3403(b)] signed by a supervisory official of a rank designated by the head of the Government authority.

(3) No financial institution, or officer, employee, or agent of such institution, shall disclose to any person that a Government authority described in paragraph (1) has sought or obtained access to a customer's financial records.

(4) The Government authority specified in paragraph (1) shall compile an annual tabulation of the occasions in which this section was used.

(b)(1) Nothing in this title shall prohibit a Government authority from obtaining financial records from a financial institution if the Government authority determines that delay in obtaining access to such records would create imminent danger of—

    (A) physical injury to any person;

    (B) serious property damage; or

    (C) flight to avoid prosecution.

(2) In the instances specified in paragraph (1), the Government shall submit to the financial institution of the certificate required in section 1103(b) [12 USCS § 3403(b)] signed by a supervisory official of a rank designated by the head of the Government authority.

(3) Within five days of obtaining access to financial records under this subsection, the Government authority shall file with the appropriate court a signed, sworn statement of a supervisory official or a rank designated by the head of the Government authority setting forth the grounds for the emergency access. The Government authority shall thereafter comply with the notice provisions of section 1109(c) [12 USCS § 3409(c)].

(4) The Government authority specified in paragraph (1) shall compile an annual tabulation of the occasions in which this section was used.

§ 3415.   COST REIMBURSEMENT

(a) Except for records obtained pursuant to section 1103(d) or 1113(a) through (h) [12 USCS § 3403(d) or 3413(a)–(h)], or as otherwise provided by law, a Government authority shall pay to the financial institution assembling or providing financial records pertaining to a customer and in accordance with procedures established by this title a fee for reimbursement for such costs as are reasonably necessary and which have been directly incurred in searching for, reproducing, or transporting books, papers, records, or other data required or requested to be produced. The Board of Governors of the Federal Reserve System shall, by regulation, establish the rates and conditions under which such payment may be made.

§ 3416.   JURISDICTION

An action to enforce any provision of this title may be brought in any appropriate United States district court without regard to the amount in controversy within three years from the date on which the violation occurs or the date of discovery of such violation, whichever is later.

§ 3417.   CIVIL PENALTIES

(a) Any agency or department of the United States or financial institution obtaining or disclosing financial records or information contained therein in violation of this title is liable to the consumer to whom such records relate in an amount equal to the sum of—

(1) $100 without regard to the volume of records involved;

(2) any actual damages sustained by the customer as a result of the disclosure;

(3) such punitive damages as the court may allow, where the violation is found to have been willful or intentional; and

(4) in the case of any successful action to enforce liability under this section, the costs of the action together with reasonable attorney's fees as determined by the court.

(b) Whenever the court determines that any agency or department of the United States has violated any provision of this title and the court finds that the circumstances surrounding the violation raise questions of whether an officer or employee of the department or agency acted willfully or intentionally with respect to the violation, the Civil Service Commission shall promptly initiate a proceeding to determine whether disciplinary action is warranted against the agent or employee who was primarily responsible for the violation. The Commission after investigation and consideration of the evidence submitted, shall submit its findings and recommendations to the administrative authority of the agency concerned and shall send copies of the findings and recommendations to the officer or employee or his representative. The administrative authority shall take the corrective action that the Commission recommends.

(c) Any financial institution or agent or employee thereof making a disclosure of financial records pursuant to this title in good-faith reliance upon a certificate by any Government authority shall not be liable to the customer for such disclosure.

(d) The remedies and sanctions described in this title shall be the only authorized judicial remedies and sanctions for violations of this title.

§.3418.   INJUNCTIVE RELIEF

In addition to any other remedy contained in this title, injunctive relief shall be available to require that the procedures of this title are complied with. In the event of any successful action, costs together with reasonable attorney's fees as determined by the court may be recovered.

§ 3419.   SUSPENSION OF STATUTES OF LIMITATIONS

If any indvidual files a motion or application under this title which has the effect of delaying the access of a Government authority to financial records pertaining to such individual, any applicable statute of limitations shall be deemed to be tolled for the period extending from the date such motion or application was filed until the date upon which the motion or application is decided.

§ 3420.   GRAND JURY INFORMATION

Financial records about a customer obtained from a financial institution pursuant to a subpoena issued under the authority of a Federal grand jury—
(1) shall be returned and actually presented to the grand jury;
(2) shall be used only for the purpose of considering whether to issue an indictment or presentment by that grand jury, or of prosecuting a crime for which that indictment or presentment is issued, or for a purpose authorized by rule 6(e) of the Federal Rules of Criminal Procedure;
(3) shall be destroyed or returned to the financial institution if not used for one of the purposes specified in paragraph (2); and
(4) shall not be maintained, or a description of the contents of such records shall not be maintained by any Government authority other than in the sealed records of the grand jury, unless such record has been used in the prosecution of a crime for which the grand jury issued an indictment or presentment or for a purpose authorized by rule 6(e) of the Federal Rules of Criminal Procedure.

§ 3421.   REPORTING REQUIREMENTS

(a) In April of each year, the Director of the Administrative Office of the United States Courts shall send to the appropriate committees of Congress a report concerning the number of applications for delays of notice made pursuant to section 1109 [12 USCS § 3409] and the number of customer challenges made pursuant to section 1110 [12 USCS § 3410] during the preceding calendar year. Such report shall include: the identity of the Government authority requesting a delay of notice; the number of notice delays sought and the number granted under each subparagraph of section 1109(a)(3) [12 USCS § 3409(a)(3)]; the number of notice delay extensions sought and the number granted; and the number of customer challenges made and the number that are successful.
(b) In April of each year, each Government authority that requests access to financial records of any customer from a financial institution pursuant to section 1104, 1105, 1106, 1107, 1108, 1109, or 1114 [12 USCS § 3404, 3405, 3406, 3407, 3408, or 3414] shall send to the appropriate committees of Congress a report describing requests made during the preceding calendar year. Such report shall include the number of requests made during the preceding calendar year. Such report shall include the number of requests

for records made pursuant to each section of this title listed in the preceding sentence and any other related information deemed relevant or useful by the Government authority.

§ 3422. SECURITIES AND EXCHANGE COMMISSION; EXEMPTION

The Securities and Exchange Commission shall not be subject to the provisions of this title for a period of two years from the date of enactment of the title [enacted Nov. 10, 1978].

APPENDIX K

DEPOSITORY INSTITUTIONS DEREGULATION AND MONETARY CONTROL ACT

TITLE I—MONETARY CONTROL ACT OF 1980

SHORT TITLE

SEC. 101. This title may be cited as the "Monetary Control Act of 1980".

REPORTING REQUIREMENTS

SEC. 102. Section 11(a) of the Federal Reserve Act (12 U.S.C. 248(a)) is amended—

(1) by inserting "(1)" after "(a)"; and

(2) by adding at the end thereof the following new paragraph:

"(2) To require any depository institution specified in this paragraph to make, at such intervals as the Board may prescribe, such reports of its liabilities and assets as the Board may determine to be necessary or desirable to enable the Board to discharge its responsibility to monitor and control monetary and credit aggregates. Such reports shall be made (A) directly to the Board in the case of member banks and in the case of other depository institutions whose reserve requirements under section 19 of this Act exceed zero, and (B) for all other reports to the Board through the (i) Federal Deposit Insurance Corporation in the case of insured State nonmember banks, savings banks, and mutual savings banks, (ii) National Credit Union Administration Board in the case of insured credit unions, (iii) Federal Home Loan Bank Board in the case of any institution insured by the Federal Savings and Loan Insurance Corporation or which is a member as defined in section 2 of the Federal Home Loan Bank Act, and (iv) such State officer or agency as the Board may designate in the case of any other type of bank, savings and loan association, or credit union. The Board shall endeavor to avoid the imposition of unnecessary burdens on reporting institutions and the duplication of other reporting requirements. Except as otherwise required by law, any

Public Law 96–221.

data provided to any department, agency, or instrumentality of the United States pursuant to other reporting requirements shall be made available to the Board. The Board may classify depository institutions for the purposes of this paragraph and may impose different requirements on each such class.".

RESERVE REQUIREMENTS

SEC. 103. Section 19(b) of the Federal Reserve Act (12 U.S.C. 461(b)) is amended to read as follows:

"(b) RESERVE REQUIREMENTS.—

"(1) DEFINITIONS.—The following definitions and rules apply to this subsection, subsection (c), section 11A, the first paragraph of section 13, and the second, thirteenth, and fourteenth paragraphs of section 16:

"(A) The term 'depository institution' means—

"(i) any insured bank as defined in section 3 of the Federal Deposit Insurance Act or any bank which is eligible to make application to become an insured bank under section 5 of such Act;

"(ii) any mutual savings bank as defined in section 3 of the Federal Deposit Insurance Act or any bank which is eligible to make application to become an insured bank under section 5 of such Act;

"(iii) any savings bank as defined in section 3 of the Federal Deposit Insurance Act or any bank which is eligible to make application to become an insured bank under section 5 of such Act;

"(iv) any insured credit union as defined in section 101 of the Federal Credit Union Act or any credit union which is eligible to make application to become an insured credit union pursuant to section 201 of such Act;

"(v) any member as defined in section 2 of the Federal Home Loan Bank Act;

"(vi) any insured institution as defined in section 401 of the National Housing Act or any institution which is eligible to make application to become an insured institution under section 403 of such Act; and

"(vii) for the purpose of section 13 and the fourteenth paragraph of section 16, any association or entity which is wholly owned by or which consists only of institutions referred to in clauses (i) through (vi).

"(B) The term 'bank' means any insured or noninsured bank, as defined in section 3 of the Federal Deposit Insurance Act, other than a mutual savings bank or a savings bank as defined in such section.

"(C) The term 'transaction account' means a deposit or account on which the depositor or account holder is permitted to make withdrawals by negotiable or transferable instrument, payment orders of withdrawal, telephone transfers, or other similar items for the purpose of making payments or transfers to third persons or others. Such term includes demand deposits, negotiable order of withdrawal accounts, savings deposits subject to automatic transfers, and share draft accounts.

"(D) The term 'nonpersonal time deposits' means a transferable time deposit or account or a time deposit or account representing funds deposited to the credit of, or in which any beneficial interest is held by, a depositor who is not a natural person.

"(E) In order to prevent evasions of the reserve requirements imposed by this subsection, after consultation with the Board of Directors of the Federal Deposit Insurance Corporation, the Federal Home Loan Bank Board, and the National Credit Union Administration Board, the Board of Governors of the Federal Reserve System is authorized to determine by regulation or order, that an account or deposit is a transaction account if such account or deposit may be used to provide funds directly or indirectly for the purpose of making payments or transfers to third persons or others.

"(2) RESERVE REQUIREMENTS.—(A) Each depository institution shall maintain reserves against its transaction accounts as the Board may prescribe by regulation solely for the purpose of implementing monetary policy—

"(i) in the ratio of 3 per centum for that portion of its total transaction accounts of $25,000,000 or less, subject to subparagraph (C); and

"(ii) in the ratio of 12 per centum, or in such other ratio as the Board may prescribe not greater than 14 per centum and not less than 8 per centum, for that portion of its total transaction accounts in excess of $25,000,000, subject to subparagraph (C).

"(B) Each depository institution shall maintain reserves against its nonpersonal time deposits in the ratio of 3 per centum, or in such other ratio not greater than 9 per centum and not less than zero per centum as the Board may prescribe by regulation solely for the purpose of implementing monetary policy.

"(C) Beginning in 1981, not later than December 31, of each year the Board shall issue a regulation increasing for the next succeeding calendar year the dollar amount which is contained in subparagraph (A) or which was last determined pursuant to this subparagraph for the purpose of such subparagraph, by an amount obtained by multiplying such dollar amount by 80 per centum of the percentage increase in the total transaction accounts of all depository institutions. The increase in such transaction accounts shall be determined by subtracting the amount of such accounts on June 30 of the preceding calendar year from the amount of such accounts on June 30 of the calendar year involved. In the case of any such 12-month period in which there has been a decrease in the total transaction accounts of all depository institutions, the Board shall issue such a regulation decreasing for the next succeeding calendar year such dollar amount by an amount obtained by multiplying such dollar amount by 80 per centum of the percentage decrease in the total transaction accounts of all depository institutions. The decrease in such transaction accounts shall be determined by subtracting the amount of such accounts on June 30 of the calendar year involved from the amount of such accounts on June 30 of the previous calendar year.

"(D) Any reserve requirement imposed under this subsection shall be uniformly applied to all transaction accounts at all depository institutions. Reserve requirements imposed under this subsection shall be uniformly applied to nonpersonal time deposits at all depository institutions, except that such requirements may vary by the maturity of such deposits.

"(3) WAIVER OF RATIO LIMITS IN EXTRAORDINARY CIRCUMSTANCES. —Upon a finding by at least 5 members of the Board that extraordinary circumstances require such action, the Board, after consultation with the appropriate committees of the Congress, may impose, with respect to any liability of depository institutions, reserve requirements outside the limitations as to ratios and as to types of liabilities otherwise prescribed by paragraph (2) for a period not exceeding 180 days, and for further periods not exceeding 180 days each by affirmative action by at least 5 members of the Board in each instance. The Board shall promptly transmit to the Congress a report of any exercise of its authority under this paragraph and the reasons for such exercise of authority.

"(4) SUPPLEMENTAL RESERVES.—(A) The Board may, upon the affirmative vote of not less than 5 members, impose a supplemental reserve requirement on every depository institution of not more than 4 per centum of its total transaction accounts. Such supplemental reserve requirement may be imposed only if—

"(i) the sole purpose of such requirement is to increase the amount of reserves maintained to a level essential for the conduct of monetary policy;

"(ii) such requirement is not imposed for the purpose of reducing the cost burdens resulting from the imposition of the reserve requirements pursuant to paragraph (2);

"(iii) such requirement is not imposed for the purpose of increasing the amount of balances needed for clearing purposes; and

"(iv) on the date on which the supplemental reserve requirement is imposed, the total amount of reserves required pursuant to paragraph (2) is not less than the amount of reserves that would be required if the initial ratios specified in paragraph (2) were in effect.

"(B) The Board may require the supplemental reserve authorized under subparagraph (A) only after consultation with the Board of Directors of the Federal Deposit Insurance Corporation, the Federal Home Loan Bank Board, and the National Credit Union Administration Board. The Board shall promptly transmit to the Congress a report with respect to any exercise of its authority to require supplemental reserves under subparagraph (A) and such report shall state the basis for the determination to exercise such authority.

"(C) The supplemental reserve authorized under subparagraph (A) shall be maintained by the Federal Reserve banks in an Earnings Participation Account. Except as provided in subsection (c)(1)(A)(ii), such Earnings Participation Account shall receive earnings to be paid by the Federal Reserve banks during each calendar quarter at a rate not more than the rate earned on the securities portfolio of the Federal Reserve System during the previous calendar quarter. The Board may prescribe rules and regulations concerning the payment of earnings on Earnings Participation Accounts by Federal Reserve banks under this paragraph.

"(D) If a supplemental reserve under subparagraph (A) has been required of depository institutions for a period of one year or more, the Board shall review and determine the need for continued maintenance of supplemental reserves and shall transmit annual reports to the Congress regarding the need, if any, for continuing the supplemental reserve.

"(E) Any supplemental reserve imposed under subparagraph (A) shall terminate at the close of the first 90-day period after such requirement is imposed during which the average amount of reserves required under paragraph (2) are less than the amount of reserves which would be required during such period if the initial ratios specified in paragraph (2) were in effect.

"(5) RESERVES RELATED TO FOREIGN OBLIGATIONS OR ASSETS.— Foreign branches, subsidiaries, and international banking facilities of nonmember depository institutions shall maintain reserves to the same extent required by the Board of foreign branches, subsidiaries, and international banking facilities of member banks. In addition to any reserves otherwise required to be maintained pursuant to this subsection, any depository institution shall maintain reserves in such ratios as the Board may prescribe against—

"(A) net balances owed by domestic offices of such depository institution in the United States to its directly related foreign offices and to foreign offices of nonrelated depository institutions;

"(B) loans to United States residents made by overseas offices of such depository institution if such depository institution has one or more offices in the United States; and

"(C) assets (including participations) held by foreign offices of a depository institution in the United States which were acquired from its domestic offices.

"(6) EXEMPTION FOR CERTAIN DEPOSITS.—The requirements imposed under paragraph (2) shall not apply to deposits payable only outside the States of the United States and the District of Columbia, except that nothing in this subsection limits the authority of the Board to impose conditions and requirements on member banks under section 25 of this Act or the authority of the Board under section 7 of the International Banking Act of 1978 (12 U.S.C.3105).

"(7) DISCOUNT AND BORROWING.—Any depository institution in which transaction accounts or nonpersonal time deposits are held shall be entitled to the same discount and borrowing privileges as member banks. In the administration of discount and borrowing privileges, the Board and the Federal Reserve banks shall take into consideration the special needs of savings and other depository institutions for access to discount and borrowing facilities consistent with their long-term asset portfolios and the sensitivity of such institutions to trends in the national money markets.

"(8) TRANSITIONAL ADJUSTMENTS.—

"(A) Any depository institution required to maintain reserves under this subsection which was engaged in business on July 1, 1979, but was not a member of the Federal Reserve System on or after that date, shall maintain reserves against its deposits during the first twelve-month period following the effective date of this paragraph in amounts equal to one-eighth of those otherwise required by this subsection, during the second such twelve-month period in amounts equal to one-fourth of those otherwise required, during the third such twelve-month period in amounts equal to three-eighths of those otherwise required, during the fourth twelve-month period in amounts equal to one-half of those otherwise required, and during the fifth twelve-month period in amounts equal to five-eighths of those otherwise required, during the sixth twelve-month period in amounts equal to three-fourths of those otherwise required, and during the seventh twelve-month period in amounts equal to seven-eigths of those otherwise required. This subparagraph does not apply to any category of deposits or accounts which are first authorized pursuant to Federal law in any State after April 1, 1980.

"(B) With respect to any bank which was a member of the Federal Reserve System during the entire period beginning on July 1, 1979, and ending on the effective date of the Monetary Control Act of 1980, the amount of required reserves imposed pursuant to this subsection on and after the effective date of such Act that exceeds the amount of reserves which would have been required of such bank if the reserve ratios in effect during the reserve computation period immediately preceding such effective date were applied may, at the discretion of the Board and in accordance with such rules and regulations as it may adopt, be reduced by 75 per centum during the first year which begins after such effective date, 50 per centum during the second year, and 25 per centum during the third year.

"(C) (i) With respect to any bank which is a member of the Federal Reserve System on the effective date of the Monetary Control Act of 1980, the amount of reserves which would have been required of such bank if the reserve ratios in effect during the reserve computation period immediately preceding such effective date were applied that exceeds the amount of reserves imposed pursuant to this subsection shall, in accordance with such rules and regulations as the Board may adopt, be reduced to 25 per centum during the first year which begins after such effective date, 50 per centum during the second year, and 75 per centum during the third year.

"(ii) If a bank becomes a member bank during the four-year period beginning on the effective date of the Monetary Control Act of 1980, and if the amount of reserves which would have been required of such bank, determined as if the reserve ratios in effect during the reserve computation period immediately preceding such effective date were applied, and as if such bank had been a member during such period, exceeds the amount of reserves required pursuant to this subsection, the amount of re-reserves required to be maintained by such bank beginning on the date on which such bank becomes a member of the Federal Reserve System shall be the amount of reserves which would have been required of such bank if it had been a member on the day before such effective date, except that the amount of such excess shall, in accordance with such rules and regulations as the Board may adopt, be reduced by 25 per centum during the first year which begins after such effective date, 50 per centum during the second year, and 75 per centum during the third year.

"(D) (i) Any bank which was a member bank on July 1, 1979, and which withdraws from membership in the Federal Reserve System during the period beginning on July 1, 1979, and ending on the day before the date of enactment of the Depository Institutions Deregulation and Monetary Control Act of 1980, shall maintain reserves beginning on such date of enactment in an amount equal to the amount of reserves it would have been required to maintain if it had been a member bank on such date of enactment. After such date of enactment, any such bank shall maintain reserves in the same amounts as member banks are required to maintain under this subsection, pursuant to subparagraphs (B) and (C)(i).

"(ii) Any bank which withdraws from membership in the Federal Reserve System on or after the date of enactment of the Depository Institutions Deregulation and Monetary Control Act of 1980 shall maintain reserves in the same amount as member banks are required to maintain under this subsection, pursuant to subparagraphs (B) and (C)(i).

"(E) This subparagraph applies to any depository institution which was engaged in business on August 1, 1978, as a depository institution organized under the laws of a State, which was not a member of the Federal Reserve System on that date, and the principal office of which was outside the continental limits of the United States on that date and has remained outside the continental limits of the United States ever since. Such a depository institution shall not be required to maintain reserves against its deposits pursuant to this subsection until the first day of the sixth calendar year which begins after the effective date of the Monetary Control Act of 1980. Such a depository institution shall maintain reserves against its deposits during the sixth calendar year which begins after such effective date in an amount equal to one-eighth of that otherwise required by paragraph (2), during the seventh such year in an amount equal to one-fourth of that otherwise required, during the eighth such year in an amount equal to three-eighths of that otherwise required, during the ninth such year in an amount equal to one-half of that otherwise required, during the tenth such year in an amount equal to five-eighths of that otherwise required, during the eleventh such year in an amount equal to three-fourths of that otherwise required, and during the twelfth such year in an amount equal to seven-eighths of that otherwise required.

"(9) EXEMPTION.—This subsection shall not apply with respect to any financial institution which—

"(A) is organized solely to do business with other financial institutions;

"(B) is owned primarily by the financial institutions with which it does business; and

"(C) does not do business with the general public.

"(10) WAIVERS.—In individual cases, where a Federal supervisory authority waives a liquidity requirement, or waives the penalty for failing to satisfy a liquidity requirement, the Board shall waive the reserve requirement, or waive the penalty for failing to satisfy a reserve requirement, imposed pursuant to this subsection for the depository institution involved when requested by the Federal supervisory authority involved."

FORM OF RESERVES

SEC. 104. (a) Section 19(c) of the Federal Reserve Act (12 U.S.C. 461) is amended to read as follows:

"(c)(1) Reserves held by a depository institution to meet the requirements imposed pursuant to subsection (b) shall, subject to such rules and regulations as the Board shall prescribe, be in the form of—

"(A) balances maintained for such purposes by such depository institution in the Federal Reserve bank of which it is a member or at which it maintains an account, except that (i) the Board may, by regulation or order, permit depository institutions to maintain all or a portion of their required reserves in the form of vault cash, except that any portion so permitted shall be identical for all depository institutions, and (ii) vault cash may be used to satisfy any supplemental reserve requirement imposed pursuant to subsection (b)(4), except that all such vault cash shall be excluded from any computation of earnings pursuant to subsection (b)(4)(C); and

"(B) balances maintained by a depository institution which is not a member bank in a depository institution which maintains required reserve balances at a Federal Reserve bank, in a Federal Home Loan Bank, or in the National Credit Union Administration Central Liquidity Facility, if such depository institution, Federal Home Loan Bank, or National Credit Union Administration Central Liquidity Facility maintains such funds in the form of balances in a Federal Reserve bank of which it is a member or at which it maintains an account. Balances received by a depository institution from a second depository institution and used to satisfy the reserve requirement imposed on such second depository institution by this section shall not be subject to the reserve requirements of this section imposed on such first depository institution, and shall not be subject to assessments or reserves imposed on such first depository institution pursuant to section 7 of the Federal Deposit Insurance Act (12 U.S.C. 1817), section 404 of the National Housing Act (12 U.S.C. 1727), or section 202 of the Federal Credit Union Act (12 U.S.C. 1782).

"(2) The balances maintained to meet the reserve requirements of subsection (b) by a depository institution in a Federal Reserve bank or passed through a Federal Home Loan Bank or the National Credit Union Administration Central Liquidity Facility or another depository institution to a Federal Reserve bank may be used to satisfy liquidity requirements which may be imposed under other provisions of Federal or State law.".

(b) The first sentence of section 5A(b)(1) of the Federal Home Loan Bank Act (12 U.S.C. 1425a(b)) is amended—

(1) by striking out "and" before "(D)"; and

(2) by inserting before the period at the end thereof the following:

"; and (E) balances maintained in a Federal Reserve bank or passed through a Federal Home Loan Bank or another depository institution to a Federal Reserve bank pursuant to the Federal Reserve Act".

MISCELLANEOUS AMENDMENTS

SEC. 105. (a) The first paragraph of section 13 of the Federal Reserve Act (12 U.S.C. 342) is amended—

(1) by inserting "or other depository institutions" after "member banks";

(2) by inserting "or other items" after "payable upon presentation" the first and third place it appears therein;

(3) by inserting "or other items" after "payable upon presentation within its district";

(4) by inserting "or other depository institution" after "nonmember bank or trust company" each place it appears therein;

(5) by striking out "sufficient to offset the items in transit held for its account by the Federal reserve bank" and inserting in lieu thereof "in such amount as the Board determines taking into account items in transit, services provided by the Federal Reserve bank, and other factors as the Board may deem appropriate"; and

(6) by inserting "or other depository institution" after "prohibiting a member or nonmember bank".

(b)(1) The second paragraph of section 16 of the Federal Reserve Act (12 U.S.C. 412) is amended—

(A) by inserting before the period at the end of the third sentence the following: ", or assets that Federal Reserve banks may purchase or hold under section 14 of this Act"; and

(B) by adding at the end thereof the following: "Collateral shall not be required for Federal Reserve notes which are held in the vaults of Federal Reserve banks.".

(2) Section 14(b)(1) of the Federal Reserve Act (12 U.S.C. 355), as such section is in effect on the effective date of this title and as it will be in effect on June 1, 1981, is amended by inserting after "reclamation districts," the following: "and obligations of, or fully guaranteed as to principal and interest by, a foreign government or agency thereof,".

(c) The thirteenth paragraph of section 16 of the Federal Reserve Act (12 U.S.C. 360) is amended—

(1) by striking out "member banks" each place it appears therein and inserting in lieu thereof "depository institutions";

(2) by striking out "member bank" each place it appears therein and inserting in lieu thereof "depository institution"; and

(3) by inserting after "checks" each place it appears therein, the following: "and other items, including negotiable orders of withdrawal and share drafts".

(d) The fourteenth paragraph of section 16 of the Federal Reserve Act

(12 U.S.C. 248(o)) is amended by striking out "its member banks" and inserting in lieu thereof "depository institutions".

(e) The first sentence of section 19(e) of the Federal Reserve Act (12 U.S.C. 463) is amended to read as follows: "No member bank shall keep on deposit with any depository institution which is not authorized to have access to Federal Reserve advances under section 10(b) of this Act a sum in excess of 10 per centum of its own paid-up capital and surplus.".

(f) The last subsection of section 19 of the Federal Reserve Act (12 U.S.C. 505) is amended by striking out "(j)(1)" and inserting in lieu thereof "(1)(1)".

ABOLITION OF PENALTY RATE

SEC. 106. Section 10(b) of the Federal Reserve Act (12 U.S.C. 374b) is amended by striking out the second sentence of the first paragraph.

PRICING OF SERVICES

SEC. 107. The Federal Reserve Act is amended by inserting after section 11 the following new section:

"PRICING OF SERVICES

"SEC. 11A. (a) Not later than the first day of the sixth month after the date of enactment of the Monetary Control Act of 1980, the Board shall publish for public comment a set of pricing principles in accordance with this section and a proposed schedule of fees based upon those principles for Federal Reserve bank services to depository institutions, and not later than the first day of the eighteenth month after the date of enactment of the Monetary Control Act of 1980, the Board shall begin to put into effect a schedule of fees for such services which is based on those principles.

"(b) The services which shall be covered by the schedule of fees under subsection (a) are—

"(1) currency and coin services;

"(2) check clearing and collection services;

"(3) wire transfer services;

"(4) automated clearinghouse services;

"(5) settlement services;

"(6) securities safekeeping services;

"(7) Federal Reserve float; and

"(8) any new services which the Federal Reserve System offers, including but not limited to payment services to effectuate the electronic transfer of funds.

"(c) The schedule of fees prescribed pursuant to this section shall be based on the following principles:

"(1) All Federal Reserve bank services covered by the fee schedule shall be priced explicitly.

"(2) All Federal Reserve bank services covered by the fee schedule shall be available to nonmember depository institutions and such services shall be priced at the same fee schedule applicable to member banks, except that nonmembers shall be subject to any other terms, including a requirement of balances sufficient for clearing purposes, that the Board may determine are applicable to member banks.

"(3) Over the long run, fees shall be established on the basis of all direct and indirect costs actually incurred in providing the Federal Reserve services priced, including interest on items credited prior to actual collection, overhead, and an allocation of imputed costs which takes into account the taxes that would have been paid and the return on capital that would have been provided had the services been furnished by a private business firm, except that the pricing principles shall give due regard to competitive factors and the provision of an adequate level of such services nationwide.

"(4) Interest on items credited prior to collection shall be charged at the current rate applicable in the market for Federal funds.

"(d) The Board shall require reductions in the operating budgets of the Federal Reserve banks commensurate with any actual or projected decline in the volume of services to be provided by such banks. The full amount of any savings so realized shall be paid into the United States Treasury.".

EFFECTIVE DATES

SEC. 108. This title shall take effect on the first day of the sixth month which begins after the date of the enactment of this title, except that the amendments regarding sections 19(b)(7) and 19(b)(8)(D) of the Federal Reserve Act shall take effect on the date of enactment of this title.

TITLE II—DEPOSITORY INSTITUTIONS DEREGULATION

SHORT TITLE

SEC. 201. This title may be cited as the "Depository Institutions Deregulation Act of 1980".

FINDINGS AND PURPOSE

SEC. 202. (a) The Congress hereby finds that—

(1) limitations on the interest rates which are payable on deposits and accounts discourage persons from saving money, create inequities for depositors, impede the ability of depository institutions to compete for funds, and have not achieved their purpose of providing an even flow of funds for home mortgage lending; and

(2) all depositors, and particularly those with modest savings, are

entitled to receive a market rate of return on their savings as soon as it is economically feasible for depository institutions to pay such rate.

(b) It is the purpose of this title to provide for the orderly phase-out and the ultimate elimination of the limitations on the maximum rates of interest and dividends which may be paid on deposits and accounts by depository institutions by extending the authority to impose such limitations for 6 years, subject to specific standards designed to ensure a phase-out of such limitations to market rates of interest.

ESTABLISHMENT AND AUTHORITY OF COMMITTEE

SEC. 203.(a) The authorities conferred by section 19(j) of the Federal Reserve Act (12 U.S.C. 371b), section 18(g) of the Federal Deposit Insurance Act (12 U.S.C. 1828(g)), and section 5B(a) of the Federal Home Loan Bank Act (12 U.S.C. 1425b(a)) or by any other provision of Federal law, other than section 117 of the Federal Credit Union Act (12 U.S.C. 1763), to prescribe rules governing the payment of interest and dividends and the establishment of classes of deposits or accounts, including limitations on the maximum rates of interest and dividends which may be paid on deposits and accounts, and the authority conferred by the provisions of section 102 of Public Law 94–200 (12 U.S.C. 461 note) are hereby transferred to the Depository Institutions Deregulation Committee (hereinafter in this title referred to as the "Deregulation Committee").

(b) The Deregulation Committee shall consist of the Secretary of the Treasury, the Chairman of the Board of Governors of the Federal Reserve System, the Chairman of the Board of Directors of the Federal Deposit Insurance Corporation, the Chairman of the Federal Home Loan Bank Board, and the Chairman of the National Credit Union Administration Board, who shall be voting members, and the Comptroller of the Currency, who shall be a nonvoting member of the Deregulation Committee. The Deregulation Committee shall hold public meetings at least quarterly. All meetings of the Deregulation Committee shall be conducted in conformity with the provisions of section 552b of title 5, United States Code. The Deregulation Committee may not take any action unless such action is approved by a majority vote of the voting members of the Deregulation Committee.

(c) The authorities conferred by this title on the Deregulation Committee and its members may not be delegated.

DIRECTIVE TO THE COMMITTEE

SEC. 204. (a) The Deregulation Committee shall, by regulation, exercise the authorities tranferred by section 203 to provide for the orderly phase-out and the ultimate elimination of the limitations on the maximum rates of interest and dividends which may be paid on deposits and accounts as rapidly as economic conditions warrant. The phase-out of such limitations may be achieved by the Deregulation Committee by the gradual increase in such limitations applicable to all existing categories of accounts, the complete elimination of the limitations applicable to particular categories of accounts, the creation of new categories of accounts not subject to limitations or with limitations set at current market rates, any combination of the above methods, or any other method.

(b) The Deregulation Committee shall work toward providing all depositors with a market rate of return on their savings with due regard for the safety and soundness of depository institutions. Pursuant to the authority granted by this title, the Deregulation Committee shall increase all limitations on the maximum rates of interest and dividends which may be paid on deposits and accounts to market rates as soon as feasible, except that the Deregulation Committee shall not increase such limitations above market rates during the six-year period beginning on the date of enactment of this title.

TARGETS

SEC. 205. (a) In order to assist the Dergulation Committee in establishing the limitations on the maximum rates of interest and dividends which may be paid on all deposits and accounts at market rates as soon as feasible and in order to provide maximum assurance that interest rate controls will be phased-out during the 6-year period following the date of enactment of this title, the Deregulation Committee shall vote, not later than 18 months after such date of enactment, on whether to increase the limitations on the maximum rates applicable to passbook and similar savings accounts by at least one-fourth of one percentage point during such 18-month period, and shall vote, not later than the end of each of the third, fourth, fifth, and sixth years after such date of enactment, on whether to increase the limitations on the maximum rates applicable to all categories of deposits and accounts by at least one-half of one percentage point.

(b) The Deregulation Committee may, consistent with the purposes of this title, adjust the limitations on the rates applicable to all categories of deposits and accounts to rates which are higher or lower than the targets set forth in this section.

REPORTS

SEC. 206. Each member of the Deregulation Committee shall separately report to the Congress annually after the date of enactment of this Act regarding the economic viability of depository institutions. Each such report shall contain—

(1) an assessment of whether the removal of any differential between the rates payable on deposits and accounts by banks and those payable by thrift institutions will adversely affect the housing finance market or the viability of the thrift industry;

(2) recommendations for measures which would encourage savings,

provide for the equitable treatment of small savers, and ensure a steady and adequate flow of funds to thrift institutions and the housing market;

(3) findings concerning disintermediation of savings deposits from insured banks and insured thrift institutions to uninsured money market innovators paying market rates to savers; and

(4) recommendations for such legislative and administrative actions as the member involved considers necessary to maintain the economic viability of depository institutions.

TERMINATIONS

SEC. 207. (a) Section 7 of Public Law 89–597 (12 U.S.C. 461 note) is hereby repealed.

(b) Effective upon the expiration of 6 years after the date of enactment of this Act—

(1) section 102 of Public Law 94–200 (12 U.S.C. 461 note) is hereby repealed;

(2) the second sentence of section 18(g)(1) of the Federal Deposit Insurance Act (12 U.S.C. 1828(g)(1)) is amended by striking out "payment and" and striking out ", including limitations on the rates of interest and dividends that may be paid";

(3) the third, fifth, and eighth sentences of section 18(g)(1) of the Federal Deposit Insurance Act (12 U.S.C. 1828(g)(1)) are hereby repealed;

(4) the first sentence of section 19(j) of the Federal Reserve Act (12 U.S.C. 371b) is amended by striking out "payment and" and by striking out ", including limitations on the rates of interest which may be paid";

(5) the second sentence of section 19(j) of the Federal Reserve Act (12 U.S.C. 371b) is hereby repealed;

(6) the third sentence of section 19(j) of the Federal Reserve Act (12 U.S.C. 371b) is amended by striking out "No member bank" and all that follows through *"Provided,* That, the" and inserting in lieu thereof "The";

(7) the first sentence of section 5B(a) of the Federal Home Loan Bank Act (12 U.S.C. 1425b(a)) is amended by striking out "payment and" and by striking out ", including limitations on the rates of interest or dividends on deposits, shares, or withdrawable accounts that may be paid";

(8) the second and fourth sentences of section 5B(a) of the Federal Home Loan Bank Act (12 U.S.C. 1425b(a)) are hereby repealed;

(9) the third sentence of section 5B(a) of the Federal Home Loan Bank Act (12 U.S.C. 1425b(a)) is amended by striking out ", including specifically the authority" and all that follows through "of that authority";

(10) section 117 of the Federal Credit Union Act (12 U.S.C. 1763) is amended by striking out ", pursuant to such regulations as may be issued by the Board,";

(11) section 501(a)(2) of the Depository Institutions Deregulation and Monetary Control Act of 1980 is amended by striking out "(A)" and by striking out subparagraph (B);

(12) second 527 of the Depository Institutions Deregulation and Monetary Control Act of 1980 is amended by striking out ", except as provided in section 501(a)(2)(B)"; and

(13) Public Law 93–123 (12 U.S.C. 371b note) is hereby repealed.

ENFORCEMENT

SEC. 208. (a) Compliance with the regulations issued by the Deregulation Committee under this title shall be enforced under—

(1) section 8 of the Federal Deposit Insurance Act (12 U.S.C. 1818), in the case of—

(A) national banks, by the Comptroller of the Currency;

(B) member banks of the Federal Reserve System (other than national banks) by the Board of Governors of the Federal Reserve System;

(C) banks insured by the Federal Deposit Insurance Corporation (other than members of the Federal Reserve System), by the Board of Directors of the Federal Deposit Insurance Corporation; and

(2) section 5(d) of the Home Owners' Loan Act of 1933 (12 U.S.C. 1464(d)), section 407 of the National Housing Act (12 U.S.C. 1730), and section 17 of the Federal Home Loan Bank Act, by the Federal Home Loan Bank Board (acting directly or through the Federal Savings and Loan Insurance Corporation), in the case of any institution subject to any of those provisions.

(b) For the purpose of the exercise by any agency referred to in subsection (a) of its powers under any Act referred to in that subsection, a violation of any regulation prescribed under this title shall be deemed to be a violation of a regulation prescribed under the Act involved. In addition to its powers under any provision of law specifically referred to in subsection (a), each of the agencies referred to in such subsection may exercise, for the purpose of enforcing compliance with any regulation prescribed under this title, any other authority conferred on it by law.

TRANSITIONAL PROVISIONS

SEC. 209. All rules and regulations issued pursuant to any authority transferred by section 203 of this title shall remain in effect until repealed, amended, or superseded by a regulation of the Deregulation Committee.

TERMINATION OF AUTHORITY

SEC. 210. Upon the expiration of six years after the date of the enactment of this Act, all authorities transferred to the Deregulation Committee by this title shall cease to be effective and the Deregulation Committee shall cease to exist.

TITLE III—CONSUMER CHECKING ACCOUNT EQUITY ACT OF 1980

SHORT TITLE

SEC. 301. This title may be cited as the "Consumer Checking Account Equity Act of 1980".

AUTOMATIC TRANSFER ACCOUNTS

SEC. 302. (a) Section 19(i) of the Federal Reserve Act (12 U.S.C. 371a) is amended by adding at the end thereof the following new sentence: "Notwithstanding any other provision of this section, a member bank may permit withdrawals to be made automatically from a savings deposit that consists only of funds in which the entire beneficial interest is held by one or more individuals through payment to the bank itself or through transfer of credit to a demand deposit or other account pursuant to written authorization from the depositor to make such payments or transfers in connection with checks or drafts drawn upon the bank, pursuant to terms and conditions prescribed by the Board."

(b) Section 18(g) of the Federal Deposit Insurance Act (12 U.S.C. 1828(g) is amended by inserting "(1)" after "(g)" and by adding at the end thereof the following new paragraph:

"(2) Notwithstanding the provisions of paragraph (1), an insured nonmember bank may permit withdrawals to be made automatically from a savings deposit that consists only of funds in which the entire beneficial interest is held by one or more individuals through payment to the bank itself or through transfer of credit to a demand deposit or other account pursuant to written authorization from the depositor to make such payments or transfers in connection with checks or drafts drawn upon the bank, pursuant to terms and conditions prescribed by the Board of Directors.".

NOW ACCOUNTS

SEC. 303. Section 2(a) of Public Law 93–100 (12 U.S.C. 1832(a)) is amended to read as follows:

"(a)(1) Notwithstanding any other provision of law but subject to paragraph (2), a depository institution is authorized to permit the owner of a deposit or account on which interest or dividends are paid to make withdrawals by negotiable or transferable instruments for the purpose of making transfers to third parties.

"(2) Paragraph (1) shall apply only with respect to deposits or accounts which consist solely of funds in which the entire beneficial interest is held by one or more individuals or by an organization which is operated primarily for religious, philanthropic, charitable, educational, or other similar purposes and which is not operated for profit."

REMOTE SERVICE UNITS

SEC. 304. Section 5(b)(1) of the Home Owners' Loan Act of 1933 (12 U.S.C. 1464(b)(1)) is amended by adding at the end thereof the following new sentence: "This section does not prohibit the establishment of remote service units by associations for the purpose of crediting savings accounts, debiting such accounts, crediting payments on loans, and the disposition of related financial transactions, as provided in regulations prescribed by the Board.".

SHARE DRAFTS

SEC. 305. (a) Section 101(5) of the Federal Credit Union Act (12 U.S.C. 1752(5)) is amended—

(1) by striking out "or share certificate" each place it appears therein and inserting in lieu thereof ", share certificate, or share draft account"; and

(2) by striking out "or 'share certificate'" and inserting in lieu thereof ", 'share certificate', or 'share draft'".

(b) Section 107(6) of the Federal Credit Union Act (12 U.S.C. 1757(6)) is amended by striking out "credit unions serving" and all that follows through the end thereof and inserting in lieu thereof "credit unions serving predominately low-income members (as defined by the Board) payments on—

"(A) shares which may be issued at varying dividend rates;

"(B) share certificates which may be issued at varying dividend rates and maturities; and

"(C) share draft accounts authorized under section 205(f); subject to such terms, rates, and conditions as may be established by the board of directors, within limitations prescribed by the Board.".

(c) Section 117 of the Federal Credit Union Act (12 U.S.C. 1763) is amended—

(1) in the first sentence—

(A) by striking out "and" the second place it appears therein and inserting in lieu thereof a comma; and

(B) by inserting ", and at different rates on different types of share draft accounts" before the period at the end thereof; and

(2) in the second sentence, by striking out "and share certificates"

and inserting in lieu thereof ", share certificates, and share draft accounts".

(d) Section 205 of the Federal Credit Union Act (12 U.S.C. 1785) is amended by adding at the end thereof the following new subsection:

"(f)(1) Every insured credit union is authorized to maintain, and make loans with respect to, share draft accounts in accordance with rules and regulations prescribed by the Board. Except as provided in paragraph (2), an insured credit union may pay dividends on share draft accounts and may permit the owners of such share draft accounts to make withdrawals by negotiable or transferable instruments or other orders for the purpose of making transfers to third parties.

"(2) Paragraph (1) shall apply only with respect to share draft accounts in which the entire beneficial interest is held by one or more individuals or members or by an organization which is operated primarily for religious, philanthropic, charitable, educational, or other similar purposes and which is not operated for profit.".

EFFECTIVE DATES

SEC. 306. The amendments made by sections 302, 304, and 305 of this title shall take effect at the close of March 31, 1980, and the amendments made by section 303 of this title shall take effect on December 31, 1980.

REPEAL OF EXISTING LAW

SEC. 307. At the close of March 31, 1980, the amendments made by sections 101 through 103 of Public Law 96–161 are hereby repealed.

DEPOSIT INSURANCE

SEC. 307. (a)(1) The following provisions of the Federal Deposit Insurance Act are amended by striking out "$40,000" each place it appears therein and inserting in lieu thereof "$100,000":

(A) The first sentence of section 3(m) (12 U.S.C. 1813(m)).

(B) The first sentence of section 7(i) (12 U.S.C. 1817(i)).

(C) The last sentence of section 11(a)(1) (12 U.S.C. 1821(a)(1)).

(D) The fifth sentence of section 11(i) (12 U.S.C. 1821(i)).

(2) The amendments made by this subsection are not applicable to any claim arising out of the closing of a bank prior to the effective date of this section.

(b)(1) The following provisions of title IV of the National Housing Act are amended by striking out "$40,000" each place it appears therein and inserting in lieu thereof "$100,000":

(A) Section 401(b) (12 U.S.C. 1724(b)).

(B) Section 405(a) (12 U.S.C. 1728(a)).

(2) The amendments made by this subsection are not applicable to any claim arising out of a default, as defined in section 401(d) of the National Housing Act (12 U.S.C. 1724(d)), where the appointment of a conservator,

receiver, or other legal custodian as set forth in that section became effective prior to the effective date of this section.

(c)(1) The second sentence of section 207(c) of the Federal Credit Union Act (12 U.S.C. 1787(c)) is amended by striking out "$40,000" and inserting in lieu thereof "$100,000".

(2) The amendment made by this subsection is not applicable to any claim arising out of the closing of a credit union for liquidation on account of bankruptcy or insolvency pursuant to section 207 of the Federal Credit Union Act (12 U.S.C. 1787) prior to the effective date of this section.

(d) Section 7(d) of the Federal Deposit Insurance Act (12 U.S.C. 1817(d)) is amended—

    (1) in the first sentence—

        (A) by inserting "(1)" after "(d)";

        (B) by striking out "December 31, 1961" and inserting in lieu thereof "December 31, 1980"; and

        (C) by striking out "33⅓ per centum" and inserting in lieu thereof "40 per centum"; and

    (2) by adding at the end thereof the following new paragraph:

"(2) Notwithstanding any other provision of this subsection—

"(A) whenever the Board of Directors determines that the ratio of the Corporation's capital account to the estimated insured deposits is ceeds 1.25 per centum, the Board of Directors may reduce the per centum of net assessment income to be transferred to the Corporation's capital account by such an amount, but not to exceed 50 per centum, as it determines will result in maintaining that ratio at not less than 1.10 per centum;

"(B) wherever the Board of Directors determines that the ratio of the Corporation's capital account to the estimated insured deposits exceeds 1.25 per centum, the Board of Directors may reduce the per centum of net assessment income to be transferred to the Corporation's capital account by such an amount as it determines will result in maintaining such ratio at not less than 1.25 per centum; and

"(C) whenever the Board of Directors determines that the ratio of the Corporation's capital account to the estimated insured deposits exceeds 1.40 per centum, the Board of Directors shall reduce the per centum of net assessment income to be transferred to the Corporation's capital account by such an amount as it determines will result in maintaining that ratio at not more than 1.40 per centum.".

(e) The amendments made by this section shall take effect on the date of enactment of this Act.

CREDIT UNION AMENDMENTS

SEC. 3.09. (a) The Federal Credit Union Act is amended—

    (1) in section 107(5)(A)(i)—

        (A) by inserting ", including an individual cooperative unit," immediately following "dwelling"; and

(B) by inserting "(except that a loan on an individual cooperative unit shall be adequately secured as defined by the Board)" after "thirty years";

(2) by striking out section 305(b)(3) and inserting in lieu thereof the following:

"(3) shall share in dividend distribution at rates determined by the Board. However, rates on the required capital stock shall be without preference; and";

(3) by striking out ", to the extent or in such amounts as are provided in advance in appropriation Acts" in section 307(15); and

(4) in title III, as so redesignated by subsection (b)(1), by striking out "Administrator" each place it appears and inserting in lieu thereof "Board".

(b) The Federal Credit Union Act is amended—

(1) by striking out the heading of subchapter III of such Act and inserting in lieu thereof "TITLE III—CENTRAL LIQUIDITY FACILITY";

(2) in title III, as so redesignated by paragraph (1), by striking out "subchapter" each place it appears therein and inserting in lieu thereof "title"; and

(3) in section 307(3), by striking out "subchapters I and II of this chapter" and inserting in lieu thereof "titles I and II of this Act".

INTEREST RATES ON CREDIT UNION LOANS

SEC. 310. Section 107(5)(A)(vi) of the Federal Credit Union Act (12 U.S.C. 1757(5)(A)(vi)) is amended to read as follows:

"(vi) the rate of interest may not exceed 15 per centum per annum on the unpaid balance inclusive of all finance charges, except that the Board may establish—

"(I) after consultation with the appropriate committees of the Congress, the Department of Treasury, and the Federal financial institution regulatory agencies, an interest rate ceiling exceeding such 15 per centum per annum rate, for periods not to exceed 18 months, if it determines that money market interest rates have risen over the preceding six-month period and that prevailing interest rate levels threaten the safety and soundness of individual credit unions as evidenced by adverse trends in liquidity, capital, earnings, and growth; and

"(II) a higher interest rate ceiling for Agent members of the Central Liquidity Facility in carrying out the provisions of title III for such periods as the Board may authorize;".

FEDERAL HOME LOAN BANK SETTLEMENT AND PROCESSING OF DRAFTS

SEC. 311. Section 11(e) of the Federal Home Loan Bank Act (12 U.S.C. 1431(e)) is amended—

(1) by inserting "(1)" after "(e)"; and

(2) by adding at the end thereof the following new paragraph:

"(2)(A) The Board may, subject to such rules and regulations, including definitions of terms used in this paragraph, as the Board shall from time to time prescribe, authorize Federal Home Loan Banks to be drawees of, and to engage in, or be agents or intermediaries for, or otherwise participate or assist in, the collection and settlement of (including presentment, clearing, and payment of, and remitting for), checks, drafts, or any other negotiable or nonnegotiable items or instruments of payment drawn on or issued by members of any Federal Home Loan Bank or by institutions which are eligible to make application to become members pursuant to section 4, and to have such incidental powers as the Board shall find necessary for the exercise of any such authorization.

"(B) A Federal Home Loan Bank shall make charges, to be determined and regulated by the Board consistent with the principles set forth in section 11A(c) of the Federal Reserve Act, or utilize the services of, or act as agent for, or be a member of, a Federal Reserve bank, clearinghouse, or any other public or private financial institution or other agency, in the exercise of any powers or functions pursuant to this paragraph.

"C) The Board is authorized, with respect to participation in the collection and settlement of any items by Federal Home Loan Banks, and with respect to the collection and settlement (including payment by the payor institution) of items payable by Federal savings and loan associations and Federal mutual savings banks, to prescribe rules and regulations regarding the rights, powers, responsibilities, duties, and liabilities, including standards relating thereto, of such Banks, associations, or banks and other parties to any such items or their collection and settlement. In prescribing such rules and regulations, the Board may adopt or apply, in whole or in part, general banking usage and practices, and, in instances or respects in which they would otherwise not be applicable, Federal Reserve regulations and operating letters, the Uniform Commercial Code, and clearinghouse rules.".

CENTRAL LIQUIDITY FACILITY SETTLEMENT AND PROCESSING OF SHARE DRAFTS

SEC. 312. Section 307 of the Federal Credit Union Act (12 U.S.C. 1795f) is amended—

(1) by inserting "(a)" after "SEC. 307."; and

(2) by adding at the end thereof the following:

"(b)(1) The Board may authorize the Central Liquidity Facility or its Agent members, subject to such rules and regulations, including definitions of terms used in this subsection, as the Board shall from time to time prescribe, to be drawees of, and to engage in, or be agents or intermediaries for, or otherwise participate or assist in, the collection and settlement of (including presentment, clearing, and payment of, and remitting for), checks, share drafts, or any other negotiable or nonnegotiable items or instruments of payment drawn on or issued by members of the Central Liquidity Facility, any of its Agent members, or any other credit union eligible to become a member of the Central Liquidity Facility, and to have such incidental powers as the Board shall find necessary for the exercise of any such authorization.

"(2) The Central Liquidity Facility or its Agent members shall make charges, to be determined and regulated by the Board consistent with the principles set forth in section 11A(c) of the Federal Reserve Act, or utilize the services of, or act as agent for, or be a member of, a Federal Reserve bank, clearinghouse, or any other public or private financial institution or other agency, in the exercise of any powers or functions pursuant to this subsection.

"(3) The Board is authorized, with respect to participation in the collection and settlement of any items by the Central Liquidity Facility or by its Agent members, and with respect to the collection and settlement (including payment by the payor institution) of items payable by members of the Central Liquidity Facility or of any of its Agent members, to prescribe rules and regulations regarding the rights, powers, responsibilities, duties, and liabilities, including standards relating thereto, of such entities and other parties to any such items or their collection and settlement. In prescribing such rules and regulations, the Board may adopt or apply, in whole or in part, general banking usage and practices, and, in instances or respects in which they would otherwise not be applicable, Federal Reserve regulations and operating letters, the Uniform Commercial Code, and clearinghouse rules.".

ALASKA USA FEDERAL CREDIT UNION

SEC. 313. Any person who is a member of the Alaska USA Federal Credit Union prior to any termination date which is contained in section 5 of the charter of such credit union and which would otherwise apply to such person may continue to be a member of such credit union on and after such date until the expiration of two years after the date of the enactment of this Act. For purposes of this section, the term "member of the Alaska USA Federal Credit Union" means any person who has an account at such credit union.

TITLE IV—POWERS OF THRIFT INSTITUTIONS AND MISCELLANEOUS PROVISIONS

FEDERAL SAVINGS AND LOAN INVESTMENT AUTHORITY

SEC. 401. Section 5(c) of the Home Owners' Loan Act of 1933 (12 U.S.C. 1464(c)) is amended to read as follows:

"(c) An association may to such extent, and subject to such rules and regulations as the Board may prescribe from time to time, invest in, sell, or otherwise deal with the following loans, or other investments:

"(1) Loans or investments without percentage of assets limitation: Without limitation as a percentage of assets, the following are permitted:

"(A) ACCOUNT LOANS.—Loans on the security of its savings accounts and loans specifically related to negotiable order-of-withdrawal accounts.

"(B) SINGLE-FAMILY AND MULTI-FAMILY MORTGAGE LOANS.— Loans on the security of liens upon residential real property in an amount which, when added to the amount unpaid upon prior mortgages, liens or encumbrances, if any, upon such real estate does not exceed the appraised value thereof, except that the amount of any such loan hereafter made shall not exceed 66⅔ per centum of the appraised value if such real estate is unimproved, 75 per centum of the appraised value if such real estate is improved by offsite improvements such as street, water, sewers, or other utilities, 75 per centum of the appraised value if such real estate is in the process of being improved by a building or buildings to be constructed or in the process of construction, or 90 per centum of the appraised value if such real estate is improved by a building or buildings. Notwithstanding the above loan-to-value ratios, the Board may permit a loan-to-value ratio in excess of 90 per centum if such real estate is improved by a building or buildings and that portion of the unpaid balance of such loan which is in excess of an amount equal to 90 per centum of such value is guaranteed or insured by a public or private mortgage insurer or in the case of any loan for the purpose of providing housing for persons of low income, as described in regulations of the Board.

"(C) UNITED STATES GOVERNMENT SECURITIES.—Investments in obligations of, or fully guaranteed as to principal and interest by, the United States.

"(D) FEDERAL HOME LOAN BANK AND FEDERAL NATIONAL MORT-GAGE ASSOCIATION SECURITIES.—Investments in the stock or bonds of a Federal home loan bank or in the stock of the Federal Mortgage Association.

"(E) FEDERAL HOME LOAN MORTGAGE CORPORATION INSTRU-MENTS.—Investments in mortgages, obligations, or other securities which are or ever have been sold by the Federal Home Loan Mortgage Corporation pursuant to section 305 or 306 of the Federal Home Loan Mortgage Corporation Act.

"(F) OTHER GOVERNMENT SECURITIES.—Investments in obligations, participations, securities, or other instruments of, or issued by, or fully guaranteed as to principal and interest by, the Federal National Mortgage Association, the Student Loan Marketing Association or the Government National Mortgage Association, or any other agency of the United States and an association may issue and sell securities which are guaranteed pursuant to section 306(g) of the National Housing Act.

"(G) BANK DEPOSITS.—Investments in the time deposits, certificates, or accounts of any bank the deposits of which are insured by the Federal Deposit Insurance Corporation.

"(H) STATE SECURITIES.—Investments in general obligations of any State or any political subdivision thereof.

"(I) PURCHASE OF INSURED LOANS.—Purchase of loans secured by liens on improved real estate which are insured under provisions of the National Housing Act, or insured as provided in the Servicemen's Readjustment Act of 1944 or chapter 37 of title 38, United States Code.

"(J) HOME IMPROVEMENT AND MANUFACTURED HOME LOANS. —Loans made for the repair, equipping, alteration, or improvement of any residential real property, and loans made for the purpose of manufactured home financing.

"(K) INSURED LOANS TO FINANCE THE PURCHASE OF FEE SIMPLE.—Loans as to which the association has the benefit of insurance under section 240 of the National Housing Act, or of a commitment or agreement therefor.

"(L) LOANS TO FINANCIAL INSTITUTIONS, BROKERS, AND DEALERS.—Loans to financial institutions with respect to which the United States or any agency or instrumentality thereof has any function of examination or supervision, or to any broker or dealer registered with the Securities and Exchange Commission, secured by loans, obligations, or investments in which the association has the statutory authority to invest directly.

"(M) LIQUIDITY INVESTMENTS.—Investments which, at the time of making, are assets eligible for inclusion toward the satisfaction of any liquidity requirement imposed by the Board pursuant to section 5A of the Federal Home Loan Bank Act, but only to the extent that the investment is permitted to be so included under regulations of the Board or is otherwise authorized.

"(N) INVESTMENT IN THE NATIONAL HOUSING PARTNERSHIP CORPORATION, PARTNERSHIPS, AND JOINT VENTURES.—Investments in shares of stock issued by a corporation authorized to be created pursuant to title IX of the Housing and Urban Development Act of 1968, and investments in any partnership, limited partnership, or joint venture formed pursuant to section 907(a) or 907(c) of such Act.

"(O) HOUSING AND URBAN DEVELOPMENT GUARANTEED INVESTMENTS.—Loans as to which the association has the benefit of any guaranty under title IV of the Housing and Urban Development

Act of 1968, under part B of the Urban Growth and New Community Development Act of 1970, or under section 802 of the Housing and Community Development Act of 1974 as in effect on or after the date of enactment of the Depository Institutions Deregulation and Monetary Control Act of 1980, or of a commitment or agreement therefor.

"(P) STATE HOUSING CORPORATION INVESTMENTS.—Investments in, commitments to invest in, loans to, or commitments to lend to any State housing corporation, provided that such obligations or loans arc secured directly, or indirectly through an agent or fiduciary, by a first lien on improved real estate which is insured under the provisions of the National Housing Act and that in the event of default, the holder of such obligations or loans would have the right directly, or indirectly through an agent or fiduciary, to cause to be subject to the satisfaction of such obligations or loans the real estate described in the first lien or the insurance proceeds under the National Housing Act.

"(Q) INVESTMENT COMPANIES.—An association may invest in, redeem, or hold shares or certificates in any open-end management investment company which is registered with the Securities and Exchange Commission under the Investment Company Act of 1940 and the portfolio of which is restricted by such management company's investment policy, changeable only if authorized by shareholder vote, solely to any such investments as an association by law or regulation may, without limitation as to percentage of assets, invest in, sell, redeem, hold, or otherwise deal with. The Board shall prescribe rules and regulations to implement the provisions of this subparagraph.

"(2) LOANS OR INVESTMENTS LIMITED TO 20 PER CENTUM OF ASSETS.—The following loans or investments are permitted, but authority conferred in the following subparagraphs is limited to not in excess of 20 per centum of the assets of the association for each subparagraph:

"(A) COMMERCIAL REAL ESTATE LOANS.—Loans on security of first liens upon other improved real estate.

"(B) CONSUMER LOANS AND CERTAIN SECURITIES.—An association may make secured or unsecured loans for personal, family, or household purposes, and may invest in, sell, or hold commercial paper and corporate debt securities, as defined and approved by the Board.

"(3) LOANS OR INVESTMENTS LIMITED TO 5 PER CENTUM OF ASSETS.—The following loans or investments are permitted, but the authority conferred in the following subparagraphs is limited to not in excess of 5 per centum of assets of the association for each subparagraph:

"(A) EDUCATION LOANS.—Loans made for the payment of expenses of college, university, or vocational education.

"(B) COMMUNITY DEVELOPMENT INVESTMENTS.—Investments in real property and obligations secured by liens on real property located within a geographic area or neighborhood receiving concentrated development assistance by a local government under title I of the Housing and Community Development Act of 1974, except that no investment under this subparagraph in such real property may exceed an aggregate investment of 2 per centum of the assets of the association.

"(C) NONCONFORMING LOANS.—Loans upon the security of or respecting real property or interests therein used for primarily residential or farm purposes that do not comply with the limitations of this subsection.

"(D) CONSTRUCTION LOANS WITHOUT SECURITY.—Investments not exceeding the greater of (A) the sum of its surplus, undivided profits, and reserves or (B) 5 per centum of the assets of the association, in loans the principal purpose of which is to provide financing with respect to what is or is expected to become primarily residential real estate where (i) the association relies substantially for repayment on the borrower's general credit standing and forecast of income without other security, or (ii) the association relies on other assurances for repayment, including but not limited to a guaranty or similar obligation of a third party. Investments under this subsection shall not be included in any percentage of assets or other percentage referred to in this subsection.

"(4) OTHER LOANS AND INVESTMENTS.—The following additional loans and other investments to the extent authorized below:

"(A) BUSINESS DEVELOPMENT CREDIT CORPORATIONS.—An association whose general reserve, surplus, and undivided profits aggregate a sum in excess of 5 percentum of its withdrawable accounts is authorized to invest in, lend to, or to commit itself to lend to, any business development credit corporation incorporated in the State in which the home office of the association is located in the same manner and to the same extent as savings and loan associations chartered by such State are authorized, but the aggregate amount of such investments, loans, and commitments of any such association shall not exceed one-half of 1 per centum of the total outstanding loans of the association or $250,000, whichever is less.

"(B) SERVICE CORPORATIONS.—Investments in the capital stock, obligations, or other securities of any corporation organized under the laws of the State in which the home office of the association is located, if the entire capital stock of such corporation is available for purchase only by savings and loan associations of such State and by Federal associations having their home offices in such State, but no association may make any investment under this subparagraph if its aggregate outstanding investment under this subparagraph would exceed 3 per centum of the assets of the association, except that not less than one-half of the investment permitted under this subparagraph which exceeds one per centum of assets shall be used primarily for community, inner-city, and community development purposes.

"(C) FOREIGN ASSISTANCE, CERTAIN GUARANTEED LOANS.—(i) Loans secured by mortgages as to which the association has the benefit of insurance under Title X of the National Housing Act or of a commitment or agreement for such insurance.

"(ii) Investments in housing project loans having the benefit of any guaranty under section 221 of the Foreign Assistance Act of 1961 or loans having the benefit of any guaranty under section 224 of such Act, or any commitment or agreement with respect to such loans made pursuant to either of such sections and in the share capital and capital reserve of the Inter-American Savings and Loan Bank. This authority extends to the acquisition, holding, and disposition of loans having the benefit of any guaranty under section 221 or 222 of such Act, or of any commitment or agreement for any such guaranty.

"(iii) Investments under clause (i) of this subparagraph shall not be included in any percentage of assets or other percentage referred to in this subsection. Investments under clause (ii) of this subparagraph shall not exceed, in the case of any association, 1 per centum of the assets of such association.

"(D) STATE AND LOCAL GOVERNMENT OBLIGATIONS.—An association whose general reserves, surplus, and undivided profits aggregate a sum in excess of that amount which is determined by the Board for the purpose of the third sentence of section 403(b) of the National Housing Act is authorized to invest in obligations which constitute prudent investments, as defined by the Board, of its home State and political subdivisions thereof (including any agency, corporation, or instrumentality) if (i) the proceeds of such obligations are to be used for rehabilitation, financing, or the construction of residential real estate, and (ii) the aggregate amount of all investments under this subparagraph shall not exceed the amount of the association's general reserves, surplus, and undivided profits.

"(6) DEFINITIONS.—As used in this subsection—

"(A) the terms 'residential real property' or 'residential real estate' mean leaseholds, homes (including condominiums and cooperatives, except in connection with loans on individual cooperative units, such loans shall be adequately secured as defined by the Board), combinations of homes and business property, other dwelling units, or combinations of dwelling units including homes and business property involving only minor or incidental business use, or property to be improved by construction of such structures;

"(B) the term 'loans' includes obligations and extensions or advances of credit; and any reference to a loan or investment includes an interest in such a loan or investment; and

"(C) the term 'State' means any State of the United States, the District of Columbia, the Commonwealth of Puerto Rico, the Virgin Islands, the Canal Zone, Guam, American Samoa, and any territory or possession of the United States.".

CREDIT CARDS

SEC. 402. Section 5(b) of the Home Owners' Loan Act of 1933 (12 U.S.C. 1464(b)) is amended by adding at the end thereof the following new paragraph:

"(4) An association is authorized, subject to such regulations as the Board may prescribe, to issue credit cards, extend credit in connection therewith, and otherwise engage in or participate in credit card operations.".

TRUST POWERS

SEC. 403. Section 5 of the Home Owners' Loan Act of 1933 (12 U.S.C. 1464) is amended by adding at the end thereof the following new subsection:

"(n)(1) The Board is authorized and empowered to grant by special permit to an association applying therefor, when not in contravention of State or local law, the right to act as trustee, executor, administrator, guardian, or in any other fiduciary capacity in which State banks, trust companies, or other corporations which come into competition with associations are permitted to act under the laws of the State in which the association is located. Subject to the rules and regulations of the Board, service corporations may invest in State or federally-chartered corporations which are located in the State in which the home office of the association is located and which are engaged in trust activities.

"(2) Whenever the laws of such State authorize or permit the exercise of any or all of the foregoing powers by State banks, trust companies, or other corporations which compete with associations, the granting to and the exercise of such powers by associations shall not be deemed to be in contravention of State or local law within the meaning of this section.

"(3) Associations exercising any or all of the powers enumerated in this section shall segregate all assets held in any fiduciary capacity from the general assets of the association and shall keep a separate set of books and records showing in proper detail all transactions engaged in under authority of this section. The State banking authority involved may have access to reports of examination made by the Board insofar as such reports relate to the trust department of such association but nothing in this section shall be construed as authorizing such State banking authority to examine the books, records, and assets of such associations.

"(4) No association shall receive in its trust department deposits of current funds subject to check or the deposit of checks, drafts, bills of exchange, or other items for collection or exchange purposes. Funds deposited or held in trust by the association awaiting investment shall be carried in a separate account and shall not be used by the association in the conduct of its business unless it shall first set aside in the trust department United States bonds or other securities approved by the Board.

"(5) In the event of the failure of such association, the owners of the funds held in trust for investment shall have a lien on the bonds or other securities so set apart in addition to their claim against the estate of the association.

"(6) Whenever the laws of a State require corporations acting in a fiduciary capacity to deposit securities with the State authorities for the protection of private or court trusts, associations so acting shall be required to make similar deposits and securities so deposited shall be held for the protection of private or court trusts, as provided by the State law. Associations in such cases shall not be required to execute the bond usually required of individuals if State corporations under similar circumstances are exempt from this requirement. Associations shall have power to execute such bond when so required by the laws of the State involved.

"(7) In any case in which the laws of a State require that a corporation acting as trustee, executor, administrator, or in any capacity specified in this section, shall take an oath or make an affidavit, the president, vice president, cashier, or trust officer of such association may take the necessary oath or execute the necessary affidavit.

"(8) It shall be unlawful for any association to lend any officer, director, or employee any funds held in trust under the powers conferred by this section. Any officer, director, or employee making such loan, or to whom such loan is made, may be fined not more than $5,000, or imprisoned not more than five years, or may be both fined and imprisoned, in the discretion of the court.

"(9) In passing upon applications for permission to exercise the powers enumerated in this section, the Board may take into consideration the amount of capital and surplus of the applying association, whether or not such capital and surplus is sufficient under the circumstances of the case, the needs of the community to be served, and any other facts and circumstances that seem to it proper, and may grant or refuse the application accordingly, except that no permit shall be issued to any association having a capital and surplus less than the capital and surplus required by State law of State banks, trust companies, and corporations exercising such powers.

"(10)(A) Any association desiring to surrender its right to exercise the powers granted under this section, in order to relieve itself of the necessity of complying with the requirements of this section, or to have returned to it any securities which it may have deposited with the State authorities for the protection of private or court trusts, or for any other purpose, may file with the Board a certified copy of a resolution of its board of directors signifying such desire.

"(B) Upon receipt of such resolution, the Board, after satisfying itself that such association has been relieved in accordance with State law of all duties as trustee, executor, administrator, guardian or other fiduciary, under court, private or other appointments previously accepted under authority of this section, may in its discretion, issue to such association a certificate certifying that such association is no longer authorized to exercise the powers granted by this section.

"(C) Upon the issuance of such a certificate by the Board, such association (i) shall no longer be subject to the provisions of this section or the regulations of the Board made pursuant thereto, (ii) shall be entitled to have returned to it any securities which it may have deposited with the State authorities for the protection of private or court trusts, and (iii) shall not exercise thereafter any of the powers granted by this section without first applying for and obtaining a new permit to exercise such powers pursuant to the provisions of this section.

"(D) The Board is authorized and empowered to promulgate such regulations as it may deem necessary to enforce compliance with the provisions of this subsection and the proper exercise of the trust powers granted by this subsection.

"(11)(A) In addition to the authority conferred by other law, if, in the opinion of the Board, an association is unlawfully or unsoundly exercising, or has unlawfully or unsoundly exercised, or has failed for a period of five consecutive years to exercise, the powers granted by this section or otherwise fails or has failed to comply with the requirements of this subsection, the Board may issue and serve upon the association a notice of intent to revoke the authority of the association to exercise the powers granted by this subsection. The notice shall contain a statement of the facts constituting the alleged unlawful or unsound exercise of powers, or failure to exercise powers, or failure to comply, and shall fix a time and place at which a hearing will be held to determine whether an order revoking authority to exercise such powers should issue against the association.

"(B) Such hearing shall be conducted in accordance with the provisions of subsection (d)(7), and subject to judicial review as therein provided, and shall be fixed for a date not earlier than thirty days and not later than sixty days after service of such notice unless an earlier or later date is set by the Board at the request of any association so served.

"(C) Unless the association so served shall appear at the hearing by a duly authorized representative, it shall be deemed to have consented to the issuance of the revocation order. In the event of such consent, or if upon the record made at any such hearing, the Board shall find that any allegation specified in the notice of charges has been established, the Board may issue and serve upon the association an order prohibiting it from accepting any new or additional trust accounts and revoking authority to exercise any and all powers granted by this subsection, except that such order shall permit the association to continue to service all previously accepted trust accounts pending their expeditious divestiture or termination.

"(D) A revocation order shall become effective not earlier than the expiration of thirty days after service of such order upon the association so served (except in the case of a revocation order issued upon consent, which shall become effective and enforceable, except to such extent as it is stayed, modified, terminated, or set aside by action of the Board or a reviewing court.".

CONVERSIONS

SEC. 404. The first sentence of section 5(i) of the Home Owners' Loan Act of 1933 (12 U.S.C. 1464(i))is amended by inserting ", and any State stock savings and loan type institution may (if such institution existed in stock form for a least the 4 years preceding the date of enactment of the Depository Institutions Deregulation and Monetary Control Act of 1980) convert its charter to a Federal stock charter under this Act," after "Federal savings and loan association under this Act".

LIQUIDITY REQUIREMENTS

SEC. 405. Section 5A(b) of the Federal Home Loan Bank Act (12 U.S.C. 1425a(b)) is amended to read as follows:

"(b)(1) Any institution which is a member or which is an insured institution as defined in section 401(a) of the National Housing Act shall maintain the aggregate amount of its assets of the following types at not less than such amount as, in the opinion of the Board, is appropriate:

"(A) cash;

"(B) to such extent as the Board may approve for the purposes of this section, time and savings deposits in Federal Home Loan Banks and commercial banks;

"(C) to such extent as the Board may so approve, such obligations, including such special obligations, of the United States, a State, any territory or possession of the United States, or a political subdivision, agency or instrumentality of any one or more of the foregoing, and bankers' acceptances, as the Board may approve; and

"(D) to such extent as the Board may so approve, shares or certificates of any open-end management investment company which is registered with the Securities and Exchange Commission under the Investment Company Act of 1940 and the portfolio of which is restricted by such investment company's investment policy, changeable only if authorized by shareholder vote, solely to any of the obligations or other investments enumerated in subparagraphs (A) through (C).

"(2) The requirement prescribed by the Board pursuant to this subsection (hereinafter in this section referred to as the 'liquidity requirement') may not be less than 5 per centum or more than 10 per centum of the obligation of the institution on withdrawable accounts and borrowings payable on demand or with unexpired maturities of one year or less, or in the case of institutions which are insurance companies, such other base or bases as the Board may determine to be comparable. The Board shall prescribe rules and regulations to implement the provisions of this subsection.".

STUDY OF MORTGAGE PORTFOLIOS

SEC. 406. (a)(1) The President shall convene an interagency task force consisting of the Secretary of the Treasury, the Secretary of Housing and Urban Development, the Federal Home Loan Bank Board, the Board of Governors of the Federal Reserve System, the Board of Directors of the Federal Deposit Insurance Corporation, the Comptroller of the Currency, and the National Credit Union Administration Board. The task force shall conduct a study and make recommendations regarding—

(A) the options available to provide balance to the asset-liability management problems inherent in the thrift portfolio structure;

(B) the options available to increase the ability of thrift institutions to pay market rates of interest in period of rapid inflation and high interest rates; and

(C) the options available through the Federal Home Loan Bank system and other Federal agencies to assist thrifts in times of economic difficulties.

(2) In carrying out such study, the task force shall solicit the views of, and invite participation by, consumer and public interest groups, business, labor, and State regulators of depository institutions.

(b) Not later than three months after the date of enactment of this Act, the task force shall transmit to the President and the Congress its findings and recommendations for such action as it deems appropriate.

MUTUAL CAPITAL CERTIFICATES

SEC. 407. (a) Section 5(b) of the Home Owners' Loan Act of 1933 (12 U.S.C. 1464(b)) is amended by adding at the end thereof the following:

"(5)(A) In accordance with rules and regulations issued by the Board, mutual capital certificates may be issued and sold directly to subscribers or through underwriters, and such certificates shall constitute part of the general reserve and net worth of the issuing association. The Board, in its rules and regulations relating to the issuance and sale of mutual capital certificates, shall provide that such certificates—

"(i) shall be subordinate to all savings accounts, savings certificates, and debt obligations;

"(ii) shall constitute a claim in liquidation on the general reserves, surplus, and undivided profits of the association remaining after the payment in full of all savings accounts, savings certificates, and debt obligations;

"(iii) shall be entitled to the payment of dividends; and

"(iv) may have a fixed or variable dividend rate.

"(B) The Board shall provide in its rules and regulations for charging losses to the mutual capital certificate, reserves, and other net worth accounts.".

(b) Section 403(b) of the National Housing Act (12 U.S.C. 1726(b)), is amended by adding at the end thereof the following: "Mutual capital certificates, subordinate to the rights of holders of savings accounts, savings certificates, and the Corporation, shall be deemed to be reserves for the purposes of this subsection in accordance with rules and regulations prescribed by the Corporation. The Corporation shall provide in its rules and regulations for charging losses to the mutual capital certificate, reserves, and other net worth accounts. In the event an insured institution fails to maintain the reserves required by this title, no payment of dividends on such certificates shall be made except with the approval of the Corporation.".

MUTUAL SAVINGS BANKS

SEC. 408. (a) Section 5(a) of the Home Owners' Loan Act of 1933 (12 U.S.C. 1464(a))is amended—

(1) by inserting "(1)" after "(a)";

(2) in the fourth and fifth sentences by striking out "(1)" and "(2)" each place they appear therein and inserting in lieu thereof "(A)" and "(B)", respectively; and

(3) by adding at the end thereof the following new paragraph:

"(2) A Federal mutual savings bank may make commercial, corporate, and business loans except that—

"(A) not more than 5 per centum of the assets of such a bank may be so loaned; and

"(B) such loans may only be made within the State where the bank is located or within 75 miles of the bank's home office.".

(b) Section 5(a) of the Home Owners' Loan Act of 1933 (12 U.S.C. 1464(a)) is amended by adding at the end thereof the following new paragraph:

"(3) In addition to the authority conferred by paragraph (1), Federal mutual savings bank may accept demand deposits in connection with a commercial, corporate, or business loan relationship.".

INSURANCE RESERVES

SEC. 409. The third sentence of section 403(b) of the National Housing Act (12 U.S.C. 1726(b)) is amended by striking out "5 per centum" and inserting in lieu thereof "an amount no greater than 6 per centum nor less than 3 per centum as determined by the Federal Home Loan Bank Board".

TITLE V—STATE USURY LAWS

Part A—Mortgage Usury Laws

MORTGAGES

SEC. 501. (a)(1) The provisions of the constitution or the laws of any State expressly limiting the rate or amount of interest, discount points, finance charges, or other charges which may be charged, taken, received, or reserved shall not apply to any loan, mortgage, credit sale, or advance which is—

(A) secured by a first lien on residential real property, by a first lien on stock in a residential cooperative housing corporation where the loan, mortgage, or advance is used to finance the acquisition of such stock, or by a first lien on a residential manufactured home;

(B) made after March 31, 1980; and

(C) described in section 527(b) of the National Housing Act (12 U.S.C. 1735f-5(b)), except that for the purpose of this section—

(i) the limitation described in section 527(b)(1) of such Act that the property must be designed principally for the occupancy of from one to four families shall not apply;

(ii) the requirement contained in section 527(b)(1) of such Act that the loan be secured by residential real property shall not apply to a loan secured by stock in a residential cooperative housing corporation or to a loan or credit sale secured by a first lien on a residential manufactured home;

(iii) the term "federally related mortgage loan" in section 527(b) of such Act shall include a credit sale which is secured by a first lien on a residential manufactured home and which otherwise meets the definitional requirements of section 527(b) of such Act, as those requirements are modified by this section:

(iv) the term "residential loans" in section 527(b)(2)(D) of such Act shall also include loans or credit sales secured by a first lien on a residential manufactured home;

(v) the requirement contained in section 527(b)(2)(D) of such Act that a creditor make or invest in loans aggregating more than $1,000,000 per year shall not apply to a creditor selling residential manufactured homes financed by loans or credit sales secured by first liens on residential manufactured homes if the creditor has an arrangement to sell such loans or credit sales in whole or in part, or if such loans or credit sales are sold in whole or in part to a lender, institution, or creditor described in section 527(b) of such Act or in this section or a creditor, as defined in section 103(f) of the Truth in Lending Act, as such section was in effect on the day preceding the date of enactment of this title, if such creditor makes or invests in residential real estate loans or loans or credit sales secured by first liens on residential manufactured homes aggregating more than $100,000 per year; and

(vi) the term "lender" in section 527(b)(2)(A) of such Act shall also be deemed to include any lender approved by the Secretary of Housing and Urban Development for participation in any mortgage insurance program under the National Housing Act.

(2)(A) The provisions of the constitution or law of any State expressly limiting the rate or amount of interest which may be charged, taken, received, or reserved shall not apply to any deposit or account held by, or other obligation of a depository institution. For purposes of this paragraph, the term "depository institution" means—

(i) any insured bank as defined in section 3 of the Federal Deposit Insurance Act (12 U.S.C. 1813);

(ii) any mutual savings bank as defined in section 3 of the Federal Deposit Insurance Act (12 U.S.C. 1813);

(iii) any savings bank as defined in section 3 of the Federal Deposit Insurance Act (12 U.S.C. 1813);

(iv) any insured credit union as defined in section 101 of the Federal Credit Union Act (12 U.S.C. 1752);

(v) any member as defined in section 2 of the Federal Home Loan Bank Act (12 U.S.C. 1422); and

(vi) any insured institution as defined in section 408 of the National Housing Act (12 U.S.C. 1730a).

(B) This paragraph shall not apply to any such deposit, account, or obligation which is payable only at an office of an insured bank, as defined in section 3 of the Federal Deposit Insurance Act, located in the Commonwealth of Puerto Rico.

(b)(1) Except as provided in paragraphs (2) and (3), the provisions of subsection (a)(1) shall apply to any loan, mortgage, credit sale, or advance made in any State on or after April 1, 1980.

(2) Except as provided in paragraph (3), the provisions of subsection (a)(1) shall not apply to any loan, mortgage, credit sale, or advance made in any State after the date (on or after April 1, 1980, and before April 1, 1983) on which such State adopts a law or certifies that the voters of such State have voted in favor of any provision, constitutional or otherwise, which states explicitly and by its terms that such States does not want the provisions of subsection (a)(1) to apply with respect to loans, mortgages, credit sales, and advances made in such State.

(3) In any case in which a State takes an action described in paragraph (2), the provisions of subsection (a)(1) shall continue to apply to—

(A) any loan, mortgage, credit sale, or advance which is made after the date such action was taken pursuant to a commitment therefor which was entered during the period beginning on April 1, 1980, and ending on the date on which such State takes such action; and

(B) any loan, mortgage, or advance which is a rollover of a loan, mortgage, or advance, as described in regulations of the Federal Home Loan Bank Board, which was made or committed to be made during the period beginning on April 1, 1980, and ending on the date on which such State takes any action described in paragraph (2).

(4) At any time after the date of enactment of this Act, any State may adopt a provision of law placing limitations on discount points or such other changes on any loan, mortgage, credit sale, or advance described in subsection (a)(1).

(c) The provisions of subsection (a)(1) shall not apply to a loan, mortgage, credit sale, or advance which is secured by a first lien on a residential manufactured home unless the terms of the conditions relating to such loan, mortgage, credit sale, or advance comply with consumer protection provisions specified in regulations prescribed by the Federal Home Loan Bank Board. Such regulations shall—

(1) include consumer protection provisions with respect to balloon payments, prepayment penalities, late charges, and deferral fees;

(2) require a 30-day notice prior to instituting any action leading to repossession or foreclosure (except in the case of abandonment or other extreme circumstances);

(3) require that upon prepayment in full, the debtor shall be entitled to a refund of the unearned portion of the precomputed finance charge in an amount not less than the amount which would be calculated by the actuarial method, except that the debtor shall not be entitled to a refund which is less than $1; and

(4) include such other provisions as the Federal Home Loan Bank Board may prescribe after a finding that additional protections are required.

(d) The provisions of subsection (c) shall not apply to a loan, mortgage, credit sale, or advance secured by a first lien on a residential manufactured home until regulations required to be issued pursuant to paragraphs (1), (2), and (3) of subsection (c) take effect, except that the provisions of subsection (c) shall apply in the case of such a loan, mortgage, credit sale, or advance made prior to the date on which such regulations take effect if the loan, mortgage, credit sale, or advance includes a precomputed finance charge and does not provide that, upon prepayment in full, the refund of the unearned portion of the precomputed finance charge is in an amount not less the amount which would be calculated by the actuarial method, except that the debtor shall not be entitled to a refund which is less than $1. The Federal Home Loan Bank Board shall issue regulations pursuant to the provisions of paragraphs (1), (2), and (3) of subsection (c) that shall take effect prospectively not less than 30 days after publication in the Federal Register and not later than 120 days from the date of enactment of this Act.

(e) For the purpose of this section—

(1) a "prepayment" occurs upon—

(A) the refinancing or consolidation of the indebtedness;

(B) the actual prepayment of the indebtedness by the consumer whether voluntarily or following acceleration of the payment obligation by the creditor; or

(C) the entry of a judgment for the indebtedness in favor of the creditor;

(2) the term "actuarial method" means the method of allocating payments made on a debt between the outstanding balance of the obligation and the precomputed finance charge pursuant to which a payment is applied first to thc accrued precomputed finance charge and any remainder is subtracted from, or any deficiency is added to, the outstanding balance of the obligation;

(3) the term "precomputed finance charge" means interest or a time price differential within the meaning of sections 106(a) (1) and (2) of the Truth in Lending Act (15 U.S.C. 1605(a) (1) and (2)) as computed by an add-in or discount method; and

(4) the term "residential manufactured home" means a mobile home as defined in section 603(6) of the National Mobile Home Construction and Safety Standards Act of 1974 which is used as a residence.

(f) The Federal Home Loan Bank Board is authorized to issue rules and regulations and to publish interpretations governing the implementation of this section.

(g) This section takes effect on April 1, 1980.

Part B—Business and Agricultural Loans

BUSINESS AND AGRICULTURAL LOANS

SEC. 511. (a) If the applicable rate prescribed in this section exceeds the rate a person would be permitted to charge in the absence of this section, such person may in the case of a business or agricultural loan in the amount of $25,000 or more, notwithstanding any State constitution or statute which is hereby preempted for the purposes of this section, take, receive, reserve, and charge on any such loan, interest at a rate of not more than 5 per centum in excess of the discount rate, including any surcharge thereon, on ninety-day commercial paper in effect at the Federal Reserve bank in the Federal Reserve district where the person is located.

(b) If the rate prescribed in subsection (a) exceeds the rate such person would be permitted to charge in the absence of this section, and such State imposed rate is thereby preempted by the rate described in subsection (a), the taking, receiving, reserving, or charging a greater rate than is allowed by subsection (a), when knowingly done, shall be deemed a forfeiture of the entire interest which the loan carries with it, or which has been agreed to be paid thereon. If such greater rate of interest has been paid, the person who paid it may recover, in a civil action commenced in a court of appropriate jurisdiction not later than two years after the date of such payment, an amount equal to twice the amount of interest paid from the person taking, receiving, reserving, or charging such interest.

EFFECTIVE DATE OF PART B

SEC. 512. The provisions of this part shall apply only with respect to business or agricultural loans in amounts of $25,000 or more made in any State during the period beginning on April 1, 1980, and ending on the earlier of—

>   (1) April 1, 1983; or
>   (2) the date, on or after April 1, 1980, on which such State adopts a law or certifies that the voters of such State have voted in favor of any provision, constitutional or otherwise, which states explicitly and by its terms that such State does not want the provisions of this part to apply with respect to loans made in such State,

except that such provisions shall apply to any loan made on or after such earlier date pursuant to a commitment to make such loan which was entered into on or after April 1, 1980, and prior to such earlier date.

Part C—Other Loans

INSURED BANKS

SEC. 521. The Federal Deposit Insurance Act (12 U.S.C. 1811 et seq.) is amended by adding at the end thereof the following new section:

"SEC. 27. (a) In order to prevent discrimination against State-chartered insured banks, including insured savings banks and insured mutual savings banks, or insured branches of foreign banks with respect to interest rates, if the applicable rate prescribed in this subsection exceeds the rate such State bank or insured branch of a foreign bank would be permitted to charge in the absence of this subsection, such State bank or such insured branch of a foreign bank may, not withstanding any State constitution or statute which is hereby preempted for the purposes of this section, take, receive, reserve, and charge on any loan or discount made, or upon any note, bill of exchange, or other evidence of debt, interest at a rate of not more than 1 per centum in excess of the discount rate on ninety-day commercial paper in effect at the Federal Reserve bank in the Federal Reserve district where such State bank or such insured branch of a foreign bank is located or at the rate allowed by the laws of the State, territory, or district where the bank is located, whichever may be greater.

"(b) If the rate prescribed in subsection (a) exceeds the rate such State bank or such insured branch of a foreign bank would be permitted to charge in the absence of this section, and such State fixed rate is thereby preempted by the rate described in subsection (a), the taking, receiving, reserving, or charging a greater rate of interest than is allowed by subsection (a), when knowingly done, shall be deemed a forfeiture of the entire interest which the note, bill, or other evidence of debt carries with it, or which has been agreed to be paid thereon. If such greater rate of interest has been paid, the person who paid it may recover in a civil action commenced in a court of appropriate jurisdiction not later than two years after the date of such payment, an amount equal to twice the amount of the interest paid from such State bank or such insured branch of a foreign bank taking, receiving, reserving, or charging such interest.".

INSURED SAVINGS AND LOAN ASSOCIATIONS

SEC. 522. Title IV of the National Housing Act (12 U.S.C. 1724 et seq.) is amended by adding at the end thereof the following new section:

"SEC. 414. (a) If the applicable rate prescribed in this section exceeds the rate an insured institution would be permitted to charge in the absence of this section, such institution may, notwithstanding any State constitution or statute which is hereby preempted for the purposes of this section, take, receive, reserve, and charge on any loan or discount made, or upon any note, bill of exchange, or other evidence of debt, interest at a rate of not more than 1 per centum in excess of the discount rate on ninety-day commercial paper in effect at the Federal Reserve bank in the Federal Reserve district where such institution is located or at the rate allowed by the laws of the State, territory, or district where such institution is located, whichever may be greater.

"(b) If the rate prescribed in subsection (a) exceeds the rate such institution would be permitted to charge in the absence of this section, and such State fixed rate is hereby preempted by the rate described in subsection (a), the taking, receiving, reserving, or charging a greater rate of interest than that prescribed by subsection (a), when knowingly done, shall be deemed a forfeiture of the entire interest which the note, bill, or other evidence of debt carries with it, or which has been agreed to be paid thereon. If such greater rate of interest has been paid, the person who paid it may recover, in a civil action commenced in a court of appropriate jurisdiction not later than two years after the date of such payment, an amount equal to twice the amount of the interest paid from the institution taking or receiving such interest."

INSURED CREDIT UNIONS

SEC. 523. Section 205 of the Federal Credit Union Act (12 U.S.C. 1785) is amended by adding at the end thereof the following new subsection:

"(g)(1) If the applicable rate prescribed in this subsection exceeds the rate an insured credit union would be permitted to charge in the absence of this subsection, such credit union may, notwithstanding any State constitution or statute which is hereby preempted for the purposes of this subsection, take, receive, reserve, and charge on any loan, interest at a rate of not more than 1 per centum in excess of the discount rate on ninety-day commercial paper in effect at the Federal Reserve bank in the Federal Reserve district where such insured credit union is located or at the rate allowed by the laws of the State, territory, or district where such credit union is located, whichever may be greater.

"(2) If the rate prescribed in paragraph (1) exceeds the rate such credit union would be permitted to charge in the absence of this subsection, and such State fixed rate is thereby preempted by the rate described in paragraph (1), the taking, receiving, reserving, or charging a greater rate than is allowed by paragraph (1), when knowingly done, shall be deemed a forfeiture of the entire interest which the loan carries with it, or which has been agreed to be paid thereon. If such greater rate of interest has been paid, the person who paid it may recover, in a civil action commenced in a court of appropriate jurisdiction not later than two years after the date of such payment, an amount equal to twice the amount of interest paid from the credit union taking or receiving such interest.".

SMALL BUSINESS INVESTMENT COMPANIES

SEC. 524. Section 308 of the Small Business Investment Act of 1958 (15 U.S.C. 687) is amended by adding at the end thereof the following new subsection:

"(i)(1) The purpose of this subsection is to facilitate the orderly and necessary flow of long-term loans and equity funds from small business investment companies to small business concerns.

"(2) In the case of a business loan, the small business investment company making such loan may charge interest on such loan at a rate which does not exceed the lowest of the rates described in subparagraphs (A), (B), and (C).

"(A) The rate described in this subparagraph is the maximum rate prescribed by regulation by the Small Business Administration for loans made by any small business investment company determined without regard to any State rate incorporated by such regulation).

"(B) The rate described in this subparagraph is the maximum rate authorized by an applicable State law or constitutional provision which is not preempted for purposes of this subsection.

"(C)(i) The rate described in this subparagraph is the higher of the Federal Reserve rate or the maximum rate authorized by applicable State law or constitutional provision (determined without regard to the preemption of such State law or constitutional provision).

(ii) For purposes of clause (i), the term 'Federal Reserve rate' means the rate equal to the sum of 1 percentage point plus the discount rate on ninety-day commercial paper in effect at the Federal Reserve bank in the Federal Reserve district in which the principal office of the small business investment company is located.

"(iii) The rate described in this subparagraph shall not apply to loans made in a State if there is no maximum rate authorized by applicable State law or constitutional provision for such loans or there is a maximum rate authorized by an applicable State law or constitutional provision which is not preempted for purposes of this subsection.

"(3) A State law or constitutional provision shall be preempted for purposes of paragraph (2)(B) with respect to any loan if such loan is made before the date, on or after April 1, 1980, on which such State adopts a law or certifies that the voters of such State have voted in favor of any provision, constitutional or otherwise, which states explicitly and by its terms that such State does not want the provisions of this subsection to apply with respect to loans made in such State, except that such State law or constitutional or other provision shall be preempted in the case of a loan made, on or after the date on which such law is adopted or such certification is made, pursuant to a commiment to make such loan which was entered into on or after April 1, 1980, and prior to the date on which such law is adopted or such certification is made.

"(4)(A) If the maximum rate of interest authorized under paragraph (2) on any loan made by a small business investment company exceeds the rate which would be authorized by applicable State law if such State law were not preempted for purposes of this subsection, the charging of interest at any rate in excess of the rate authorized by paragraph (2) shall be deemed a forfeiture of the greater of (i) all interest which the loan carries with it, or (ii) all interest which has been agreed to be paid thereon.

"(B) In the case of any loan with respect to which there is a forfeiture of interest under subparagraph (A), the person who paid the interest may recover from a small business investment company making such loan an amount equal to twice the amount of the interest paid on such loan. Such interest may be recovered in a civil action commenced in a court of appropriate jurisdiction no later than two years after the most recent payment of interest.".

EFFECTIVE DATE

SEC. 525. The amendments made by sections 521 through 523 of this title shall apply only with respect to loans made in any State during the period beginning on April 1, 1980, and ending on the date, on or after April 1, 1980, on which such State adopts a law or certifies that the voters of such State have voted in favor of any provision, constitutional or otherwise, which states explicitly and by its terms that such State does not want the amendments made by such sections to apply with respect to loans made in such State, except that such amendments shall apply to a loan made on or after the date such law is adopted or such certification is made if such loan is made pursuant to a commitment to make such loan which was entered into on or after April 1, 1980, and prior to the date on which such law is adopted or such certification is made.

SEVERABILITY

SEC. 526. If any provision of this Act or the application of such provision to any person or circumstance shall be held invalid, the remainder of this Act and the application of such provision to any person or circumstance other than that as to which it is held invalid shall not be affected thereby.

DEFINITION

SEC. 527. For purposes of this title, the term "State" includes the several States, the Commonwealth of Puerto Rico, the District of Columbia, Guam, the Trust Territories of the Pacific Islands, the Northern Mariana Islands, and the Virgin Islands, except as provided in section 501(a)(2)(B).

EFFECT ON OTHER LAW

SEC. 528. In any case in which one or more provisions of, or amendments made by, this title, section 529 of the National Housing Act, or any other provision of law, including section 5197 of the Revised Statutes (12 U.S.C. 85), apply with respect to the same loan, mortgage, credit sale, or advance, such loan, mortgage, credit sale, or advance may be made at the highest applicable rate.

REPEAL OF EXISTING LAW

SEC. 529. Effective at the close of March 31, 1980, Public Law 96–104, section 105(a)(2) of Public Law 96–161, and the amendments made by and the provisions of title II of Public Law 96–161 are hereby repealed, except that the provisions of such Public Law, the provisions of such section, the amendments made by such title, and the provisions of such title shall continue to apply to any loan made, any deposit made, or any obligation issued in any State during any period when those provisions or amendments were in effect in such State.

TITLE VI—TRUTH IN LENDING SIMPLIFICATION

SHORT TITLE

SEC. 601. This title may be cited as the "Truth in Lending Simplification and Reform Act".

DEFINITIONS

SEC. 602. (a) Section 103(f) of the Truth in Lending Act (15 U.S.C. 1602(f)) is amended—

(1) by striking out the first sentence and inserting in lieu thereof the following: "The term 'creditor' refers only to a person who both (1) regularly extends, whether in connection with loans, sales of property

or services, or otherwise, consumer credit which is payable by agreement in more than four installments or for which the payment of a finance charge is or may be required; and (2) is the person to whom the debt arising from the consumer credit transaction is initially payable on the face of the evidence of indebtedness or, if there is no such evidence of indebtedness, by agreement. Notwithstanding the previous sentence, a person who regularly arranges for the extension of consumer credit, which is payable in more than four installments or for which the payment of a finance charge is or may be required, from persons who are not creditors is a creditor, and in the case of an open end credit plan involving a credit card, the card issuer and any person who honors the credit card and offers a discount which is a finance charge are creditors."; and

(2) by redesignating the references to sections 127(a)(6), 127(a)(7), 127(a)(8), 127(b)(9), and 127(b)(11) in the next succeeding sentence as references to sections 127(a)(5), 127(a)(6), 127(a)(7), 127(b)(8), and 127(b)(10), respectively.

(b) The first sentence of section 103(g) of the Truth in Lending Act (15 U.S.C. 1602(g)) is amended to read as follows: "The term 'credit sale' refers to any sale in which the seller is a creditor.".

EXEMPTED TRANSACTIONS

SEC. 603. (a) Section 103(h) of the Truth in Lending Act (15 U.S.C. 1602(h)) is amended by striking out "household, or agricultural" and inserting in lieu thereof "or household".

(b) Section 103 of the Truth in Lending Act (15 U.S.C. 1602) is amended by redesignating subsections (s) and (t) as subsections (x) and (y), respectively, and by inserting after subsection (r) the following new subsections:

"(s) The term 'agricultural purposes' includes the production, harvest, exhibition, marketing, transportation, processing, or manufacture of agricultural products by a natural person who cultivates, plants, propagates, or nurtures those agricultural products, including but not limited to the acquisition of farmland, real property with a farm residence, and personal property and services used primarily in farming.

"(t) The term 'agricultural products' includes agricultural, horticultural, viticultural, and dairy products, livestock, wildlife, poultry, bees, forest products, fish and shellfish, and any products thereof, including processed and manufactured products, and any and all products raised or produced on farms and any processed or manufactured products thereof."

(c) Section 104 of the Truth in Lending Act (15 U.S.C. 1603) is amended—

(1) by amending paragraph (1) to read as follows:

"(1) Credit transactions involving extensions of credit primarily for business, commercial, or agricultural purposes, or to government or governmental agencies or instrumentalities, or to organizations.";

(2) by amending paragraph (3) to read as follows:

"(3) Credit transactions, other than those in which a security interest is or will be acquired in real property, or in personal property used or expected to be used as the principal dwelling of the consumer, in which the total amount financed exceeds $25,000."; and

(3) by striking out paragraph (5).

OPEN END CREDIT PLAN

SEC. 604. Section 103(i) of the Truth in Lending Act (15 U.S.C. 1602(i)) is amended to read as follows:

"(i) The term 'open end credit plan' means a plan under which the creditor reasonably contemplates repeated transactions, which prescribes the terms of such transactions, and which provides for a finance charge which may be computed from time to time on the outstanding unpaid balance. A credit plan which is an open end credit plan within the meaning of the preceding sentence is an open end credit plan even if credit information is verified from time to time.".

MODEL FORMS

SEC. 605. Section 105 of the Truth in Lending Act (15 U.S.C. 1605) is amended by inserting "(a)" before "The", and by adding at the end thereof the following:

"(b) The Board shall publish model disclosure forms and clauses for common transactions to facilitate compliance with the disclosure requirements of this title and to aid the borrower or lessee in understanding the transaction by utilizing readily understandable language to simplify the technical nature of the disclosures. In devising such forms, the Board shall consider the use by creditors or lessors of data processing or similar automated equipment. Nothing in this title may be construed to require a creditor or lessor to use any such model form or cause prescribed by the Board under this section. A creditor or lessor shall be deemed to be in compliance with the disclosure provisions of this title with respect to other than numerical disclosures if the creditor or lessor (1) uses any appropriate model form or clause as published by the Board, or (2) uses any such model form or clause and changes it by (A) deleting any information which is not required by this title, or (B) rearranging the format, if in making such deletion or rearranging the format, the creditor or lessor does not affect the substance, clarity, or meaningful sequence of the disclosure.

"(c) Model disclosure forms and clauses shall be adopted by the Board after notice duly given in the Federal Register and an opportunity for public comment in accordance with section 553 of title 5, United States Code.

"(d) Any regulation of the Board, or any amendment or inerpretation thereof, requiring any disclosure which differs from the disclosures previously required by this chapter, chapter 4, or chapter 5, or by any regulation of the Board promulgated thereunder shall have an effective date of that October 1 which follows by at least six months the date of promulgation, except that the Board may at its discretion take interim action by regulation, amendment, or inerpretation to lengthen the period of time permitted for creditors or lessors to adjust their forms to accommodate new requirements or shorten the length of time for creditors or lessors to make such adjustments when it makes a specific finding that such action is necessary to comply with the findings of a court or to prevent unfair or deceptive disclosure practices. Notwithstanding the previous sentence, any creditor or lessor may comply with any such newly promulgated disclosure requirements prior to the effective date of the requirements.".".

COMPONENTS OF FINANCE CHARGE

SEC. 606. (a) Section 106(a) of the Truth in Lending Act (15 U.S.C. 1605(a)) is amended by striking out ", including any of the following types of charges which are applicable" and inserting in lieu thereof the following: ". The finance charge does not include charges of a type payable in a comparable cash transaction. Examples of charges which are included in the finance charge include any of the following types of charges which are applicable".

(b) Section 106(d) of the Truth in Lending Act (15 U.S.C. 1605(d)) is amended by striking out paragraphs (3) and (4).

ACCURACY OF ANNUAL PERCENTAGE RATE

SEC. 607. (a) Section 107(c) of the Truth in Lending Act (15 U.S.C. 1606(c)) is amended to read as follows:

"(c) The disclosure of an annual percentage rate is accurate for the purpose of this title if the rate disclosed is within a tolerance not greater than one-eighth of 1 per centum more or less than the actual rate or rounded to the nearest one-fourth of 1 per centum. The Board may allow a greater tolerance to simplify compliance where irregular payments are involved.".

(b) Section 107(e) of the Truth in Lending Act (15 U.S.C. 1606(e)) is amended by striking out "(c) or".

(c) Section 107(f) of the Truth in Lending Act (15 U.S.C. 1606(f)) is hereby repealed.

RESTITUTION

SEC. 608. (a) Section 108 of the Truth in Lending Act (15 U.S.C. 1607) is amended by adding at the end thereof the following:

"(e)(1) In carrying out its enforcement activities under this section, each agency referred to in subsection (a) or (c), in cases where an annual percentage rate or finance charge was inaccurately disclosed, shall notify the creditor of such disclosure error and is authorized in accordance with the provisions of this subsection to require the creditor to make an adjustment to the account of the person to whom credit was extended, to assure that such person will not be required to pay a finance charge in excess of the finance charge actually disclosed or the dollar equivalent of the annual percentage rate actually disclosed, whichever is lower. For the purposes of this subsection, except where such disclosure error resulted from a willful violation which was intended to mislead the person to whom credit was extended, in determining whether a disclosure error has occurred and in calculating any adjustment, (A) each agency shall apply (i) with respect to the annual percentage rate, a tolerance of one-quarter of 1 percent more or less than the actual rate, determined without regard to section 107(c) of this title, except in the case of an irregular mortgage lending transaction, and (ii) with respect to the finance charge, a corresponding numerical tolerance as generated by the tolerance provided under this subsection for the annual percentage rate; except that (B) with respect to transactions consummated after two years following the effective date of section 608 of the Truth in Lending Simplification and Reform Act, each agency shall apply (i) for transactions that have a scheduled amortization of ten years or less, with respect to the annual percentage rate, a tolerance not to exceed one-quarter of 1 percent more or less than the actual rate, determined without regard to section 107(c) of this title, but in no event a tolerance of less than the tolerances allowed under section 107(c), (ii) for transactions that have a scheduled amortization of more than ten years, with respect to the annual percentage rate, only such tolerances as are allowed under section 107(c) of this title, and (iii) for all transactions, with respect to the finance charge, a corresponding numerical tolerance as generated by the tolerances provided under this subsection for the annual percentage rate.

"(2) Each agency shall require such an adjustment when it determines that such disclosure error resulted from (A) a clear and consistent pattern or practice of violations, (B) gross negligence, or (C) a willful violation which was intended to mislead the person to whom the credit was extended. Notwithstanding the preceding sentence, except where such disclosure error resulted from a willful violation which was intended to mislead the person to whom credit was extended, an agency need not require such an adjustment if it determines that such disclosure error—

"(A) resulted from an error involving the disclosure of a fee or charge that would otherwise be excludable in computing the finance charge, including but not limited to violations involving the disclosures described in sections 106(b), (c) and (d) of this title, in which event the agency may require such remedial action as it determines to be equitable, except that for transactions consummated after two years after the effective date of section 608 of the Truth in Lending Simplification and Reform Act, such an adjustment shall be ordered for violations of section 106(b);

"(B) involved a disclosed amount which was 10 per centum or less of the amount that should have been disclosed and (i) in cases where the error involved a disclosed finance charge, the annual percentage rate was disclosed correctly, and (ii) in cases where the error involved a disclosed annual percentage rate, the finance charge was disclosed correctly; in which event the agency may require such adjustment as it determines to be equitable;

"(C) involved a total failure to disclose either the annual percentage rate or the finance charge, in which event the agency may require such adjustment as it determines to be equitable; or

"(D) resulted from any other unique circumstance involving clearly technical and nonsubstantive disclosure violations that do not adversely affect information provided to the consumer and that have not misled or otherwise deceived the consumer.

In the case of other such disclosure errors, each agency may require such an adjustment.

"(3) Notwithstanding paragraph (2), no adjustment shall be ordered (A) if it would have a significantly adverse impact upon the safety or soundness of the creditor, but in any such case, the agency may require a partial adjustment in an amount which does not have such an impact, except that with respect to any transaction consummated after the effective date of section 608 of the Truth in Lending Simplification and Reform Act, the agency shall require the full adjustment, but permit the creditor to make the required adjustment in partial payments over an extended period of time which the agency considers to be reasonable, (B) if the amount of the adjustment would be less than $1, except that if more than one year has elapsed since the date of the violation, the agency may require that such amount be paid into the Treasury of the United States, or (C) except where such disclosure error resulted from a willful violation which was intended to mislead the person to whom credit was extended, in the case of an open-end credit plan, more than two years after the violation, or in the case of any other extension of credit, as follows:

"(i) with respect to creditors that are subject to examination by the agencies referred to in paragraphs (1) through (3) of section 108(a) of this title, except in connection with violations arising from practices identified in the current examination and only in connection with transactions that are consummated after the date of the immediately preceding examination, except that where practices giving rise to violations identified in earlier examinations have not been corrected, adjustments for those violations shall be required in connection with transactions consummated after the date of the examination in which such practices were first identified;

"(ii) with respect to creditors that are not subject to examination by such agencies, except in connection with transactions that are consummated after May 10, 1978; and

"(iii) in no event after the later of (I) the expiration of the life of the credit extension, or (II) two years after the agreement to extend credit was consummated.

"(4)(A) Notwithstanding any other provision of this section, an adjustment under this subsection may be required by an agency referred to in subsection (a) or (c) only by an order issued in accordance with cease and desist procedures provided by the provision of law referred to in such subsections.

"(B) In the case of an agency which is not authorized to conduct cease and desist proceedings, such an order may be issued after an agency hearing on the record conducted at least thirty but not more than sixty days after notice of the alleged violation is served on the creditor. Such a hearing shall be deemed to be a hearing which is subject to the provisions of section 8(h) of the Federal Deposit Insurance Act and shall be subject to judicial review as provided therein.

"(5) Except as otherwise specifically provided in this subsection and notwithstanding any provision of law referred to in subsection (a) or (c), no agency referred to in subsection (a) or (c) may require a creditor to make dollar adjustments for errors in any requirements under this title, except with regard to the requirements of section 165.

"(6) A creditor shall not be subject to an order to make an adjustment, if within sixty days after discovering a disclosure error, whether pursuant to a final written examination report or through the creditor's own procedures, the creditor notifies the person concerned of the error and adjusts the account so as to assure that such person will not be required to pay a finance charge in excess of the finance charge actually disclosed or the dollar equivalent of the annual percentage rate actually disclosed, whichever is lower.

"(7) Nothwithstanding the second sentence of subsection (e)(1), subsection (a)(3)(C)(i), and subsection (e)(3)(C)(ii), each agency referred to in subsection (a) or (c) shall require an adjustment for an annual percentage rate disclosure error that exceeds a tolerance of one quarter of one percent less than the actual rate, determined without regard to section 107(c) of this title, except in the case of an irregular mortgage lending transaction, with respect to any transaction consummated between January 1, 1977, and the effective date of section 608 of the Truth in Lending Simplification and Reform Act.".

(b) This section shall take effect on the date of enactment of the Truth in Lending Simplification and Reform Act.

(c) Effective one year after the date of enactment of the Truth in Lending Simplification and Reform Act, section 108(e)(1)(A)(i) and section 108(e)(7) of the Truth in Lending Act are amended by striking out ", except in the case of an irregular mortgage lending transaction".

EFFECT ON OTHER LAWS

SEC. 609. Section 111(a) of the Truth in Lending Act (15 U.S.C. 1610(a)) is amended to read as follows:

"(a)(1) Chapters 1, 2, and 3 do not annul, alter, or affect the laws of any State relating to the disclosure of information in connection with credit transactions, except to the extent that those laws are inconsistent with the provisions of this title, and then only to the extent of the inconsistency. Upon its own motion or upon the request of any creditor, State, or other interested party which is submitted in accordance with procedures prescribed in regulations of the Board, the Board shall determine whether any such inconsistency exists. If the Board determines that a State-required disclosure is inconsistent, creditors located in that State may not make disclosures using the inconsistent term or form, and shall incur no liability under the law of that State for failure to use such term or form, notwithstanding that such determination is subsequently amended, rescinded, or determined by judicial or other authority to be invalid for any reason.

"(2) Upon its own motion or upon the request of any creditor, State, or other interested party which is submitted in accordance with procedures prescribed in regulations of the Board, the Board shall determine whether any disclosure required under the law of any State is substantially the same in meaning as a disclosure required under this title. If the Board determines that a State-required disclosure is substantially the same in meaning as a disclosure required by this title, then creditors located in that State may make such disclosure in compliance with State law in lieu of the disclosure required by this title, except that the annual percentage rate and finance charge shall be disclosed as required by section 122.".

ANNUAL REPORTS

SEC. 610. (a) Section 114 of the Truth in Lending Act (15 U.S.C. 1613) is amended by striking out "Not later than January 3 of each year after 1969," and inserting in lieu thereof "Each year".

(b) Section 18(f)(6) of the Federal Trade Commission Act (15 U.S.C. 57a(f)(6)) is amended by striking out "not later than March 15 of".

(c) Section 707 of the Equal Credit Opportunity Act (15 U.S.C. 1691f) is amended by striking out "Not later than February 1 of each year after 1976" and inserting in lieu thereof "Each year".

GENERAL DISCLOSURE REQUIREMENTS

SEC. 611. Sections 121 and 122 of the Truth in Lending Act (15 U.S.C. 1631 and 1632) are amended to read as follows:

"§ 121. GENERAL REQUIREMENT OF DISCLOSURE

"(a) Subject to subsection (b), a creditor or lessor shall disclose to the person who is obligated on a consumer lease or a consumer credit transaction the information required under this title. In a transaction involving more than one obligor, a creditor or lessor, except in a transaction under section 125, need not disclose to more than one of such obligors if the obligor given disclosure is a primary obligor.

"(b) If a transaction involves one creditor as defined in section 103(f), or one lessor as defined in section 181(3), such creditor or lessor shall make the disclosures. If a transaction involves more than one creditor or lessor, only one creditor or lessor shall be required to make the disclosures. The Board shall by regulation specify which creditor or lessor shall make the disclosures.

"(c) The Board may provide by regulation that any portion of the information required to be disclosed by this title may be given in the form of estimates where the provider of such information is not in a position to know exact information.

"(d) The Board shall determine whether tolerances for numerical disclosures other than the annual percentage rate are necessary to facilitate compliance with this title, and if it determines that such tolerances are necessary to facilitate compliance, it shall by regulation permit disclosures within such tolerances. The Board shall exercise its authority to permit tolerances for numerical disclosures other than the annual percentage rate so that such tolerances are narrow enough to prevent such tolerances from resulting in misleading disclosures or disclosures that circumvent the purposes of this title.

"§ 122. FORM OF DISCLOSURE; ADDITIONAL INFORMATION

"(a) Information required by this title shall be disclosed clearly and conspicuously, in accordance with regulations of the Board. The terms 'annual percentage rate' and 'finance charge' shall be disclosed more conspicuously than other terms, data, or information provided in connection with a transaction, except information relating to the identity of the creditor. Regulations of the Board need not require that disclosures pursuant to this title be made in the order set forth in this title and, except as otherwise provided, may permit the use of terminology different from that employed in this title if it conveys substantially the same meaning.

"(b) Any creditor or lessor may supply additional information or explanation with any disclosures required under chapters 4 and 5 and, except as provided in section 128(b)(1), under this chapter.".

RESCISSION

Sec. 612. (a)(1) Section 125(a) of the Truth in Lending Act (15 U.S.C. 1635(a)) is amended to read as follows:

"(a) Except as otherwise provided in this section, in the case of any consumer credit transaction (including opening or increasing the credit limit for an open end credit plan) in which a security interest, including any such interest arising by operation of law, is or will be retained or acquired in any property which is used as the principal dwelling of the person to whom credit is extended, the obligor shall have the right to rescind the transaction until midnight of the third business day following the consummation of the transaction or the delivery of the information and rescission forms required under this section together with a statement containing the material disclosures required under this title, whichever is later, by notifying the creditor, in accordance with regulations of the Board, of his intention to do so. The creditor shall clearly and conspicuously disclose, in accordance with regulations of the Board, to any obligor in a transaction subject to this section the rights of the obligor under this section. The creditor shall also provide, in accordance with regulations of the Board, appropriate forms for the obligor to exercise his right to rescind any transaction subject to this section.".

(2) Section 103 of the Truth in Lending Act (15 U.S.C. 1602), as amended by section 603(b), is amended by adding at the end thereof the following:

"(u) The term 'material disclosures' means the disclosure, as required by this title, of the annual percentage rate, the method of determining the finance charge and the balance upon which a finance charge will be imposed, the amount of the finance charge, the amount to be financed, the total of payments, the number and amount of payments, and the due dates or periods of payments scheduled to repay the indebtedness.".

(3) Section 125(b) of the Truth in Lending Act (15 U.S.C. 1635(b)) is amended by striking out "ten days" each place it appears therein and inserting in lieu thereof "20 days".

(4) Section 125(b) of the Truth in Lending Act (15 U.S.C. 1635(b)) is amended by adding at the end thereof the following new sentence: "The procedures prescribed by this subsection shall apply except when otherwise ordered by a court.".

(5) Section 125(c) of the Truth in Lending Act (15 U.S.C. 1635(c)) is amended by inserting "information, forms, and" after "whom".

(6) Section 125 of the Truth in Lending Act (15 U.S.C. 1635) is amended by striking out subsections (e) and (f) and inserting in lieu thereof the following:

(e)(1) This section does not apply to—

"(A) a residental mortgage transaction as defined in section 103(w);

"(B) a transaction which constitutes a refinancing or consolidation (with no new advances) of the principal balance then due and any accrued and unpaid finance charges of an existing extension of credit by the same creditor secured by an interest in the same property;

"(C) a transaction in which an agency of a State is the creditor; or

"(D) advances under a preexisting open end credit plan if a security interest has already been retained or acquired and such advances are in accordance with a previously established credit limit for such plan.

"(2) The provision of paragraph (1)(D) shall cease to be effective 3 years after the effective date of the Truth in Lending Simplification and Reform Act.

"(f) An obligor's right of rescission shall expire three years after the date of consummation of the transaction or upon the sale of the property, whichever occurs first, notwithstanding the fact that the information and forms required under this section or any other disclosures required under this chapter have not been delivered to the obligor, except that if (1) any agency empowered to enforce the provisions of this title institutes a proceeding to enforce the provisions of this section within three years after the date of consummation of the transaction, (2) such agency finds a violation of section 125, and (3) the obligor's right to rescind is based in whole or in part on any matter involved in such proceeding, then the obligor's right of rescission shall expire three years after the date of consummation of the transaction or upon the earlier sale of the property, or upon the expiration of one year following the conclusion of the proceeding, or any judicial review or period for judicial review thereof, whichever is later.

"(g) In any action in which it is determined that a creditor has violated this section, in addition to rescission the court may award relief under section 130 for violations of this title not relating to the right to rescind.".

(b) Section 103 of the Truth in Lending Act (15 U.S.C. 1602) is amended by inserting after subsection (u) the following:

"(v) The term 'dwelling' means a residential structure or mobile home which contains one to four family housing units, or individual units of condominiums or cooperatives.

"(w) The term 'residential mortgage transaction' means a transaction in which a mortgage, deed of trust, purchase money security interest arising under an installment sales contract, or equivalent consensual security interest is created or retained against the consumer's dwelling to finance the acquisition or initial construction of such dwelling.".

OPEN END DISCLOSURES

SEC. 613. (a)   Section 127(a) of the Truth in Lending Act (15 U.S.C. 1637(a)) is amended—

(1) by adding at the end of paragraph (1) the following new sentence: "If no such time period is provided, the creditor shall disclose such fact.";

(2) by striking out paragraph (5) and redesignating paragraphs (6), (7), and (8) as paragraphs (5), (6), and (7), respectively; and

(3) by amending paragraphs (5) and (6), as redesignated by paragraph (2), to read as follows:

"(5) Identification of other charges which may be imposed as part of the plan, and their method of computation, in accordance with regulations of the Board.

"(6) In cases where the credit is or will be secured, a statement that a security interest has been or will be taken in (A) the property purchased as part of the credit transaction, or (B) property not purchased as part of the credit transaction identified by item or type.".

(b) Section 127(b)(2) of the Truth in Lending Act (15 U.S.C. 1637(b)(2)) is amended to read as follows:

"(2) The amount and date of each extension of credit during the period, and a brief identification, on or accompanying the statement of each extension of credit in a form prescribed by the Board sufficient to enable the obligor either to identify the transaction or to relate it to copies of sales vouchers or similar instruments previously furnished, except that a creditor's failure to disclose such information in accordance with this paragraph shall not be deemed a failure to comply with this chapter or this title if (A) the creditor maintains procedures reasonably adapted to procure and provide such information, and (B) the creditor responds to and treats any inquiry for clarification or documentation as a billing error and an erroneously billed amount under section 161. In lieu of complying with the requirements of the previous sentence, in the case of any transaction in which the creditor and seller are the same person, as defined by the Board, and such person's open end credit plan has fewer than 15,000 accounts, the creditor may elect to provide only the amount and date of each extension of credit during the period and the seller's name and location where the transaction took place if (A) a brief identification of the transaction has been previously furnished, and (B) the creditor responds to and treats any inquiry for clarification or documentation as a billing error and an erroneously billed amount under section 161.".

(c) Section 127(b) of the Truth in Lending Act (15 U.S.C. 1637) is amended by striking out paragraph (7) and by redesignating paragraphs (8), (9), (10), and (11) as paragraphs (7), (8), (9), and (10), respectively.

(d) Section 127(a)(7) of the Truth in Lending Act (15 U.S.C. 1637(a)), as redesignated by subsection (a)(2), is amended by striking out "each of two billing cycles per year, at semiannual intervals" and inserting in lieu thereof "one billing cycle per calendar year, at intervals of not less than six months or more than eighteen months".

(e) Section 127(c) of the Truth in Lending Act (15 U.S.C. 1637(c)) is hereby repealed.

(f) Section 143 of the Truth in Lending Act (15 U.S.C. 1663) is amended by striking out "or the appropriate rate determined under section 127(a)(5)".

(g) Section 161(a) of the Truth in Lending Act 15 (U.S.C. 1666(a)) is amended by redesignating the references to sections 127(b)(11) and 127(a)(8) as references to sections 127(b)(10) and 127(a)(7), respectively.

OTHER THAN OPEN END DISCLOSURES

SEC. 614. (a) Section 128(a) of the Truth in Lending Act (15 U.S.C. 1638(a)) is amended to read as follows:

"(a) For each consumer credit transaction other than under an open end credit plan, the creditor shall disclose each of the following items, to the extent applicable:

"(1) The identity of the creditor required to make disclosure.

"(2)(A) The 'amount financed', using that term, which shall be the amount of credit of which the consumer has actual use. This amount shall be computed as follows, but the computations need not be disclosed and shall not be disclosed with the disclosures conspicuously segregated in accordance with subsection (b)(1):

　　"(i) take the principal amount of the loan or the cash price less downpayment and trade-in;

　　"(ii) add any charges which are not part of the finance charge or of the principal amount of the loan and which are financed by the consumer, including the cost of any items excluded from the finance charge pursuant to section 106; and

　　"(iii) subtract any charges which are part of the finance charge but which will be paid by the consumer before or at the time of the consummation of the transaction, or have been withheld from the proceeds of the credit.

"(B) In conjunction with the disclosure of the amount financed, a creditor shall provide a statement of the consumer's right to obtain, upon a written request, a written itemization of the amount financed. The statement shall include spaces for a 'yes' or 'no' indication to be initialed by the consumer to indicate whether the consumer wants a written itemization of the amount financed. Upon receiving an affirmative indication, the creditor shall provide, at the time other disclosures are required to be furnished, a written itemization of the amount financed. For the purposes of this subparagraph, 'itemization of the amount financed' means a disclosure of the following items, to the extent applicable:

　　"(i) the amount that is or will be paid directly to the consumer;

　　"(ii) the amount that is or will be credited to the consumer's account to discharge obligations owed to the creditor;

　　"(iii) each amount that is or will be paid to third persons by the creditor on the consumer's behalf, together with an identification of or reference to the third person; and

　　"(iv) the total amount of any charges described in the preceding subparagraph (A)(iii).

"(3) The 'finance charge,' not itemized, using that term.

"(4) The finance charge expressed as an 'annual percentage rate', using that term. This shall not be required if the amount financed does not exceed $75 and the finance charge does not exceed $5, or if the amount financed exceeds $75 and the finance charge does not exceed $7.50.

"(5) The sum of the amount financed and the finance charge, which shall be termed the 'total of payments'.

"(6) The number, amount, and due dates or period of payments scheduled to repay the total of payments.

"(7) In a sale of property or services in which the seller is the creditor required to disclose pursuant to section 121(b), the 'total sale price', using that term, which shall be the total of the cash price of the property or services, additional charges, and the finance charge.

"(8) Descriptive explanations of the terms 'amount financed', 'finance charge', 'annual percentage rate', 'total of payments', and 'total sale price' as specified by the Board. The descriptive explanation of 'total sale price' shall include reference to the amount of the downpayment.

"(9) Where the credit is secured, a statement that a security interest has been taken in (A) the property which is purchased as part of the credit transaction, or (B) property not purchased as part of the credit transaction identified by item or type.

"(10) Any dollar charge or percentage amount which may be imposed by a creditor solely on account of a late payment, other than a deferral or extension charge.

"(11) A statement indicating whether or not the consumer is entitled to a rebate of any finance charge upon refinancing or prepayment in full pursuant to acceleration or otherwise, if the obligation involves a precomputed finance charge. A statement indicating whether or not a penalty will be imposed in those same circumstances if the obligation involves a finance charge computed from time to time by application of a rate to the unpaid principal balance.

"(12) A statement that the consumer should refer to the appropriate contract document for any information such document provides about nonpayment, default, the right to accelerate the maturity of the debt, and prepayment rebates and penalties.

"(13) In any residential mortgage transaction, a statement indicating whether a subsequent purchaser or assignee of the consumer may assume the debt obligation on its original terms and conditions.".

(b) Section 128(b) of the Truth in Lending Act (15 U.S.C. 1638(b)) is amended to read as follows:

"(b)(1) Except as otherwise provided in this chapter, the disclosures required under subsection (a) shall be made before the credit is extended. Except for the disclosures required by subsection (a)(1) of this section, all disclosures required under subsection (a) and any disclosure provided for in subsection (b), (c), or (d) of section 106 shall be conspicuously segregated from all other terms, data, or information provided in connection with a transaction, including any computations or itemization.

"(2) In the case of a residential mortgage transaction, as defined in section 103(w), which is also subject to the Real Estate Settlement Procedures Act, good faith estimates of the disclosures required under subsection (a) shall be made in accordance with regulations of the Board under section 121(c) before the credit is extended, or shall be delivered or placed in the mail not later than three business days after the creditor receives the consumer's written application, whichever is earlier. If the disclosure statement furnished within three days of the written application contains an annual percentage rate which is subsequently rendered inaccurate within the meaning of section 107(c), the creditor shall furnish another statement at the time of settlement or consummation.".

(c) Section 128(c) of the Truth in Lending Act (15 U.S.C. 1638(c)) is amended—

  (1) by inserting "(1)" after "(c)";
  (2) by striking out "deferred payment price" and inserting in lieu thereof "total sale price"; and
  (3) by adding at the end thereof the following new paragraph:

"(2) If a creditor receives a request for a loan by mail or telephone without personal solicitation and the terms of financing, including the annual percentage rate for representative amounts of credit, are set forth in the creditor's printed material distributed to the public, or in the contract of loan or other printed material delivered to the obligor, then the disclosures required under subsection (a) may be made at any time not later than the date the first payment is due.".

(d)(1) Section 129 of the Truth in Lending Act (15 U.S.C. 1639) is hereby repealed.

(2) The table of sections at the beginning of chapter 2 of the Truth in Lending Act is amended by striking out the item relating to section 129 and inserting in lieu thereof the following:

"129. [Repealed].".

(e)(1) Section 126 of the Truth in Lending Act (15 U.S.C. 1636) is hereby repealed.

(2) The table of sections at the beginning of chapter 2 of the Truth in Lending Act is amended by striking out the item relating to section 126 and inserting in lieu thereof the following:

"126. [Repealed].".

(f)(1) The table of sections at the beginning of chapter 2 of the Truth in Lending Act is amended by striking out the item relating to section 128 and inserting in lieu thereof the following:

"128. Consumer credit not under open end credit plans.".

(2) The section heading for section 128 of the Truth in Lending Act (15 U.S.C. 1638) is amended by striking out "SALES" and inserting in lieu thereof "CONSUMER CREDIT".

CIVIL LIABILITY

SEC. 615. (a) Section 130 of the Truth in Lending Act (15 U.S.C. 1640) is amended—

(1) in subsection (a)(2)(B), by striking out "in such action" and inserting in lieu thereof "under this subparagraph in any class action or series of class actions arising out of the same failure to comply by the same creditor";

(2) in subsection (a)(3), by inserting "or in any action in which a person is determined to have a right of rescission under section 125" after "liability";

(3) by amending subsections (b), (c), and (d) to read as follows:

"(b) A creditor or assignee has no liability under this section or section 108 or section 112 for any failure to comply with any requirement imposed under this chapter or chapter 5, if within sixty days after discovering an error, whether pursuant to a final written examination report or notice issued under section 108(e)(1) or through the creditor's or assignee's own procedures, and prior to the institution of an action under this section or the receipt of written notice of the error from the obligor, the creditor or assignee notifies the person concerned of the error and makes whatever adjustments in the appropriate account are necessary to assure that the person will not be required to pay an amount in excess of the charge actually disclosed, or the dollar equivalent of the annual percentage rate actually disclosed, whichever is lower.

"(c) A creditor or assignee may not be held liable in any action brought under this section or section 125 for a violation of this title if the creditor or assignee shows a preponderance of evidence that the violation was not intentional and resulted from a bona fide error notwithstanding the maintenance of procedures reasonably adapted to avoid any such error. Examples of a bona fide error include, but are not limited to, clerical, calculation, computer malfunction and programing, and printing errors, except that an error of legal judgement with respect to a person's obligations under this title is not a bona fide error.

"(d) When there are multiple obligors in a consumer credit transaction or consumer lease, there shall be no more than one recovery of damages under subsection (a)(2) for a violation of this title.";

(4) in subsection (e), by adding at the end thereof the following new sentence: "This subsection does not bar a person from asserting a violation of this title in an action to collect the debt which was brought more than one year from the date of the occurrence of the violation as a matter of defense by recoupment or set-off in such action, except as otherwise provided by State law.";

(5) in subsection (f), by inserting ", section 108(b), section 108(c), section 108(e)," after "this section";

(6) in subsection (g), by adding at the end thereof the following

new sentence: "This subsection does not bar any remedy permitted by section 125."; and

(7) by amending subsection (h) to read as follows:

"(h) A person may not take any action to offset any amount for which a creditor or assignee is potentially liable to such person under subsection (a)(2) against any amount owed by such person, unless the amount of the creditor's or assignee's liability under this title has been determined by judgment of a court of competent jurisdiction in an action of which such person was a party. This subsection does not bar a consumer then in default on the obligation from asserting a violation of this title as an original action, or as a defense or counterclaim to an action to collect amounts owed by the consumer brought by a person liable under this title.".

(b) Section 130(a) of the Truth in Lending Act (15 U.S.C. 1640(a)) is amended—

(1) by inserting ", including any requirement under section 125," immediately after "this chapter"; and

(2) by adding at the end thereof the following: "In connection with the disclosures referred to in section 127, a creditor shall have a liability determined under paragraph (2) only for failing to comply with the requirements of section 125, section 127(a), or of paragraph (4), (5), (6), (7), (8), (9), or (10) of section 127(b) or for failing to comply with disclosure requirements under State law for any term or item which the Board has determined to be substantially the same in meaning under section 111(a)(2) as any of the terms or items referred to in section 127(a) or any of those paragraphs of section 127(b). In connection with the disclosures referred to in section 128, a creditor shall have a liability determined under paragraph (2) only for failing to comply with the requirements of section 125 or of paragraph (2) (insofar as it requires a disclosure of the 'amount financed'), (3), (4), (5), (6), or (9) of section 128(a), or for failing to comply with disclosure requirements under State law for any term which the Board has determined to be substantially the same in meaning under section 111(a)(2) as any of the terms referred to in any of those paragraphs of section 128(a). With respect to any failure to make disclosures required under this chapter or chapter 4 or 5 of this title, liability shall be imposed only upon the creditor required to make disclosure, except as provided in section 131.".

LIABILITY OF ASSIGNEES

SEC. 616. (a) Section 131 of the Truth in Lending Act (15 U.S.C. 1641) is amended to read as follows:

"§ 131. LIABILITY OF ASSIGNEES

"(a) Except as otherwise specifically provided in this title, any civil action for a violation of this title or proceeding under section 108 which may be brought against a creditor may be maintained against any assignee of such creditor only if the violation for which such action or proceeding is brought is apparent on the face of the disclosure statement, except where the assignment was involuntary. For the purpose of this section, a violation apparent on the face of the disclosure statement includes, but is not limited to (1) a disclosure which can be determined to be incomplete or inaccurate from the face of the disclosure statement or other documents assigned, or (2) a disclosure which does not use the terms required to be used by this title.

"(b) Except as provided in section 125(c), in any action or proceeding by or against any subsequent assignee of the original creditor without knowledge to the contrary by the assignee when he acquires the obligation, written acknowledgement of receipt by a person to whom a statement is required to be given pursuant to this title shall be conclusive proof of the delivery thereof and, except as provided in subsection (a), of compliance with this chapter. This section does not affect the rights of the obligor in any action against the original creditor.

"(c) Any consumer who has the right to rescind a transaction under section 125 may rescind the transaction as against any assignee of the obligation.".

(b) Section 115 or the Truth in Lending Act (15 U.S.C. 1614) is hereby repealed.

(c)(1) The table of sections at the beginning of chapter 1 of the Truth in Lending Act is amended by striking out the item relating to section 115 and inserting in lieu thereof the following:

"115. [Repealed].".

(2) The table of sections at the beginning of chapter 2 of the Truth in Lending Act is amended by striking out the item relating to section 131 and inserting in lieu thereof the following:

"131. Liability of assignees.".

LIABILITY OF CREDIT CARDHOLDER

SEC. 617. Section 133(a) of the Truth in Lending Act (15 U.S.C. 1643(a)) is amended to read as follows:

"(a)(1) A cardholder shall be liable for the unauthorized use of a credit card only if—

"(A) the card is an accepted credit card;

"(B) the liability is not in excess of $50;

"(C) the card issuer gives adequate notice to the cardholder of the potential liability;

"(D) the card issuer has provided the cardholder with a description of a means by which the card issuer may be notified of loss or theft of the card, which description may be provided on the face or reverse side of the statement required by section 127(b) or on a separate notice accompanying such statement;

"(E) the unauthorized use occurs before the card issuer has been notified that an unauthorized use of the credit card has occurred or may occur as the result of loss, theft, or otherwise; and

"(F) the card issuer has provided a method whereby the user of such card can be identified as the person authorized to use it.

"(2) For purposes of this section, a card issuer has been notified when such steps as may be reasonably required in the ordinary course of business to provide the card issuer with the pertinent information have been taken, whether or not any particular officer, employee, or agent of the card issuer does in fact receive such information.".

DISSEMINATION OF ANNUAL PERCENTAGE RATES

SEC. 618.   (a)   Chapter 2 of the Truth in Lending Act (15 U.S.C. 1631 et seq.) is amended by adding at the end thereof the following new section:

"§ 136.   DISSEMINATION OF ANNUAL PERCENTAGE RATES

"(a) The Board shall collect, publish, and disseminate to the public, on a demonstration basis in a number of standard metropolitan statistical areas to be determined by the Board, the annual percentage rates charged for representative types of nonsale credit by creditors in such areas. For the purpose of this section, the Board is authorized to require creditors in such areas to furnish information necessary for the Board to collect, publish, and disseminate such information.

"(b) The Board is authorized to enter into contracts or other arrangements with appropriate persons, organizations, or State agencies to carry out its functions under subsection (a) and to furnish financial assistance in support thereof."

(b) The table of sections contained at the beginning of such chapter is amended by adding at the end thereof the following new item:

"136. Dissemination of annual perentage rates.".

CREDIT ADVERTISING

SEC. 619.   (a)   Section 143 of the Truth in Lending Act (15 U.S.C. 1662) is amended to read as follows:

"§ 143.   ADVERTISING OF OPEN END CREDIT PLANS

"No advertisement to aid, promote, or assist directly or indirectly the extension of consumer credit under an open end credit plan may set forth any of the specific terms of that plan unless it also clearly and conspicuously sets forth all of the following items:

"(1) Any minimum or fixed amount which could be imposed.

"(2) In any case in which periodic rates may be used to compute the finance charge, the periodic rates expressed as annual percentage rates.

"(3) Any other term that the Board may by regulation require to be disclosed.".

(b) Section 144(d) of the Truth in Lending Act (15 U.S.C. 1664) is amended by striking out paragraphs (1) through (4) thereof, and inserting in lieu thereof the following:

"(1) The downpayment, if any.

"(2) The terms of repayment.

"(3) The rate of the finance charge expressed as an annual percentage rate.".

CORRECTION OF BILLING ERRORS

SEC. 620. (a) Section 161(b) of the Truth in Lending Act (15 U.S.C. 1666(b)) is amended—

(1) by redesigning paragraph (6) as paragraph (7); and

(2) by inserting after paragraph (5) the following:

"(6) Failure to transmit the statement required under section 127(b) of this Act to the last address of the obligor which has been disclosed to the creditor, unless that address was furnished less than twenty days before the end of the billing cycle for which the statement is required.".

(b) Section 161(c) of the Truth in Lending Act (15 U.S.C. 1666(c)) is amended by inserting ", which may include finance charges on amounts in dispute," after "statements of account".

CREDIT BALANCES

SEC. 621. (a) Section 165 of the Truth in Lending Act (15 U.S.C. 1666d) is amended to read as follows:

"§ 165. TREATMENT OF CREDIT BALANCES

"Whenever a credit balance in excess of $1 is created in connection with a consumer credit transaction through (1) transmittal of funds to a creditor in excess of the total balance due on an account, (2) rebates of unearned finance charges or insurance premiums, or (3) amounts otherwise owed to or held for the benefit of an obligor, the creditor shall—

"(A) credit the amount of the credit balance to the consumer's account:

"(B) refund any part of the amount of the remaining credit balance, upon request of the consumer; and

"(C) make a good faith effort to refund the consumer by cash, check, or money order any part of the amount of the credit balance remaining in the account for more than six months, except that no further action is required in any case in which the consumer's current location is not known by the creditor and cannot be traced through the consumer's last known address or telephone number.".

(b) The table of sections at the beginning of chapter 4 of the Truth in Lending Act is amended by striking out the item relating to section 165 and inserting in lieu thereof the following:

"165. Treatment of credit balances.".

GOVERNMENT EXEMPTION

SEC. 622. (a) Setcion 113 of the Truth in Lending Act (15 U.S.C. 1612) is amended to read as follows:

"§ 113.   EFFECT ON GOVERNMENTAL AGENCIES

"(a) Any department or agency of the United States which administers a credit program in which it extends, insures, or guarantees consumer credit and in which it provides instruments to a creditor which contain any disclosures required by this title shall, prior to the issuance or continued use of such instruments, consult with the Board to assure that such instruments comply with this title.

"(b) No civil or criminal penalty provided under this title for any violation thereof may be imposed upon the United States or any department or agency thereof, or upon any State or political subdivision thereof, or any agency of any State or political subdivision.

"(c) A creditor participating in a credit program administered, insured, or guaranteed by any department or agency of the United States shall not be held liable for a civil or criminal penalty under this title in any case in which the violation results from the use of an instrument required by any such department or agency.

"(d) A creditor participating in a credit program administered, insured, or guaranteed by any department or agency of the United States shall not be held liable for a civil or criminal penalty under the laws of any State (other than laws determined under section 111 to be inconsistent with this title) for any technical or procedural failure, such as failure to use a specific form, to make information available at a specific place on an instrument, or to use a specific typeface, as required by State law, which is caused by the use of an instrument required to be used by such department or agency.".

(b) The table of sections at the beginning of chapter 1 of the Truth in Lending Act is amended by striking out the item relating to section 113 and inserting in lieu thereof the following:

"113. Effect on governmental agencies.".

ORAL DISCLOSURES

Sec. 623. (a) Section 146 of the Truth in Lending Act (15 U.S.C. 1665a) is amended to read as follows:

"§ 146. USE OF ANNUAL PERCENTAGE RATE IN ORAL DISCLOSURES

"In responding orally to any inquiry about the cost of credit, a creditor, regardless of the method used to compute finance charges, shall state rates only in terms of the annual percentage rate, except that in the case of an open end credit plan, the periodic rate also may be stated and, in the case of an other than open end and credit plan where a major component of the finance charge consists of interest computed at a simple annual rate, the simple annual rate also may be stated. The Board may, by regulation, modify the requirements of this section or provide an exception from this section for a transaction or class of transactions for which the creditor cannot determine in advance the applicable annual percentage rate.".

(b) The table of sections at the beginning of chapter 3 of the Truth in Lending Act is amended by striking out the item relating to section 146 and inserting in lieu thereof the following:

"146. Use of annual percentage rate in oral disclosures.".

CONSUMER LEASING

Sec. 624. Section 185(b) of the Truth in Lending Act (15 U.S.C. 1667(b)) is amended by striking out "sections 115, 130, and 131" and inserting in lieu thereof "sections 130 and 131."

EFFECTIVE DATE

Sec. 625. (a) Except as provided in section 608(b), the amendments made by this title shall take effect upon the expiration of two years after the date of enactment of this title.

(b) All regulations, forms, and clauses required to be prescribed under the amendments made by this title shall be promulgated at least one year prior to such effective date.

(c) Notwithstanding subsections (a) and (b), any creditor may comply with the amendments made by this title, in accordance with the regulations, forms, and clauses prescribed by the Board, prior to such effective date.

TITLE VII—AMENDMENTS TO THE NATIONAL BANKING LAWS

Part A—National Banking Laws

POWER TO HOLD REAL PROPERTY OR INTERESTS IN REAL PROPERTY

Sec. 701. (a) Section 5137 of the Revised Statutes (12 U.S.C. 29) is amended—

(1) by inserting before the period at the end of the last paragraph thereof the following: "except as otherwise provided in this section"; and

(2) by adding at the end thereof the following new paragraph:

"For real estate in the possession of a national banking association upon application by the association, the Comptroller of the Currency may approve the possession of any such real estate by such association for a period longer than five years, but not to exceed an additional five years, if (1) the association has made a good faith attempt to dispose of the real estate within the five-year period, or (2) disposal within the five-year period would be detrimental to the association. Upon notification by the association to the Comptroller of the Currency that such conditions exist that require the expenditure of funds for the development and improvement of such real estate, and subject to such conditions and limitations as the Comptroller of the Currency shall prescribe, the association may expend such funds as are needed to enable such association to recover its total investment.".

(b) Section 4(a) of the Bank Holding Company Act of 1956 (12 U.S.C. 1843(a)) is amended by adding at the end thereof the following: "Notwithstanding any other provision of this Act, the period ending December 31, 1980, referred to in paragraph (2) above, may be extended by the Board of Governors to December 31, 1982, but only for the divestiture by a bank holding company of real estate or interests in real estate lawfully acquired for investment or development. In making its decision whether to grant such extension, the Board shall consider whether the company has made a good faith effort to divest such interests and whether such extension is necessary to avert substantial loss to the company.".

DIVIDENDS ON PREFERRED STOCK

SEC. 702. The first sentence of subsection (a) of section 302 of the Act entitled "An Act to provide relief in the existing national emergency in banking, and for other purposes", approved March 9, 1933 (12 U.S.C. 51b), is amended by striking out "at a rate not exceeding 6 per cent per annum".

CONSIDERATION OF PREFERRED STOCK IN DETERMINING IMPAIRMENT OF CAPITAL

SEC. 703. The third sentence of section 345 of the Banking Act of 1935 (12 U.S.C. 51b–1) is amended by striking out "at a rate not exceeding six per centum per annum".

REVOCATION OF TRUST POWERS

SEC. 704. The first section of the Act of September 28, 1962 (76 Stat. 668; 12 U.S.C. 92a), is amended by adding at the end thereof the following new subsection:

"(k)(1) In addition to the authority conferred by other law, if, in the opinion of the Comptroller of the Currency, a national banking association is unlawfully or unsoundly exercising, or has unlawfully or unsoundly exercised, or has failed for a period of five consecutive years to exercise, the powers granted by this section or otherwise fails or has failed to comply with the requirements of this section, the Comptroller may issue and serve upon the association a notice of intent to revoke the authority of the association to exercise the powers granted by this section. The notice shall contain a statement of the facts constituting the alleged unlawful or unsound exercise of powers, or failure to exercise powers, or failure to comply, and shall fix a time and place at which a hearing will be held to determine whether an order revoking authority to exercise such powers should issue against the association.

"(2) Such hearing shall be conducted in accordance with the provisions of subsection (h) of section 8 of the Federal Deposit Insurance Act (12 U.S.C. 1818(h)), and subject to judicial review as provided in such section, and shall be fixed for a date not earlier than thirty days nor later than sixty days after service of such notice unless an earlier date or later date is set by the Comptroller at the request of any association so served.

"(3) Unless the association so served shall appear at the hearing by a duly authorized representative, it shall be deemed to have consented to the issuance of the revocation order. In the event of such consent, or if upon the record made at any such hearing, the Comptroller shall find that any allegation specified in the notice of charges has been established, the Comptroller may issue and serve upon the association an order prohibiting it from accepting any new or additional trust accounts and revoking authority to exercise any and all powers granted by this section, except that such order shall permit the association to continue to service all previously accepted trust accounts pending their expeditious divestiture or termination.

"(2) A revocation order shall become effective not earlier than the expiration of thirty days after service of such order upon the association so served (except in the case of a revocation order issued upon consent, which shall become effective at the time specified therein), and shall remain effective and enforceable, except to such extent as it is stayed, modified, terminated, or set aside by action of the Comptroller or a reviewing court.".

EMERGENCY LIMITATIONS AND RESTRICTIONS ON BUSINESS OF MEMBER BANKS

SEC. 705. Section 4 of the Act of March 9, 1933 (48 Stat. 2; 12 U.S.C. 95), is amended—

    (1) by inserting "(a)" after "SEC. 4."; and

    (2) by adding at the end thereof the following:

"(b)(1) In the event of natural calamity, riot, insurrection, war, or other emergency conditions occurring in any State whether caused by acts or nature or of man, the Comptroller of the Currency may designate by proclamation any day a legal holiday for the national banking associations located in that State. In the event that the emergency conditions affect only part of a State, the Comptroller of the Currency may designate the part so affected and may proclaim a legal holiday for the national banking associations located in that affected part. In the event that a State or a State official authorized by law designates any day as a legal holiday for either emergency or ceremonial reasons for all banks chartered by that State to do business within that State, that same day shall be a legal holiday for all national banking associations chartered to do business within that State unless the Comptroller of the Currency shall by written order permit all national banking associations located in that State to remain open.

"(2) For the purpose of this subsection, the term 'State' means any of the several States, the District of Columbia, the Commonwealth of Puerto Rico, the Northern Mariana Islands, Guam, the Virgin Islands, American Samoa, the Trust Territory of the Pacific Islands, or any other territory or possession of the United States.".

PROCEDURE FOR CONVERSION, MERGER, OR CONSOLIDATION

SEC. 106. The second sentence of subsection (b) of section 2 of the Act of August 17, 1950 (64 Stat. 456; 12 U.S.C. 214a(b)), is amended by striking out "unanimous" and inserting in lieu thereof "majority".

DELEGATION OF AUTHORITY

SEC. 707. (a) Chapter 9 of title VII of the Revised Statutes (12 U.S.C. 1 et seq.) is amended by inserting after section 327 the following new section:

"SEC. 327A. The Comptroller of the Currency may delegate to any duly authorized employee, representative, or agent any power vested in the office by law.".

(b) The table of contents contained at the beginning of chapter 9 of title VII of the Revised Statutes is amended by inserting after the item relating to section 327 the following new item:

"327A. Delegation of authority.".

AUTHORITY TO PRESCRIBE REGULATIONS

SEC. 708. Chapter 4 of title LXII of the Revised Statutes (12 U.S.C. 21 et seq.) is amended by inserting immediately following section 5239 a new section 5239A to read as follows:

"SEC. 5329A. Except to the extent that authority to issue such rules and regulations has been expressly and exclusively granted to another regulatory agency, the Comptroller of the Currency is authorized to prescribe rules and regulations to carry out the responsibilities of the office, except that the authority conferred by this section does not apply to section 5155 of the Revised Statutes or to securities activities of National Banks under the Act commonly known as the 'Glass-Steagall Act'.".

EXAMINATION OF NATIONAL BANKING ASSOCIATIONS

SEC. 709. (a) Section 5240 of the Revised Statutes (12 U.S.C. 481) is amended by striking out the first two sentences and inserting in lieu thereof the following: "The Comptroller of the Currency, with the approval of the Secretary of the Treasury, shall appoint examiners who shall examine every national bank as often as the Comptroller of the Currency shall deem necessary.".

( ) Section 5240 of the Revised Statutes (12 U.S.C. 481) is amended by adding at the end thereof the following new sentence: "The Comptroller of the Currency, upon the request of the Board of Governors of the Federal Reserve System, is authorized to assign examiners appointed under this section to examine foreign operations of State banks which are members of the Federal Reserve System.".

OWNERSHIP INTEREST OF DIRECTORS OF NATIONAL BANKS

SEC. 710. The second sentence of section 5146 of the Revised Statutes (12 U.S.C. 72) is amended by striking out the second sentence and inserting in lieu thereof the following: "Every director must own in his or her own right either shares of the capital stock of the association of which he or she is a director the aggregate par value of which is not less than $1,000, or an equivalent interest, as determined by the Comptroller of the Currency, in any company which has control over such association within the meaning of section 2 of the Bank Holding Company Act of 1956 (12 U.S.C. 1841). If the capital of the bank does not exceed $25,000, every director must own in his or her own right either shares of such capital stock the aggegrate par value of which is not less than $500, or an equivalent interest, as determined by the Comptroller of the Currency, in any company which has control over such association within the meaning of section 2 of the Bank Holding Company Act of 1956 (12 U.S.C. 1841).".

PURCHASE OF STOCK IN BANKERS' BANKS

SEC. 711. The paragraph numbered "Seventh" of section 5136 of the Revised Statutes (12 U.S.C. 24(7)) is amended by inserting before the period at the end thereof the following: "*: Provided further,* That, notwithstanding any other provision of this paragraph, the association may purchase for its own account shares of stock of a bank insured by the Federal Deposit Insurance Corporation if the stock of such bank is owned exclusively by other banks (except to the extent State law requires directors qualifying shares) and if such bank is engaged exclusively in providing banking services for other banks and their officers, directors, or employees, but in no event shall the total amount of such stock held by the association exceed at any time 10 per centum of its capital stock and paid in and unimpaired surplus, and in no event shall the purchase of such stock result in the association's acquiring more than 5 per centum of any class of voting securities of such bank".

INTERSTATE TRUST OPERATIONS

SEC. 712. (a) Section 5169 of the Revised Statutes (12 U.S.C. 27) is amended by adding at the end thereof the following: "Notwithstanding the provisions of the preceding sentence, a national banking association the operations of which are limited as provided in the preceding sentence shall be deemed an additional bank within the contemplation of section 3 of the Bank Holding Company Act of 1956.".

(b) Section 3(d) of the Bank Holding Company Act of 1956 (12 U.S.C. 1842(d)) is amended by inserting "(1)" after "(d)" and by adding at the end thereof the following:

"(2)(A) Except as provided in subparagraph (B), the restrictions contained in paragraph (1) regarding the acquisition of shares or assets of, or interests in, an additional bank shall apply to the acquisition of shares or assets of, or interests in, a trust company.

"(B) Subparagraph (A) shall not apply with respect to the acquisition of shares or assets of, or interests in, a trust company if such acquisition was approved by the Board on or before March 5, 1980, and if such trust company opened for business and was operating on on before March 5, 1980.

"(C) For the purpose of this paragraph, the term 'trust company' means any company whose powers are limited to the powers specified in subsection (a) of the first section of the Act entitled 'An Act to place authority over the trust powers of national banks in the Comptroller of the Currency', approved September 28, 1962 (12 U.S.C. 92a), for a national bank located in the same State in which such trust company is located.".

(c) The amendments made by this section are hereby repealed on October 1, 1981.

LOANS FOR THE FORMATION OF A ONE-BANK HOLDING COMPANY

SEC. 713. Section 3(c) of the Bank Holding Company Act of 1956 (12 U.S.C. 1842(c)) is amended by adding at the end thereof the following: "Notwithstanding any other provision of law, the Board shall not follow any practice or policy in the consideration of any application for the formation of a one-bank holding company if following such practice or policy would result in the rejection of such application solely because the transaction to form such one-bank holding company involves a bank stock loan which is for a period of not more than twenty-five years. The previous sentence shall not be construed to prohibit the Board from rejecting any application solely because the other financial arrangements are considered unsatisfactory. The Board shall consider transactions involving bank stock loans for the formation of a one-bank holding company having a maturity of twelve years or more on a case by case basis and no such transaction shall be approved if the Board believes the safety or soundness of the bank may be jeopardized.".

Part B—Termination of National Bank Closed Receivership Fund

PURPOSE

SEC. 721. The purpose of this part is to terminate the closed receivership fund by—

(1) providing final notice of availability of liquidating dividends to creditors of national banks closed on or before January 22, 1934;

(2) barring rights of creditors to collect liquidating dividends from the Comptroller of the Currency after a reasonable period of time following such final notice; and

(3) refunding to the Comptroller the principal amount of such fund and any income earned thereon.

DEFINITIONS

SEC. 722. For purposes of this part—

(1) the term "closed receivership fund" means the aggregation of undisbursed liquidating dividends from national banks closed on or before January 22, 1934, held by the Comptroller in his capacity as successor to receivers of those banks;

(2) the term "Comptroller" means the Comptroller of the Currency;

(3) the term "claimant" means a depositor or other creditor who asserts a claim against a closed national bank for a liquidating dividend; and

(4) the term "liquidating dividend" means an amount of money in the closed receivership fund determined by a receiver of a closed national bank or by the Comptroller to be owed by that bank to a depositor or other creditor.

TERMINATION OF CLOSED RECEIVERSHIP FUND

SEC. 723. (a) The Comptroller shall publish notice once a week for four weeks in the Federal Register that all rights of depositors and other creditors of closed national banks to collect liquidating dividends from the closed receivership fund shall be barred after twelve months following the last date of publication of such notice.

(b) The Comptroller shall pay the principal amount of a liquidating dividend, exclusive of any income earned thereon, to a claimant presenting a valid claim, if the claimant applies to collect within twelve months following the late date notice is published.

(c) If a creditor shall fail to apply to collect a liquidating dividend within twelve months after the last date notice is published, all rights of the claimant against the closed receivership fund with respect to the liquidating dividend shall be barred.

(d) The principal amount of any liquidating dividends (1) for which claims have not been asserted within twelve months following the last date notice is published or (2) for which the Comptroller has determined a valid claim has not been submitted shall, together with any income earned on liquidating dividends and other moneys, if any, remaining in the closed receivership fund, be covered into the general funds of the Comptroller.

TITLE VIII—REGULATORY SIMPLIFICATION

SHORT TITLE

SEC. 801. This title may be cited as the "Financial Regulation Simplification act of 1980".

FINDINGS

SEC. 802. The Congress hereby finds that many regulations issued by the Board of Governors of the Federal Reserve System, the Board of Directors of the Federal Deposit Insurance Corporation, the Comptroller of the Currency, the Federal Home Loan Bank Board, and the National Credit Union Administation Board (hereinafter in this title referred to as the "Federal financial regulatory agencies") often impose costly, duplicative, and unnecessary burdens on both financial institutions and consumers. Regulations should be simple and clearly written. Regulations should achieve legislative goals effectively and efficiently. Regulations should not impose unnecessary costs and paperwork burdens on the economy, on financial institutions, or on consumers.

POLICY

SEC. 803. Any regulation issued by the Federal financial regulatory agencies shall, to the maximum extent practicable, insure that—

(1) the need for and purpose of such regulation is established clearly;

(2) meaningful alternatives to the promulgation of such regulations are considered before such regulation is issued;

(3) compliance costs, paperwork, and other burdens on the financial institutions, consumers, and public are minimized;

(4) conflicts, duplication, and inconsistencies between the regulations issued by the Federal financial regulatory agencies are to be avoided to the extent possible taking into account differences in statutory responsibilities, the classes of financial institutions' regulation and methods of implementation of statutory or policy objectives;

(5) timely participation and comment by other Federal agencies, ap-

propriate State and local agencies, financial institutions, and consumers are available; and

(6) any regulation issued shall be as simple and clearly written as possible and understandable by those who are subject to such regulation.

REVIEW OF EXISTING REGULATIONS

SEC. 804. The Federal financial regulatory agencies shall establish a program which assures periodic review of existing regulations to determine whether those regulations achieve the policies stated in section 803. Those regulations which are not in keeping with such policies shall be revised accordingly.

REPORTING

SEC. 805. Not later than six months after the date of enactment of this title and in subsequent annual reports, each Federal financial regulatory agency shall submit a report of its progress in implementing this title to the Committee on Banking, Finance and Urban Affairs of the House of Representatives and the Committee on Banking, Housing, and Urban Affairs of the Senate.

TERMINATION DATE

SEC. 806. This title is hereby repealed five years after the date of enactment of this title.

TITLE IX—FOREIGN CONTROL OF UNITED STATES FINANCIAL INSTITUTIONS

DEFINITIONS

SEC. 901. For purposes of this title—

(1) the term "domestic financial institution" means any bank, mutual savings bank, or savings and loan association organized under the laws of any State or of the United States;

(2) the term "foreign person" means any foreign organization or any individual resident in a foreign country or any organization or individual owned or controlled by such an organization or individual; and

(3) the term "takeover" means any acquisition of the stock or assets of any domestic financial institution if, after such acquisition, the amount of stock or assets held is 5 per centum or more of the institution's stock or assets.

MORATORIUM

SEC. 902. The Board of Governors of the Federal Reserve System, the Comptroller of the Currency, the Board of Directors of the Federal Deposit

Insurance Corporation, and the Federal Home Loan Bank Board may not approve any application relating to the takeover of any domestic financial institution by a foreign person until July 1, 1980, unless—

(1) such takeover is necessary to prevent the bankruptcy or insolvency of the domestic financial institution involved;

(2) the application was initially submitted for filing on or before March 5, 1980;

(3) the domestic financial institution has deposits of less than $100,000,000;

(4) the application relates to a takeover of shares or assets pursuant to a foreign person's intrafirm reorganization of its interests in a domestic financial institution, including specifically any application to establish a bank holding company pursuant to such reorganization;

(5) the application relates to a takeover of the assets or shares of a domestic financial institution if such assets or shares are owned or controlled by a foreign person; or

(6) the application relates to the takeover of a domestic financial institution which is a subsidiary of a bank holding company under an order to divest by December 31, 1980.

Approved March 31, 1980.

APPENDIX L
FOREIGN CORRUPT
PRACTICES ACT

§ 78DD-1. FOREIGN CORRUPT PRACTICES BY ISSUERS—
PROHIBITED PRACTICES

(a) It shall be unlawful for any issuer which has a class of securities registered pursuant to section 78*l* of this title or which is required to file reports under section 78*o*(d) of this title, or for any officer, director, employee, or agent of such issuer or any stockholder thereof acting on behalf of such issuer, to make use of the maîls or any means or instrumentality of interstate commerce corruptly in furtherance of an offer, payment, promise to pay, or authorization of the payment of any money, or offer, gift, promise to give, or authorization of the giving of anything of value to—

    (1) any foreign official for purposes of—

        (A) influencing any act or decision of such foreign official in his official capacity, including a decision to fail to perform his official functions; or

        (B) inducing such foreign official to use his influence with a foreign government or instrumentality thereof to affect or influence any act or decision of such government or instrumentality,

in order to assist such issuer in obtaining or retaining business for or with, or directing business to, any person;

    (2) any foreign political party or official thereof or any candidate for foreign political office for purposes of—

        (A) influencing any act or decision of such party, official, or candidate in its or his official capacity, including a decision to fail to perform its or his official functions; or

        (B) inducing such party, official, or candidate to use its or his influence with a foreign government or instrumentality thereof to affect or influence any act or decision of such government or instrumentality,

in order to assist such issuer in obtaining or retaining business for or with, or directing business to, any person; or

15 U.S.C. 78dd–1, 78dd–2, and 78ff.

(3) any person, while knowing or having reason to know that all or a portion of such money or thing of value will be offered, given, or promised, directly or indirectly, to any foreign official, to any foreign political party or official thereof, or to any candidate for foreign political office, for purposes of—

>   (A) influencing any act or decision of such foreign official, political party, party official, or candidate in his or its official capacity, including a decision to fail to perform his or its official functions; or

>   (B) inducing such foreign official, political party, party official, or candidate to use his or its influence with a foreign government or instrumentality thereof to affect or influence any act or decision of such government or instrumentality,

in order to assist such issuer in obtaining or retaining business for or with, or directing business to, any person.

DEFINITION

(b) As used in this section, the term "foreign official" means any officer or employee of a foreign government or any department, agency, or instrumentality thereof, or any person acting in an official capacity for or on behalf of such government or department agency, or instrumentality. Such term does not include any employee of a foreign government or any department, agency, or instrumentality thereof whose duties are essentially ministerial or clerical.

§ 78DD–2. FOREIGN CORRUPT PRACTICES BY DOMESTIC CONCERNS

(a) It shall be unlawful for any domestic concern, other than an issuer which is subject to section 78dd–1 of this title, or any officer, director, employee, or agent of such domestic concern or any stockholder thereof acting on behalf of such domestic concern, to make use of the mails or any means or instrumentality of interstate commerce corruptly in furtherance of an offer, payment, promise to pay, or authorization of the payment of any money, or offer, gift, promise to give, or authorization of the giving of anything of value to—

>   (1) any foreign official for purposes of—

>>   (A) influencing any act or decision of such foreign official in his official capacity including a decision to fail to perform his official functions; or

>>   (B) inducing such foreign official to use his influence with a foreign government or instrumentality thereof to affect or influence any act or decision of such government or instrumentality,

in order to assist such domestic concern in obtaining or retaining business for or with, or directing business to, any person;

(2) any foreign political party or official thereof or any candidate for foreign political office for purposes of—

(A) influencing any act or decision of such party, official, or candidate in its or his official capacity, including a decision to fail to perfom its or his official functions; or

(B) inducing such foreign official, political party, party official, or candidate to use his or its influence with a foreign government or instrumentality thereof to affect or influence any act or decision of such government or instrumentality,

in order to assist such domestic concern in obtaining or retaining business for or with, or directing business to, any person; or

(3) any person, while knowing or having reason to know that all of a portion of such money or thing of value will be offered, given, or promised, directly or indirectly, to any foreign official, to any foreign political party or official thereof; or to any candidate for foreign political office, for purposes of—

(A) influencing any act or decision of such foreign official, political party, party official, or candidate in his or its official capacity, including a decision to fail to perform his or its official functions; or

(B) inducing such party, official, or candidate to use its or his influence with a foreign government or instrumentality thereof to affect or influence any act or decision of such government or instrumentality,

in order to assist such domestic concern in obtaining or retaining business for or with, or directing business to, any person.

PENALTIES

(b) (1) (A) Except as provided in subparagraph (B), any domestic concern which violates subsection (a) of this section shall, upon conviction, be fined not more than $1,000,000.

(B) Any individual who is a domestic concern and who willfully violates subsection (a) of this section shall, upon conviction, be fined not more than $10,000, or imprisoned not more than five years, or both.

(2) Any officer or director of a domestic concern, or stockholder acting on behalf of such domestic concern, who willfully violates subsection (a) of this section shall, upon conviction, be fined not more than $10,000, or imprisoned not more than five years, or both.

(3) Whenever a domestic concern is found to have violated subsection (a) of this section, any employee or agent of such domestic concern who is a United States citizen, national, or resident or is otherwise subject to the jurisdiction of the United States (other than an officer, director, or stock

holder acting on behalf of such domestic concern), and who willfully carried out the act or practice constituting such violation shall, upon conviction, be fined not more than $10,000, or imprisoned not more than five years, or both.

(4) Whenever a fine is imposed under paragraph (2) or (3) of this subsection upon any officer, director, stockholder, employee, or agent of a domestic concern, such fine shall not be paid, directly or indirectly, by such domestic concern.

CIVIL ACTION BY ATTORNEY GENERAL TO PREVENT VIOLATIONS

(c) Whenever it appears to the Attorney General that any domestic concern, or officer, director, employee, agent, or stockholder thereof, is engaged, or is about to engage, in any act or practice constituting a violation of subsection (a) of this section, the Attorney General may, in his discretion, bring a civil action in an appropriate district court of the United States to enjoin such act or practice, and upon a proper showing a permanent or temporary injunction or a temporary restraining order shall be granted without bond.

DEFINITIONS

(d) As used in this section:
    (1) the Term "domestic concern" means (A) any individual who is a citizen, national, or resident of the United States; or (B) any corporation, partnership, association, joint-stock company, business trust, unincorporated organization, or sole proprietorship which has its principal place of business in the United States, or which is organized under the laws of a State of the United States or a territory, possession, or commonwealth of the United States.
    (2) The term "foreign official" means any officer or employee of a foreign government or any department, agency, or instrumentality thereof, or any person acting in an official capacity for or on behalf of any such government or department, agency, or instrumentality. Such term does not include any employee of a foreign government or any department, agency, or instrumentality thereof whose duties are essentially ministerial or clerical.
    (3) The term "interstate commerce" means trade, commerce, transportation, or communication among the several States, or between any foreign country and any State or between any State and any place or ship outside thereof. Such term includes the intrastate use of (A) a telephone or other means of communication, or (B) any other interstate instrumentality.

78FF. PENALTIES

(a) Any person who willfully violates any provision of this chapter (other than section 78dd–1 of this title), or any rule or regulation thereunder the violation of which is made unlawful or the observance of which is required under the terms of this chapter, or any person who willfully and knowingly makes, or causes to be made, any statement in any application, report, or document required to be filed under this chapter or any rule or regulation thereunder or any undertaking contained in a registration statement as provided in subsection (d) of section 78*o* of this title or by any self-regulatory organization in connection with an application for membership or participation therein or to become associated with a member thereof, which statemnet was false or misleading with respect to any material fact, shall upon conviction be fined not more than $10,000, or imprisoned not more than five years, or both, except that when such person is an exchange, a fine not exceeding $500,000 may be imposed; but no person shall be subject to imprisonment under this section for the violation of any rule or regulation if he proves that he had no knowledge of such rule or regulation.

BIBLIOGRAPHY

Abrams, Marshall D., and Philip G. Stein. *Computer Hardware Software: An Interdisciplinary Introduction*. New York: Addison-Wesley, 1973.

Ackoff, Russell. *Redesigning the Future*. New York: John Wiley & Sons, 1974.

Adams, D. L., and Mullarkey, J. F. "A Survey of Audit Software." *Journal of Accountancy* (September 1972): 39–66.

AFIPS. *System Review Manual on Security*. Montvale, N.J., 1974.

"All About Minocomputers." Delran, N.J.: Datapro Research Corporation (September 1977).

"All About Small Business Computers." Delran, N.J.: Datapro Research Corporation (September 1977).

Allen, Brandt R. "Embezzler's Guide to the Computer." *Harvard Business Review*. **53** (July 1975): 79–89.

American Institute of Certified Public Accountants. *Audit Guide: Audits of Service-Center-Produced Records*. New York: The American Institute of Certified Public Accountants, 1974.

Arthur D. Little, Inc. *The Consequences of Electronic Funds Transfer—A Technology Assessment of Movement Towards A Less Check/Less Cash Society*. Report submitted to and for review by the National Science Foundation, Washington, D.C., 1975.

Baird, Lindsay L. "An Analytical Approach to Identifying Computer Vulnerability." *Security Management* (May 1974): 6–11.

Bank Administration Institute. *Auditing Bank EDP Systems*. Chicago: Bank Administration Institute, 1968.

Baruch, Hurd. *Wall Street Security Risk*. Washington, D.C.: Acropolis Books, 1971.

Bequai, August. *Computer Crime*. Lexington, Mass.: D. C. Heath, 1977.

Bequai, August. "Crooks and Computers." *Trial Magazine,* **12** (August 1976): 48–53.

Bequai, August. "Legal Problems in Prosecuting Computer Crimes." *Security Management,* **21** (July 1977): 26–27.

Bequai, August. "Litigation under the EFTS." *Federal Bar News,* **23** (June 1976): 174–177.

Bequai, August. "The Electronic Criminal." *Barrister,* **4** (Winter 1977): 8–12.

Bequai, August. "Wanted: The White Collar Ring." *Student Lawyer,* **5** (May 1977): 44–48.

Bjork, L. A., Jr., "Generalized Audit Trail Requirements and Concepts for Data Base Applications." *IBM Systems Journal,* **14**: 3 (1975).

Brandon, Dick H., and Sidney Segelstein. *Data Processing Contracts: Structure, Contents, and Negotiation*. New York: Van Nostrand-Reinhold, 1976.

Brinch, Hansen P. *Operating System Principles*. Englewood Cliffs, N.J.: Prentice-Hall, 1973.

Brown, Foster. "Auditing Control and System Design." *Journal of Systems Management*. (April 1975): 24–31.

Bylinsky, Gene. "Here Comes the Second Computer Revolution." *Fortune* (November 1975).

Cadmus, Bradford. *Operational Auditing Handbook*. New York: The Institute of Internal Auditors, Inc., 1964.

Canadian Institute of Chartered Accountants. *Computer Audit Guidelines*. Toronto, Ontario, 1971.

Canning, Richard G. "Computer Fraud and Embezzlement." *EDP Analyzer,* **2**: 9 (September 1973).

Carke, Thurstan, and John J. Tigue, Jr. *Dirty Money—Swiss Banks, The Mafia, Money Laundering and White Collar Crime*. New York: Simon & Schuster, 1975.

Carmier, Frank. *Wall Street's Shady Side*. Washington, D.C.: Public Affairs Press, 1962.

Carper, Jean. *Not with a Gun*. New York: Grossman, 1973.

Cassell, Stephen A. "Floppy Disk Drives and Systems." *Modern Data* (August 1975).

Corsiglia, Jack. "Matching Computer to the Job: First Step Towards Selection." *Data Processing* (December 1970).

Crowley, Thomas H. *Understanding Computers*. New York: McGraw-Hill, 1967.

Davis, Gordon B. *Auditing and EDP*. New York: American Institute of Certified Public Accountants, 1968.

Dirks, Raymond L., and Leonard Gross. *The Great Wall Street Scandal*. New York: McGraw-Hill, 1974.

Ditri, Arnold E., John C. Shaw, and William Atkins. *Managing the EDP Function*. New York: McGraw-Hill, 1971.

Edelhertz, Herbert. *The Nature, Impact, and Prosecution of White Collar Crime*. Washington, D.C.: Government Printing Office, 1970.

Eldin, Hamed K., and F. Max Croft. *Information Systems: A Management Science Approach*. New York: Petrocelli, 1974.

Ernst, Morris. "Management, the Computer, and Society." *Computers and Automation* (September 1971).

Farr, M. A. L., B. Chadwick, and K. K. Wonk. *Security for Computer Systems*. Manchester, U.K.: The National Computing Centre, Limited (NCC publications), 1972.

Farr, Robert. *The Electronic Criminals*. New York: McGraw-Hill, 1975.

Fouri, William M. *Introduction to the Computer: The Tool of Business*. Englewood Cliffs, N.J.: Prentice-Hall, 1977.

Geis, Gilbert. *The White Collar Criminal*. New York: Atherton Press, 1968.

Georgen, W. Donald. "Rating Internal Controls." *Financial Executive* (April 1975): 42–50.

Gladney, H. M., et al. "An Access Control Mechanism for Computing Resources." *IBM Systems Journal,* **14**: 3 (1975).

Greenawalt, Kent. *Legal Protections of Privacy.* Washington, D.C.: Office of Telecommunications Policy, 1975.

Griblin, August. "Beware—Computerniks at Work." *The National Observer* (May 23, 1977): 1, 15.

Grimes, John A. "Equity Funding: Fraud by Computer." *American Federationist,* **80** (December 1973): 7–9.

Gruenberger, Fred, and David Babcock. *Computing with Mini-Computers.* Los Angeles: Melville Publishing Company, 1973.

Hudes, Albert. "Behind the Scenes at Equity Funding." *TEMPO,* **19**: 1 (1973): 12–19.

IBM Corporation. *The Considerations of Data Security in a Computer Environment.* G520–2169, 1972.

IBM Corporation. *The Considerations of Physical Security in a Computer Environment.* G520–2700, 1970.

The Institute of Internal Auditors. *Modern Concepts of Internal Auditing, Establishing the Internal Audit Function EDP–Job Descriptions.* Orlando, Fla., 1974.

Jancura, Elise G., and Arnold H. Berger. *Computers: Auditing and Control.* Philadelphia: Auerbach Publishers, 1973.

Knight, Kenneth E. "Changes in Computer Performance." *Datamation* (September 1966).

Knuth, Donald. *The Art of Computer Programming.* New York: Addison-Wesley, 1975.

Kohn, E. J. *Fraud.* New York: Harper & Row, 1973.

Larsen, Kent S. *Privacy, A Public Concern: A Resource Document Based on the Proceedings of a Seminar on Privacy Sponsored by the Domestic Council Committee on the Right of Privacy and the Council of State Governments.* Washington, D.C.: U.S. Government Printing Office, 1975.

Laudon, Kenneth C. *Computers and Bureaucratic Reform.* New York: John Wiley & Sons, 1974.

Lettieri, Larry. "Negotiating the Contract Maze." *Computer Decisions* (April 1977).

Lipson, Milton. *On Guard: The Business of Private Security.* New York: Times, 1975.

Martin, James. *Design of Real-Time Computer Systems.* Englewood Cliffs, N.J.: Prentice-Hall, 1976.

Martin, James. *Security Accuracy and Privacy in Computer Systems.* Englewood Cliffs, N.J.: Prentice-Hall, 1973.

Maurer, Ward D. *Programming: An Introduction to Computer Languages and Techniques.* San Francisco: Holden-Day, 1968.

McKnight, Gerald. *Computer Crime.* New York: Walker, 1973.

McPhee, W. S. "Operating System Integrity in OS/VS 2." *IBM Systems Journal,* **13**: 3 (1974): 230–252.

Meigs, Walter B., E. John Larsen, and Robert F. Meigs. *Principles of Auditing.* Homewood, Ill.: Richard D. Irwin, 1973.

Michie, Donald. *On Machine Intelligence.* New York: Halsted Press, 1974.

Miller, Arthur R. *The Assault on Privacy.* Ann Arbor: University of Michigan Press, 1971.

Munyan, Jack. *So You're Going to Automate.* New York: Petrocelli, 1975.

Parker, Donn B. *Crime by Computer.* New York: Scribner, 1976.

Porter, W. Thomas. *EDP Controls and Auditing.* Belmont, Calif.: Wadsworth Publishing Company, 1974.

Porter, W. Thomas. "Evaluating Internal Controls in EDP Systems." *Journal of Accountancy* (August 1974): 34–40.

Reid, G. F., and J. A. Demiak. "EDP Implementation with General Purpose Software." *Journal of Accountancy* (July 1971): 35–46.

Sackman, Harold. *Man–Computer Problem Solving.* Princeton, N.J.: Auerbach Publishers, 1970.

Scalletta, Walsh. *Understanding Computer Contracts.* New York: Data Processing Management Association, 1976.

Sharpe, William F. *The Economics of Computers.* New York: Columbia University Press, 1969.

Shaw, John C., and William Atkins. *Managing Computer System Projects.* New York: McGraw-Hill, 1970.

Short, G. F. *Establishing a Company Security Program.* IBM Data Security Forum, Denver, 1974.

Solomon, Martin B. "Economics of Scale and Computer Personnel." *Datamation* (March 1970.)

Soucek, Branko. *Microprocessors and Microcomputers.* New York: Wiley-Interscience, 1976.

Steffen, Roswell, as told to Curt Miller. "How I Embezzled $1.5 Million—And Nearly Got Away With It." *Bank Systems and Equipment* (June 1974): 26–28.

Stone, H. S. *Introduction to Computer Organization and Data Structures.* New York: McGraw-Hill, 1972.

Sutherland, Edwin H. *White Collar Crime.* New York: Holt, Rinehart & Winston, 1949.

Tausworthe, Robert C. *Standardized Development of Computer Software.* Englewood Cliffs, N.J.: Prentice-Hall, 1977.

Turn, Rein. *Computers in the 1980s.* New York: Columbia University Press, 1974.

U.S. Department of Health, Education and Welfare. *Records, Computers and Rights of Citizens.* Washington, D.C. 1973.

Wasserman, J. J. "Data Security in an On-Line Computer Environment." *The EDP Auditor* (1974).

Weinberg, Gerald M. *The Psychology of Computer Programming.* New York: Van Nostrand-Reinhold, 1971.

Weinberg, Gerald M. *An Introduction to General Systems Thinking.* New York: John Wiley & Sons, 1975.

Westin, Alan. *Privacy and Freedom.* New York, Atheneum, 1967.

Westin, Alan, and Michael Baker. *Databanks in a Free Society.* New York: Quadrangle Books, 1973.

Wheeler, Stanton, ed. *On Record.* New York: Russell Sage Foundation, 1969.

Whiteside, Thomas. "Annals of Crime (Computers–II)." *New Yorker* (August 29,

Wilensky, Harold. *Organizational Intelligence.* New York, Basic Books, 1967.
1977): 34–64.

Wooldridge, Susan, Colin Corder, and Claude Johnson. *Security Standards for Data Processing.* New York: John Wiley & Sons, 1973.

Wu, Margaret S. *Introduction to Computer Data Processing.* New York: Harcourt, Brace, Jovanovich, 1975.

"Your Finances Bared (But Who's Looking)." *Money Magazine,* **6** (May 1977): 85–88.

Yourdon, Edward. *Design of On-Line Computer Systems.* Englewood Cliffs, N.J.: Prentice-Hall, 1973.

Yourdon, Edward. "Reliability of Real Time Systems." *Modern Data* (January 1972).

INDEX